Adios

Adios to Tears

The Memoirs of a Japanese-Peruvian
Internee in U.S. Concentration Camps

SEIICHI HIGASHIDE

Foreword by C. Harvey Gardiner
Preface by Elsa H. Kudo
Epilogue by Julie Small

UNIVERSITY OF WASHINGTON PRESS
Seattle and London

A Note to Readers

We, the eight children of Seiichi Higashide, were deeply moved by the
account of our father's life and experiences in his recollection, *Adios to Tears*.
With feelings of gratitude and much love, we cooperated to make possible
English and Spanish translations of that volume. We hope that the
translations will grant a larger audience an awareness of his extraordinary
experiences and an understanding of our different types of relatedness.
We dedicate this book to our dear parents.

Elsa Yukiko Kudo
Carlos Shuichi Higashide
Irma Setsuko Kudo
Arthur Hideki Higashide
Martha Yoko Shigio
Richard Daisuke Higashide
Deanna Mitsuko Aspengren
Mark Yoshio Higashide

Contents

Foreword by C. Harvey Gardiner   vii

Preface to the Year 2000 Edition by Elsa H. Kudo   3

Preface to the Original Edition   7

Chapter One. The Fall of the Higashide Family   9

Chapter Two. Pursuing a Dream of Success Overseas   27

Chapter Three. My New World, Peru   44

Chapter Four. Moving Toward Financial Independence   68

Chapter Five. Approaching Storm Clouds   88

Chapter Six. Fierce Winds of Oppression   113

Chapter Seven. The Pitiful "Japanese People's
Army of Peru"   133

Chapter Eight. The Ordeal of "Utopia"   155

Chapter Nine. From a Barbed-wire "Town"
to a Chain-link Town   176

Chapter Ten. A Concrete Frontier   193

Chapter Eleven. Becoming Americanized   213

Chapter Twelve. Hawaii—A Paradise of Sea and Sun   233

Afterword   245

Bibliography   247

Epilogue by Julie Small   249

Index   254

Foreword

We met in Chicago in 1981, a triangle of strangers in quest of justice.

The distinguished members of the U.S. Commission on Wartime Relocation and Internment of Civilians, one side of the triangle, represented the American government's effort to resolve one of its major World War II aberrations: the treatment dealt the Japanese American internees. In its coast-to-coast investigations, the Commission was focusing on 110,000 Japanese Americans, as though they were its sole concern.

In Chicago, the second and third sides of the justice-seeking triangle cropped up: an historian much interested in Japanese–Latin American relations and a civilian, Peruvian Japanese wartime internee.

Network television cameras rolled as dignitaries and local personalities (Studs Terkel was one) welcomed the Commission. When the welcoming din subsided and the session opened, I was called first as an expert witness on the Peruvian Japanese wartime experience. Granted fifteen minutes to speak, I used every second to document the kidnapping and imprisoning of 1,800 civilians, none of whom had had any charge levied against them. Former Justice Arthur J. Goldberg of the U.S. Supreme Court, who led the questioning, concluded by agreeing that American agencies, including the Executive Department, the Department of State, the U.S. Army, the FBI, and the Immigration and Naturalization Service had violated the civil rights of those Latin American Japanese. At the conclusion of my presentation, I gave a copy of my fresh-off-the press book, *Pawns in a Triangle of Hate: The Peruvian Japanese and the United States,* to each member of the Commission.

The next witness, Seiichi Higashide, seventy-two years old and one of those 1,800 people seized in Peru in 1942–44, represented the final side of the justice-seeking triangle. Ably assisted by family members, including his eldest child, Elsa, also an internee, a determined Higashide recounted his own nightmarish experience. His story became a case study of the abuse and violation of elementary human rights thrust upon all the Peruvian Japanese internees.

Made aware, in Chicago and again in New York City, of those internees, the Commission continued to pursue its labors. A year later, its massive report, titled *Personal Justice Denied,* appeared. The Latin American Japanese won mention in the Appendix.

While millions awaited the reaction of the U.S. government to that report, Seiichi Higashide and Elsa, again aided by family members, undertook the recollection, research, and writing that grew into a remarkable biographical-historical account: *Adios to Tears: The Memoirs of a Japanese-Peruvian Internee in U.S. Concentration Camps.* The book is an archetypal narration of the unvoiced wartime travail of innocent thousands.

Born into rural poverty in a remote mountain village in Hokkaido, young Higashide eventually made his way to Tokyo. Engulfed there in a struggle to survive that included collecting and reselling bottles, selling newspapers, and performing hard manual labor, he engaged in night-school studies in engineering and architecture, fields yielding him no opportunity in Japan. Always a student and contemplating migration to Peru, he studied Spanish to ease his immersion into a strange world. Tears marked his sailing from his homeland in 1930, at the age of twenty-one.

Inured to hard work and uncertainty in Japan, Higashide encountered both in Peru, in addition to a language barrier, prejudice, and countless points of cultural collision. He labored many months, room and board his only remuneration. He taught school. His work ethic, earnestness, and other positive qualities gradually won him helpful contacts and advancement. In 1935 he married Angelica Yoshinaga, a Nisei eight years his junior. Launching into shopkeeping and family building, he prospered in both. By the late 1930s he was a community leader in Ica, a provincial town five hundred miles south of Lima. But just when he was savoring success and some affluence in his adopted homeland, storm clouds gathered.

Anti-Japanese rioting and the approaching collision of Japan and the United States skewed Higashide's prospects. Events of December 7, 1941, and the swift issuance by the United States of the Proclaimed List of Certain Blocked Nationals (blacklist) hit home when his name, as a community leader, appeared on the initial list. For a long time, however, he evaded deportation.

Seized finally early in January 1944 by four policemen while he dined with his family, Higashide was spirited north to a urine-soaked jail cell in Lima. Ten days later, his distraught wife, pregnant with their fifth child, saw him forced aboard ship in Callao by Peruvian police and American soldiers. Sailing away a second time, he again shed tears.

Temporarily ashore in Panama, he and his fellow deportees labored, unpaid. Upon learning that families could be reunited with internees, he telegraphed Angelica. A frail twenty-seven-year-old, by then the mother of five, she had to close out business interests and ready the children, not one of whom was yet eight years old, for a trip into the unknown.

The family was reunited in July 1944 at the Immigration and Naturalization Service facility (guarded with barbed wire, watchtowers, and armed personnel) in Crystal City, Texas, and the prospects of the seven bewildered Higashides quickly improved. Work was optional; if indulged, a wage was paid. Recreation facilities and schools occupied the children. As the months multiplied, the outlook and attitude of the adults changed, along with the changing world. For the Higashides, Peru gradually faded. America loomed larger in their future. Subtly but steadily, elementary Americanization was underway.

Released, provisionally, after more than two years of internment, the Higashides moved cautiously, haltingly into mainstream American life, another bumpy beginning in a strange land. Years mounted into decades; roots deepened. Citizenship, schooling, hard work— all contributed to their pursuit of the American dream.

Adios to Tears mingles suffering with success. It is a very personal story, not a definitive history. Its structure—occasional disjunctions and repetitions, flashbacks, anticipations and heartfelt outbursts—add an extemporaneous and emotionally rich quality that is priceless and sincere. The story mirrors one life in three countries on as many continents, relating family, immigrant community, and the wider world of radically differing cultures.

In the meantime, that triangle of strangers in Chicago in 1981, representing government, historical perspective, and personal experience, awaits, at the close of the twentieth century, the redress due the Peruvian Japanese.

Adios to Tears does cry . . . for justice.

C. HARVEY GARDINER
November 1999

MAP 1. South America

MAP 2. Peru

Adios to Tears

Preface to the Year 2000 Edition

More than five years have passed since my husband and I first published *Adios to Tears*. Love and perhaps a feeling of filial piety were what plunged me into the unknown waters of self-publishing. In 1993, with my father's health deteriorating, my one big dream was to present to him an English version of his memoirs. There were times when I felt I couldn't go on. I didn't know what to do or where to turn! Yes, there are "how to" books and seminars, but nothing seemed to answer my own particular questions. In fact, I received negative responses from family members as well as "experts": "Don't do it. You don't know anything about publishing." Also, time was of the essence. I was often desperate, but the need to fulfill the dream was more pressing.

Recalling those years, it is with deep gratitude and affection that I give thanks in this second edition to those who became my mentors and actively helped to make the first edition possible. Simply and humbly, I thank Aiko and Jack Herzig (archival researchers); Bill Hohri *(Repairing America);* the late Michi N. Weglyn *(Years of Infamy)* and her husband, Walter, for their constant support and special friendship; Grace Shimizu and Stephanie Moore, who willingly and expertly handled nearly all public-relations and sales matters on the mainland and, in spite of their own busy schedules, also managed to be our chauffeurs in San Francisco; John and Masako Kobayashi for their many acts of kindness; and Barbara Marumoto (Representative, Hawaii), for initiating on the floor of the House of Representatives a special certificate of honor for the author. My gratitude also goes to Auntie Fumiko Yoshinaga, Kay Uno Kaneko, John and Kumiko Stall, and Mr. Iwao Tomita (founder of Tohmatsu and Company) for their enthusiastic endorsement of my father's book and for their active support. I want to make special mention of a gentle soul, the late Ben Sanematsu *(Light from Within),* for making the Braille form of *Adios to Tears* available.

The list is too long to name all those who passed the word along, including journalists, friends, family members, and kind readers who took the time to call or write, but I do want to say again, thank you, mahalo, arigato, gracias.

As the publisher of the first English edition of *Adios to Tears,* we are most happy and proud that an updated, second English edition will now be available from the University of Washington Press. It has been a source of comfort and trust to work with Naomi Pascal, editor-in-chief, and I wish to express my gratitude for her patience and understanding in making this second edition a reality. I am aware that there are many people in the background who contributed to "producing" the book, and I say to them, thank you most kindly for all the hard work and dedication.

Dr. C. Harvey Gardiner *(Pawns in a Triangle of Hate)* made a scholarly contribution to the Hearings in Chicago in 1981, which helped give credence to our personal testimonies. I want to thank him for contributing the Foreword for this second edition.

My deepest appreciation goes to my partner and husband, Eigo, for his support and help. He didn't complain about my quest to turn hundreds of loose pages of translation into a bona fide book to present to my father. He was the order taker, shipping clerk, bookkeeper, cook, and dishwasher, and he brought me tea just when I needed it.

Since publication of the first edition, much has happened in the world around us and in our own lives. One gigantic loss has been the passing of Seiichi Higashide in 1997 at the age of eighty-eight. His fight for redress for the Japanese Latin Americans (the JLAs) is now generally known to at least his fellow internees (Peru-Kai members). He continued to hope that the United States would apologize and offer monetary compensation to every JLA who experienced loss of civil and human rights, worldly possessions, and good reputation during the war.

Less than a year after the reunion in San Francisco in 1990, some Peru-Kai members founded the Japanese Peruvian Oral History Project (JPOHP), with Grace Shimizu as its coordinator. They began to tape Japanese Peruvian oral histories and to educate others about this little known episode of American history. In retrospect, it was a brilliant and timely idea to have formed JPOHP before all our elders perish, for it is they who remember most intensely because their lives were so irreparably ripped apart.

With the tremendous help and support of the internees living in mainland Japan (under the conscientious and dedicated leadership of Kazu Hayashida and Mitsuaki Oyama), in Okinawa (with the guidance of Keiko Kawata), and in Peru (through the generosity of the late Kishiro Hayashi and son Tomas), and of participants in the United States, JPOHP has conducted more than fifty oral histories.

Countless volunteers are continually endeavoring to translate into English transcriptions from the spoken Japanese, Spanish, and a hodgepodge of the three languages. It is a daunting undertaking. A great debt of gratitude goes to the many volunteers who contribute their talents, time, and energy to make this project viable.

The JLAs began to connect with other Americans who sympathized with them as their story became known through the work of JPOHP, the Committee hearings and subsequent publication of *Personal Justice Denied,* research papers, books and articles by scholars such as Edward N. Barnhart, Roger Daniels, C. Harvey Gardiner, Michi Weglyn, Ellen Carson (Esq.), and the memoirs of John K. Emmerson and Seiichi Higashide, as well as from the internees themselves who began to share their stories. Invigorated by the help and support of ordinary folks, students, activists, churches, and various other groups, the Campaign for Justice was born when the JLAs decided to sue the government for redress.

Along with so many others, Grace Shimizu and Julie Small have worked tirelessly for JLA redress. Shimizu is director of JPOHP, a founding member of Campaign for Justice, and the daughter of former internee, ninety-three-year-old Susumu Shimizu. Julie Small is a founding member and co-chair of Campaign for Justice. She learned about the wartime kidnapping and incarceration of JLAs through the slow unveiling of the story at family gatherings of a friend who was interned as a child with his family from Peru. She felt the injustice and suffering that this family had gone through, quit her job in finance, and has devoted most of her waking hours to the Campaign for Justice.

Shimizu and Small have cooperated to write the Epilogue for this new edition of *Adios to Tears.* By sharing their expertise gained through the redress struggles, they give the reader an insight into the continuing fight for justice for the JLAs, a glimpse of the difficulty of suing the most powerful country in the world, and an understanding of why a small group of people (with the help of many concerned Americans) has dared to do this. Certainly, they help to make real our democratic form of government, which professes to champion the civil and human rights of world citizens.

The JLA's redress fight continues under the most trying circumstances. We hope it will end in victory. Our country will have shown true greatness to the world, and these almost forgotten internees can finally have a sense of closure. All peoples in the United States of America will be able to feel more secure that the concentration camps cannot be so easily duplicated in the future . . . better still, that such denial of justice will never happen again to anyone.

ELSA H. KUDO
September 1999

Preface to the Original Edition

I feel that in my life I have come to have "three motherlands." Although I am aware that a person can't have three motherlands, please allow me to say so because that is truly how I feel.

My first motherland is Japan, where I was born in 1909 on the island of Hokkaido. There I spent the greater part of my youth in quiet discontent, yearning for greater opportunities than my remote village in the wooded mountains could provide.

At long last, in the midst of the Great Depression, I was able to escape to Tokyo. As fate would have it, my life there likewise became too small and confining for me. Earlier I had dreamed of escaping from Hokkaido; again I dreamed of a more open society and my dreams extended outward beyond the seas. I dreamed of going to the outside world.

The new world I discovered came to be Peru. However, contrary to my dreams and visions of a larger, more exciting world of opportunities, I found myself in the year 1930, embedded in the small, closed world of Japanese immigrants in South America. Their world was even more narrow than the society I had left!

But life is strange and filled with unexpected developments. By chance, I was given the opportunity to develop relationships with the Peruvian community at large. From this point, my vision expanded as new perspectives and possibilities began to build one upon the other. I chased my dreams, extending toward my new horizons. In this manner I put down roots in the land of Peru, and with my life's blood nurturing the soil, my tree of life expanded to include a wife and five children. Deep are my feelings for the Latin country I call my "second motherland."

Unexpected developments became my lot in life. In 1941, war between the United States and Japan was formally declared. Early the next year, Peru severed all relations with Japan. Everyone of Japanese ancestry came to be seen as "enemy aliens" and were pressured and badgered by government authorities.

Finally, what at first could not even be imagined became reality. We of Japanese ancestry were kidnapped in the night by armed detectives, deported to the United States, and forced to spend a long period of detention in internment camps.

Eventually the war ended, but for those of us who had been kidnapped and held hostage in this strange land, it only marked the beginning of new hardships. Two alternatives were left to us: return to Japan, or remain in America. Fully aware of the hardships that lay before us, I chose the latter. As a result, my family and I were branded "illegal aliens on conditional release" and tossed out into the fiercely competitive American society.

As expected, life became a series of hardships. Somehow, I managed to survive those ordeals. Putting down roots again in this, my "third motherland," I formally became a citizen in 1958—an American both in name and reality.

Although I have been away from Japan for over half a century, I still feel that spiritually I am Japanese. At the same time, I believe if the war had not interfered, my roots would have remained planted in Peru. I would have acquired citizenship there and would have had my bones buried in its soil. Such was my love for Peru.

Now I assess my feelings again and find that they have not changed, but have grown to encompass more of the world—for surely I love this country as well, as deeply as my first and second "motherlands." I feel proud and honored to be a citizen of the United States of America.

Each of these three countries evokes in me a deep, penetrating longing to return when I am away. And in each I enjoy the comfortable sense of ease that can only come when one is at home. Thus, I am tied emotionally to these countries by a sense of belonging. To cut off any of them would be like losing part of my identity. So while I agree it is strange to say I have three motherlands, for me there is no other way to express what I feel.

The urging of my children to leave a record of my life for them has led me to write this work. I began by writing down whatever came to mind. Since this is written by an old immigrant with very little literary experience, I am sure there are many passages in which I fail to get my point across. In such instances I can only lower my head and ask for your indulgence. The events recorded here are all true. The names of people and places are real, except in a few instances where I felt offense might be taken.

Chapter One. The Fall of the Higashide Family

Higashide is the family into which I was born. It was, I have been told, a family long situated in what is presently Torikoshi Village in the Ishikawa District of Ishikawa Prefecture, Japan. There, for successive generations, members of our family had been village leaders. Documents that would authenticate this, however, were scattered and lost during my grandfather's time and it is now impossible to trace the lineage beyond my great-grandfather.

My great-grandfather, Shinyuemon Higashide, lived through the last decades of the Edo period, when Japan ended its long isolation and began to open itself up to the modern world. He had only one daughter, Riyo. Because he had no son, he adopted Riyo's husband Shinzaemon so the Higashide line could be continued.

According to my mother, grandfather Shinzaemon was "an amiable man, but a great adventurer who was very free with money." He undertook a massive project to dam the gorge in the foothills of Mt. Haku, hoping to create an irrigation source for the entire foothills area. He made repeated attempts, but failed. I have also heard that he donated lands for the village's Hachiman deity and that he tried to have a shrine built in its honor.

Had his generosity been limited to such matters it might still have been acceptable to the family, but Grandfather also freely guaranteed loans for friends and acquaintances and, as might be expected, frequently had to make good on such loans. It comes as no surprise that the family's assets were gradually transferred to other hands. According to a cousin, there are several passages concerning Grandfather in works such as *The History of Ishikawa Prefecture* and *The History of Torikoshi Village*. Without a doubt, he left behind many colorful anecdotes.

We now can accept such incidents as lighthearted topics of conversation, but for my mother, who lived in the household, Grandfather's imprudence could not be looked upon dispassionately. Mother's maiden name was Yonu Itakura. She was, as was my father, born in Torikoshi Village. She had come to the Higashide family by marrying Iwamatsu, the oldest son of Shinzaemon. Weak and prone to illnesses from childhood, she experienced the ruin of the Higashide family first-hand, and lived through depths of poverty and hardship. During my early childhood I often heard Mother let fly resentful words about Grandfather. . . . and I knew those words were justified.

Following Grandfather's failure, my father gathered the entire family, boarded a small boat, and sailed northward through the Japan Sea to Hokkaido. There, we became one of the pioneering settlers of Japan's northernmost island. From my father's standpoint, having taken responsibility for a family reduced to bankruptcy, there was no other choice. Grandmother had already died by that time, but Grandfather was still alive. Besides Grandfather, the fate of my father's two younger brothers, his younger sister, and their first son weighed heavily on the shoulders of my now penniless parents.

Tears often streamed down Mother's face as she told us of the hardships they suffered when they first settled in Hokkaido. Her tear-streaked face remains burned in my memory, never to be erased. As I grew older, Mother stopped speaking of such days of hardship, but perhaps because I retained memories from early childhood I never felt any affection for my grandfather, for he had only brought suffering to my mother.

My Father, My Pride

My father, Iwamatsu, grew up during a time when the Higashide family was still prosperous and, by the standards of his time, received an exceptional education. Because of this, even after the family moved to Otoe Village in Hokkaido, he was respected by the surrounding community and was even seen as a local "treasure." People in the neighborhood often came to him for help with letters and complex documents they had to submit to government offices. Father would read and explain these to them and frequently wrote necessary replies.

Father taught me the basics of writing and arithmetic when I was only 3 or 4. He would use *konpeito*, a type of rice candy, as counters to teach me addition and subtraction. Since he would reward me with a piece of *konpeito* for each correct answer, I was determined to get as many correct as I could.

Even after I entered elementary school, Father would direct my studies from time to time. I learned to use the abacus and the multiplication tables much earlier than other children, so when we studied those subjects in school I could already do them better than anyone else. By the time I reached the fifth grade, to my great elation, I sometimes did sums on the abacus faster than my teacher.

I respected my father's fine education, but I took even greater pride in the deep trust given him by the people of our community. He had close relationships with the owner of the Tsuda Company in Fukagawa Township and with the owner of the Hato-Masamune

Sake Brewery in Museushi Township. When it was necessary for them to be away from their businesses for extended periods, they always asked Father to oversee affairs during their absences. He often took me along to the shops and, while we spent our days there, he single-handedly managed everything from bookkeeping to directing the daily activities of the employees. Seeing this through a child's eyes, I came to have great pride in my father, who was entrusted with the operations of such large businesses.

Father was also a good friend of the head of Otoe Village, Kichihei Fukazawa. As a child I often went along on visits to the Fukazawa home. Mr. Fukazawa was an agricultural specialist who had earlier studied in Europe. When I was about 12 he was elected to the Prefectural Assembly. After serving a number of terms there, he was elected to the National Diet, where for many years he worked hard to improve Japanese agriculture.

In part because of his deep friendship with Mr. Fukazawa, Father was often urged by people in the area to become a member of the Village Assembly or to become the head of our neighborhood association. For whatever reason, however, he always declined public office. I believe, now, that this was because responsibilities as head of a large, extended family weighed heavily upon him.

Father had many people to care for. Just raising his four surviving children would have been a difficult task for a farmer just barely managing to survive. But he was also obligated to provide for his two younger brothers and his younger sister until they could establish their own independent households. He accomplished this, somehow, and even found a wife for our widowed grandfather.

He also provided Grandfather with the satisfaction of having subsidiary branch families. My uncle had been set up as an independent household, but he came to lose everything because of miscalculations in the grain market. Father then had to take in and see to the needs of his brother's entire household. My older brother died at an early age and Father was left with the responsibility for his grandson. As head of the family, he had to bear these responsibilities. But it is also clear that it would have been an impossible burden had Father not been a man of exceptional character.

I believe one factor that sustained Father's strength was his deep faith in Buddhism. Every day without fail, no matter how busy he was, he gathered everyone before our Buddhist altar in the morning and again in the evening. Only after he had read the prescribed sutras were meals partaken. I now have completely forgotten them, but in my youth I had been a proper lay believer and could recite those sutras from memory.

Life of Poverty in Hokkaido

My father, Iwamatsu, and my mother, Yonu, had six children. Their first son, Yoshitaka, was born in Ishikawa Prefecture, but the other five children were born in Otoe Village in Sorachi District in Hokkaido. I was born on January 18, 1909 as their fourth son. Although called their fourth son, their second and third sons had died soon after birth so, in actuality, I became their second son. The other two in our family were my older sister, Misao, and my younger sister, Shizue.

Otoe Village was so remote that it had no doctor until I was 5 or 6. When we caught a cold, had a stomach ache, or any other illnesses, we could only take the potions left by the medicine peddlers, who came once a year from Toyama Prefecture, and hoped for the best. When I look back, it seems miraculous that children were raised under such conditions. My two older brothers were lost, but it was our good fortune that the remaining four of us grew up without major illnesses.

In those days, every able body in every farming household had to work in the fields. Infants, soon after birth, were placed in straw baskets called *izuko* and were left at home, their tiny bodies bound firmly to those baskets. From dawn to noon and from noon to dusk, infants were left without milk or water. Screaming and crying, they simply worked themselves to sleep. As pitiful as the infants' conditions were, imagine how unbearable it was for their parents. They, mindful of the infants they had left at home, were yet compelled to work in the fields.

Today, mechanization has brought some free time to farming life, but in those earlier days farmers had nothing worth calling "a time of rest." During peak agricultural periods women and children had to work. Entire families went out in the darkness before dawn and worked into the gloom of night until they could no longer see what was before them. Days passed into each other as they worked to finish off the requirements of the season.

Although they did not go out to the fields in winter, they still had no respite. Winter was time to "catch up" on miscellaneous household chores: maintenance of agricultural equipment, gathering of firewood, repair of homes, care of farm animals, straw work (making ropes, baskets, sandals, etc.).

Although they endured such heavy physical labor, farm meals

were truly meager. It is often said that farmers never lack food, but that is not true. In those days in Hokkaido crops were frequently destroyed by unseasonable and abrupt changes in weather, resulting in great numbers of deaths by starvation.

Government programs had to be devised to try to prevent deaths by starvation. One such program provided for "guidance counselors" to travel from village to village to teach villagers how to prepare and preserve potatoes. Potatoes are hardy enough to withstand unfavorable climatic changes. When I was a child, every family in our area had potatoes as its staple food. Potatoes that were peeled and diced, then blanched and dried, could be kept over long periods. When it was to be eaten, it was mixed in equal measure with crushed barley and then boiled. In the early days this was what we called our *gohan,* our "rice."

The crushed barley we put into our "rice" was different from what we see today. It needed a great deal of preparation. First, the barley was soaked in water overnight, then it had to be crushed with a hand-turned roller. At our home, crushing the barley was a daily chore for my older sister. Every day, as soon as she came home from school, she began processing the barley.

When I was about 12 or 13, we were able to have some actual rice added to what we had been calling our "rice." It was not a fully refined and polished rice, but still I thought real rice was delicious. As the mixture cooked, the heavier rice kernels would sink to the bottom of the pot, so the scorched portion on the bottom of the pot was almost all rice. We children competed to get that scorched part of the mixture.

To accompany the rice mixture, we almost always ate miso soup, pickled vegetables, garden vegetables, or wild greens. When wild greens were available, we had a variety of dishes and the dinner table was quite bountiful. But during winters, days often passed with only miso soup and pickled vegetables. At our home we pickled long, white radishes in large tubs. When winter came, these appeared on our dinner table daily. The green tops that were cut off the radishes when the pickles were made were dried and preserved to be added as a filler for our miso soup during the winter.

When I think of the food, I recall the lunch box that I took to school. It always contained the rice mixture and pickled radishes or pickled greens. On rare occasions when I found a small slice of salted salmon in my lunch box, I considered it a great feast.

The salted salmon was, of course, "home-made." When Otoe Village was first being settled, during the spawning season salmon still swam upstream, eagerly vying and spilling over each other, in the Ishigari River which flowed through our village. With long rods tipped with large nails, the settlers would snare the salmon and pull them up onto the riverbank. The salmon were cleaned and then packed and covered over with salt. Thus prepared, the salmon could literally be preserved for years.

The native Ainu people who lived in our village wore tonged slippers made from the cured skin of the salmon, but we settlers ate the salmon skin. We even thought that the salt used to preserve the salmon was delicious, as the flavor of the salmon came to permeate the salt. One of my mother's special dishes was pressed sushi made with salted salmon. The salmon sushi was a dish that could not be omitted during the New Year holidays and during the harvest festival in autumn; we children looked forward to those times when Mother made salmon sushi for us.

Salmon was our most prized dish and an important source of protein. Another source of animal protein was a tiny fish called iriko. Dried whole, we would use *iriko* to make the stock for our miso soup. Our hens laid a few eggs every day, but we ate them only when we were ill, because eggs were one of the few products that could be sold for cash. Vegetable protein was relatively plentiful. We soaked large green soy beans in water overnight and, having mashed them flat with a wooden mallet, put them in our miso soup. The mashing of soy beans was also one of my older sister's daily chores.

Winters in Hokkaido

Winters in Hokkaido are severe, especially in the central region where our village was located. I hated winters more than anything. Our home was no more than a thatched hut that readily let in the bitter cold. We had nothing like the highly developed protective winter clothing and heating devices available today. At night, hugging the cat, I would nestle my feet into the *kotatsu,* a crude charcoal warmer set into the floor, and slept with quilts covering my head. During blizzards at night, snow would blow in through gaps in the window frames and we would often awake with mounds of snow on our quilts.

The blizzards caused a number of frightening incidents. One exceptionally furious blizzard happened when I was in the first or second grade; it remains, even today, etched in my mind. We were in school, studying as usual, when suddenly the weather changed drastically and we found ourselves in the midst of a fierce snowstorm so thick we could not see an inch ahead of us. It was obvious the children could not return home alone under those conditions, so from every family in the community fathers and older brothers came to the schoolhouse to take the children home. For safety, the children were placed between adults and tied firmly with rope to form a single file. Snow buffeted them from all sides. The adults carried shovels to clear the snow, and they advanced along the roadway, crouching as if about to be toppled over.

I do not know how many times we were about to be blown over. If we had fallen and were trapped in the snow, the blizzard was so fierce that even an adult would have been instantly buried in the snow. That we returned home that day was a miracle.

The following day the blizzard passed as suddenly as it had arrived; it was a clear, calm day. But a sudden, tragic report darkened our hearts. We learned that the Kinoshita sisters, who lived in a place even more remote and difficult to reach than our home, had not returned since the previous day. Neighbors in the entire area were notified and everyone immediately turned out to search the roads and lanes. Eventually, in a low area along a roadside, two frozen forms were discovered, their bodies tightly clasped together. The sisters had probably crossed paths with their parents, who had gone out to bring them home. Struggling toward home, the girls must have been caught in the fierce winds and blown over into the snowbanks. Unable to crawl back up to the road, they had been buried in the snow.

When I heard the report of the two sisters, it was so pitiful that I let out a loud wail and tears tumbled down my face. Such fierce blizzards were commonplace. The sad fate of the Kinoshita sisters was not simply "something that happened to other people"; we knew it could happen to any of us at any time.

Most of my recollections of winters in Hokkaido are of hardships, but I also have some pleasant memories—some of them so much so as to be like dreams. Among these are the times I went out with Father to remote mountains to cut firewood during my winter holidays from school.

Back then, there were vast tracts of nationally owned forests in Hokkaido which we villagers called "government forests." These forests contained areas such as those used for windbreaks and areas owned directly by the Imperial Family, where the felling of trees was completely prohibited; but, in other areas, the cutting of trees by the general public was conditionally allowed.

Forest overseers were sent into the mountains at regular intervals to mark trees that had value only as firewood or to mark off trees needed to be removed in order to thin out overgrown areas. Each tree was marked with a number to be assigned for removal by the general public. Those who wished to remove them went to their village offices and, by lottery, were assigned the numbers of particular trees. They could then seek out those trees and fell them for firewood.

Cutting firewood was one of the most important winter tasks in our family, for it was our major source of fuel for heating. During school holidays, on days when the weather was fair, I would accompany Father into the mountains. I would follow behind him, carrying our lunch boxes. Even in mid-winter, to walk into snowy mountains on a fine day is an expansive experience that raises one's spirits.

The trees which had been selected out for purposes of forest management were large trees, greater around than an adult could embrace. To cut them down required great effort. Even that, however, I found exhilarating. The crashing sounds of the falling trees seemed to move the earth itself—echoing through the mountains in every direction, reverberating endlessly. Snow accumulated on the trees flew up, scattering over the area. Colored by the rays of the sun, the snow fell sparkling and dancing down in slow descent.

The downed trees were cut into lengths of about three feet, then were split and stacked. They were to be hauled down from the mountain with the coming of spring. Gathering firewood required such great physical labor that every day we came down from the mountains exhausted to the point of trembling.

Even in that state, however, before we returned home we would set up simple wire snares. Baited with pieces of cabbage, these snares noosed the necks of wild rabbits. The anticipation of checking the snares provided great pleasure as we climbed into the mountains the next morning. Overnight, we might even snare two or three rabbits.

Splitting the logs into firewood took several days. Stacked and buried under snow, the firewood was left in the mountains until early spring. It was to be brought down from the mountains when the snow began to give way. Cutting the firewood was bone-breaking work, but the task of bringing it down from the mountains was by no means a lesser one.

Removing the firewood from the mountains first required making a path over the deeply piled snow so that a horse-drawn sledge could pass over. On a warm, sunny day in early spring, with "snow shoes" attached to our straw boots, we would stamp down the snow which had begun to melt. By the next morning the stamped out path would have frozen into solid ice capable of holding up a horse-drawn sledge.

We would load the sledge with firewood in the early morning and descend the mountain before the ice-packed track melted. When the sun rose and loosened the snow, we simply had to stop work for that day. Many times the sledge swerved off of the trail and into places where the snow had not been packed and fell over sideways. On steep slopes we had to attach a chain to the sledge and, while braking it, carefully lower it down. This was extremely difficult work that required both strength and technique. Yet, when I look back on it now, those times seem encased in dream-like enchantment.

The Yoshimura Farm and Tenant Farmers

About 1919, a person named Nishimichi, who had been an office worker for a copper mine in either Ishikawa or Toyama prefectures, was left jobless when the mine closed down. I don't know what connection existed between our family and the Nishimichi family, but his family of four came over to Hokkaido to seek Father's help. Father began looking for a clerical type of job for Mr. Nishimichi in Fukagawa and nearby areas, but he was unable to find an opening. The Nishimichi family was forced to accept a role as tenant farmers in the Yoshimura farming complex in Otoe Village.

The Yoshimura farm was a large operation that occupied a broad stretch of fertile flatlands in Otoe Village. Almost all of its lands were in paddy fields of rice and many tenant farmers had already been contracted. There was one site, however, that no one had wanted to take. It was to that site that the Nishimichi family, with no farming experience at all, entered as tenant farmers. In the beginning it must have been extremely difficult but after a while they were somehow able to maintain a livelihood.

Misfortune came, however, in the third year after the Nishimichis had contracted for that site. Bad weather brought a disastrously poor harvest to the central areas of Hokkaido. Not even half of the rice plants matured to the bearing stage and farmers faced days when they did not know whether they could eat or not. Still, they had to deliver the annual quota of produce which they had contracted with their landlords. For the Nishimichi family, this simply meant that they faced death by starvation. Nishimichi and his family suddenly fled in the night, crossed over to the Asahikawa area of Hokkaido.

When I heard of this, I felt that those tenant farmers were truly pitiful. Yet, at the same time, I also felt that Nishimichi had acted in a cowardly manner. But, more than anything, I felt an inexpressible resentment toward the owner of that huge farming operation who had insisted on strictly enforcing the collection of his annual in-kind rental obligation. How in the world did those farm owners come to control almost all of the best lands of the village? With a child's questionings, I thought it extremely suspicious and could not accept the situation. We were at the lowest economic strata ourselves, so my feelings for those pathetic tenant farmers were aroused and I burned with resentment toward the great landowners who dwelled in houses that were like castles and lived as if they were great lords.

The Laborers Who Built the Irrigation System

In Hokkaido from the beginning to about the middle of the Taisho period (1912-1925), some massive irrigation projects were undertaken in many areas. Around 1916 or 1917, one such construction project took place in our village.

On my way with my father or older sister to make purchases in Fukagawa on the opposite side of the Ishikari River, I often stopped to watch the construction work. A large group of laborers dug the earth with shovels and pickaxes, filled large straw baskets called *mokko,* and carried them up an embankment more than 30 feet high.

Even in the bitterest cold of winter, with snow falling, the laborers were naked from the waist up. I thought that very strange and asked Father about it. He explained that the laborers were not allowed to wear clothes so they would work as hard as they could in order to survive the cold. I was stunned to hear of such heartless practices.

According to father, nearly all of the laborers were young Koreans who had been tricked into coming there from Tokyo. At the construction site they were placed in "detention huts." Essentially, they had been robbed of their freedom. Father explained, "They are told that all travel costs would be paid, that clothing, food and housing were provided without charge, and that they would be paid irresistibly high wages. But when they finally arrive in Hokkaido they are placed in 'detention huts.' Those who become ill and cannot work and those who are caught attempting to escape are beaten to death by the 'patrol stick' foremen and buried under that stone wall over there."

It was true. Spread out across the construction site big, tough-looking men carrying long staves watched over the laborers. Those overseers were called "patrol stick" foremen.

When I heard this, I was so shocked that the hair on my arms stirred and stood up as I came to realize what a fearful place the construction site was. I felt a deep sorrow for the laborers who worked there and could not help feeling a bond of fellowship with them. According to father, the work required such hard labor that no one would work there for those wages. Thus, even the government authorities and the police overlooked such forced "slave labor," in essence providing their "consent through silence."

After I heard about this, I could not put those pitiful laborers out of my mind for some time. Not long after that, on a summer's day, two laborers escaped from the nearby construction site and suddenly appeared at our home seeking help. With their palms placed together in prayerful request, they pleaded for help. Since their Japanese was poor, they were probably Koreans. Father silently took them over to the stable and hid them in the loft which had been filled with hay and dried rice straw. Alert for any changes, I went outside and, after making sure that there were no pursuers, took some rice balls over to them.

The two stayed hidden until dusk. When it became dark, they came out of the stable. Bowing their heads they said repeatedly, "Thank you, thank you!"

Before they left for an unknown fate, Father gave them some old shirts and pants and, handing over one or two yen in cash, warned them to be extremely careful. That night our family spoke only of those two men and hoped that they would not be caught.

Some time after this incident there was a ceremony to celebrate the completion of the irrigation facilities in the neighboring village of Ichiyan. Father took me with him to the ceremony. While we walked on the splendid stone embankment, Father said, "We shall never know how many Korean laborers are buried under these stones. This irrigation channel was built on such sacrifices."

More than 10 years later, when I left Hokkaido and got off the train at Ueno Station in Tokyo, the first thing that caught my eyes was a huge sign recruiting workers for Hokkaido. It was an advertisement that indeed would have made young men in search of jobs immediately leap at the opportunity. It seemed so attractive that, had I been in such a situation, even I would probably have gone to Hokkaido or any other destination. I thought about the construction site and the two Korean laborers who had escaped and come to our home. Tokyo, I thought to myself intently, must be a fearsome place.

My Older Brother, Older Sister and Younger Sister

I have many memories of my older brother from our time together in Hokkaido. Among these the most intense is the time he was seriously injured in an accident. I was still only 6 or 7, but that incident still remains vivid in my memory. My brother then was about 17 or 18. It was a cold winter day when he went out to work as a temporary laborer to do maintenance on electrical lines. A fellow worker who had been up on an electric pole accidentally dropped a spanner and, disastrously, it hit my brother on the head. The pure white snow became stained with blood and my brother lost consciousness. He was carried back to our house and when we saw him in that state the whole family was stunned.

There were no doctors nearby, so we could only wait helplessly for some change in his condition. Mother, in particular, feared that he would not recover. Weeping, she held him desperately throughout the night. For a time we truly felt the worst might happen. But, fortunately, it seems the injury did not affect any vital points and eventually my brother recovered fully. My brother never again showed any interest in taking such work.

Other than that incident, my memories of my older brother are mainly happy ones. By nature he seemed to be the type of person who was good at whatever he undertook and I learned many things from him. I do not know where he acquired them, but he had marvelous horticultural skills and knew how to create and maintain Japanese gardens; he often was out in the garden doing such work.

He was very good at grafting plants and had brought in and cared for many unusual trees and shrubs. Among other things, he also sharpened and evened out the teeth of the saw I used when cutting firewood. Once, when I was free at home during the summer break from school, he took me out to build a paddy field in an unused section of land. Even that task, which required special techniques to control water levels, was successful. Looking back at our youthful years, I also remember that once he got hold of a camera lens and painstakingly made a box camera. But even he, as talented as he was, could not make the dry-plate.

My older brother was not only naturally skillful, he was also a highly motivated and diligent student. Although he attended school only up to the fourth grade, he then used middle school lecture notes to study and eventually became a substitute teacher at the village elementary school. But he was not satisfied with that. He continued to study wholeheartedly and eventually passed the national examinations in each subject area one by one until he finally became a regular teacher. He then earned the qualifications for administration of secondary education and rose to the position of school principal.

Because he was such a conscientious, straightforward person, he gained the trust and confidence of both the authorities who controlled the schools as well as the local people. At a time when it was normal for teachers to be ordered to move from one school to another every two or three years, his case was a significant exception. From the time he became a substitute teacher until he died from illness, he was never ordered to transfer to another school.

Having lived such frugal and modest lives, all of us children thought it natural to work hard and contribute to the livelihood of the family. My older brother, of course, was no exception. From time to time he would buy a used Western-styled suit and joyously showed it off to all of us, but I don't recall his ever having a new suit made for himself. His monthly salary was almost always given directly to my father completely untouched.

My sister, seven years older than I, did the same. She worked hard and humbly endured our poverty. After she completed the second level of post-elementary studies she left school to accept a life of farm work in order to help our parents. In winter, she commuted to a Buddhist nunnery to learn how to sew Japanese clothing. In the severe winters of Otoe Village, to walk to sewing classes a mile away was not a casual task. Yet she persevered, became certified as a sewing teacher, and began teaching neighborhood girls in order to add to the family income. As with my older brother, my sister never indulged in extravagance.

Compared to her older brothers and sister, my younger sister was a degree more fortunate. Although I left Hokkaido when she was still very young and have very little direct knowledge of her experience, by the time she was born our family had come to enjoy some financial stability. Compared to earlier conditions, I do not believe she tasted the severe hardships undergone by her older three siblings.

School Years

I passed through the then-mandatory six years of elementary school and two years of post-elementary courses at the head of my class and graduated with honors. On the day of the graduation ceremony for the secondary courses, our neighbors all congratulated me, but I did not feel particularly happy about it. My father seemed to be more elated. Smiling broadly, he would say to every person he met, "Our Seiichi never once opened his textbooks at home. If he had prepared and reviewed carefully as other children do, I don't know how much he might have accomplished."

It was true. I never studied at home. Yet, my grades were good and I had always been at the head of the class. The year I graduated, I became what is now known as class president. Every morning when we paid respect to the emperor and recited our obligations, I stood with the teachers before the entire school to call out the required orders of procedure.

I hated to miss school. Walking the nearly two miles to and from school in winter was a major effort. Yet, even under those conditions, I never missed a day. The only exception occured in the second grade, when I missed a week because of the measles. Every year I received the award for endeavor.

In those days, everyone wore wooden clogs in summer and straw boots in winter. The first time I had rubber boots bought for me was when I was in the fifth or sixth grade. It was about that time that we used homemade skis to commute to school in winter.

It had been decided that after I graduated from the post-elementary courses I would help the family by working on our farm. I had hoped to go on to higher schooling, but our family finances would not allow it. The year I graduated my teacher made a special visit to our home in order to persuade Father to allow me to advance to higher education. But even at that, it was not to be. When I learned that several classmates who had poorer grades than I were planning to go on to higher school I felt bitter, resentful and filled with frustration.

I grew distant and would spend days without saying a word. I was also just at the usual age of rebelliousness. Perhaps my parents felt sorry about my situation, for they never scolded me for such behavior. At this time it was always my older brother's wife who was kind and consoling. From her point of view, her husband, as the oldest son, should have taken the responsibility of carrying on the farm. Instead, he had become a school teacher and turned over the role of successor to me. She felt badly about that. I worked for about a year on the farm, but I could not give up the idea of higher schooling and every day was filled with silent discontent.

Running Away to Sapporo

One day I could bear my situation no longer and impulsively decided to run off to Sapporo. Without hesitation, I left home and walked about a mile to the Fukagawa Station to take a train to Sapporo. Following up on an advertisement I had seen in a newspaper, I went to apply for a job at the Hasegawa Company, a lacquer and chinaware wholesale company located across from Sapporo Station.

I had chosen the company because in their advertisement there was a line that read, "We allow attendance of night school."

My main goal was to work at the company and continue my studies at night school—nothing else crossed my mind. I fervently appealed to the owner of the shop by telling him of my long-held hopes of going to night school. Fortunately, the owner took a liking to me and said, "All right, I'll hire you." When I heard that, my heart jumped with joy. I bowed my head repeatedly and thanked him by saying, "*Arigato-gozaimasu*. Please accept my efforts and guide my efforts."

But it happened that the shop owner's final question was to undo me. "You did come here with the permission of your parents, I assume?" I was suddenly brought to earth. If I had answered, "Yes, they agree," it would have been passed over; but I was a country-bred youth of 15 and lies did not come readily to my lips. I confessed, "I thought that even if I spoke with them they would never allow it, so I came without telling them."

That was what upended the situation. The owner earnestly began to lecture me about my actions and the affair ended with my returning to Fukagawa on the next train. I was so disappointed and discouraged that I felt as if my heart had been torn open.

On the train back I considered what the owner of the shop had just told me. According to him, many young people came to the large cities with great aspirations but because there were so many temptations in the city most fell into evil ways and ruined their precious opportunities in life. "Even in our shop," he said, "a number of young people have fallen in with no-good companions and abandoned their dreams. To struggle for an education is quite literally that: to undertake an extraordinary struggle. It is not as easy as you seem to think. If you don't have resolve and perseverance, it will not come about." I suddenly became fearful of the city and ashamed of my own impetuous behavior.

It was near dawn the next day when I reached home. Without saying a word, I kept my outward composure and pretended that everything was normal. My parents, too, did not badger me with questions. As parents they must have worried that their son just out of the post-secondary courses had suddenly disappeared but, on the other hand, they must have been relieved that I returned right away. At any rate, it was left at that and they did not scold me at all. Even so, I again, as earlier, continued to pass each day with a sense of unfulfillment.

Employment at the Butter Processing Plant

After that incident, Father must have felt the need to reconsider his plan to make me the successor to our farm. My getting employment at the dairy plant in Otoe was surely a result of my father's change of heart. He sought out the help of the village head, Fukazawa Kichihei, and having made a special effort found a position for me at the butter processing plant operated by the village dairy "co-op." Father must have finally concluded that he could not chain me only to farm work. Perhaps if I were employed it would keep me there with them, rather than having me go out to the city.

In any event, four or five months after my attempt at "running away," I began working at the butter processing plant. The plant had been built in Otoe through the efforts of Mr. Fukazawa and was the first butter processing plant in Japan. Its head technician was a person named Shibazaki Matabei, who had been sent out by the Hokkaido prefectural offices. I was to be his assistant.

My starting salary was 30 yen per month, an extremely high amount in those days. Even the head technician received only 50 yen per month, so it was an excessively high salary for a youth of only 15 or 16. I was much envied by everyone, although I handed over my salary untouched to my father. I did so with no feelings of resistance at all.

When I worked at the plant, butter was produced on a cycle that began at about midnight and ended in the late morning hours. At about six in the morning we received the milk carried over by women from the neighboring areas and, having evaluated the cream content, began extracting the cream with a separating device. The skimmed milk that remained after the cream was extracted was then returned to those who had brought the milk. That was used for family consumption, given to calves, or used to make cheese.

My job usually ended in the morning and my afternoons were free. I did not dislike the job, but I still was not satisfied. At about this time I began reading accounts of successful self-made men in Japan and America. The more I read such books, the more my desire for education was aroused and I could not stand the disappointment of remaining in the obscurity of the countryside.

Like the characters in those "Horatio Alger" stories, I wanted to pursue my studies no matter what hardships I faced. But that dream seemed impossible to fulfill. With no other alternatives, I attempted to satisfy my ever growing desire for education with the study groups and lecture series sponsored by the village Youth Organization.

Opportunities Offered by the Youth Organization

When I had completed the second year of the post-elementary curriculum, I joined the Youth Organization of Otoe Village, as was customary at that time. Almost all the young men of the village belonged to it, so it flourished with activity. Especially in winter, when farming requirements noticeably lessened, young men gathered to expend their youthful energy in study groups and sports. This was especially true in our mountain village, where there were no real sources of amusement. The young people of that time were also exceedingly straightforward and earnest in their participation. They joined the Japan National Youth Improvement Organization and always proudly wore the triangularly shaped emblem of membership on their chests.

Every year, after entering the relatively slow agricultural period between harvesting and planting, the Youth Organization sponsored courses they called "night classes." The wide variety of subjects included civics, Japanese language, mathematics, animal husbandry, agricultural techniques, maintenance of farm equipment, and more. The classes were mostly taught by local teachers or those who had gone to school elsewhere and had returned to the village. At times, however, well-known personages from Tokyo were invited to present lectures on various subjects.

The Youth Organization also organized sports classes. For judo and kendo we mainly had local middle school teachers come over to instruct us. Once or twice a year we invited physical education teachers from Asahikawa Normal School and received instruction from them in the major types of sports approved for the Olympic Games. As a result we trained, if only in form, in representative areas such as one-to-one "combat sports," different types of ball games, track and field, gymnastics, etc.

Later, after I emigrated to Peru and became a teacher in an elementary school, the different sports I had learned and practiced during that period in Hokkaido brought much pleasure to the children there. I then came to realize that any effort to acquire skills and knowledge is never a loss or a "waste of time."

I greatly enjoyed the night school classes and lectures sponsored by the Youth Organization and learned much from them. Yet, this did not satisfy my burning desire for education—rather, the effect was like pouring oil on an already roaring flame. It is only human nature, I feel, that when one hears of something new one wants to know more about it. More and more, I wanted to study by commuting to night school, but it did not seem that I would be able to do so. Agitated by a desire that seemed never to be satisfied, I spent my days moody and discontent.

Yet, "happenstance" is one of the inexplicable factors of life. One may seek out something with all one's effort and never attain it; but, there are other times when one does not seek out something and yet it comes of itself. For me, too, that finally was about to happen.

Father Iwamatsu, age 50.

The author, Seiichi, at age 20.

Chapter Two. Pursuing a Dream of Success Overseas

Days of Struggle for an Education in Tokyo

I had been working at the butter processing plant for a while when my older sister, Misao, who had gone to Tokyo as a bride, did not recover well after giving birth to her first child. She returned home to Otoe to convalesce and be cared for by our family.

She had been away from our home for some time. It seemed that life in Tokyo was, for her, overwhelming. Perhaps that was to be expected. Raised in a remote country area of Hokkaido, she had gone to Tokyo, where even more sophisticated people can become bewildered.

To make matters worse, she had entered a complex household, which included her husband's father and younger sister. Her husband, Sotojiro Sakaguchi, owned a lumber supply business in the Honjo district of Tokyo, so she also had to oversee the needs of their live-in employees and receive customers as well.

My sister's emotional burdens were worsened because she did not have a close friend or relative with whom she could share her feelings, and she felt she could not reveal her problems to her husband, who was always extremely busy. With concerns layered on other concerns she finally reached a state close to a nervous breakdown. When she came home to us she was completely exhausted both physically and mentally.

She stayed at home for five or six months. Fortunately, she recovered and eventually the time came for her to return to Tokyo. It seems, however, that my parents were still concerned about sending their delicately constituted daughter back to Tokyo alone. Since I remained frustrated with my circumstances in Otoe, they decided that I should accompany Misao to Tokyo and stay with her to provide emotional support. They felt if she had her brother with her she would be better able to face her many responsibilities.

Of course I had no objections to the plan. In all honesty, it was less out of concern for my sister and more for my own future that I jumped at the opportunity and immediately agreed to their proposal. Perhaps I'd be able to commute to night school, I thought. I immediately quit my job at the butter processing plant and accompanied my sister to Tokyo.

When we reached Tokyo, I was taken to the site in Honjo that served as both my brother-in-law's home and place of business. It was decided that I would live-in and work for them during the interim.

In the beginning I was not much help in watching over my sister. Rather, it took everything I had to simply handle my own affairs. For someone such as I, who had been raised deep in the mountains of Hokkaido, such a large metropolis as Tokyo was a wonder beyond wonders. Everything was new. I was dazzled and lost my bearings, like a person tossed out into a great sea who had not yet learned to swim.

Along with the other live-in employees I got up early in the morning and worked all day, with almost no time to catch a breath. My duties ranged from simply sweeping up the storefront and arranging merchandise in the warehouse, to the exhausting work of stacking up lumber and delivering it. In those days, the owners of lumberyards in Fukagawa were called *taisho,* or "general," and employees were addressed with the honorific "-don" added as a suffix to part of their personal names. My name is Seiichi so I was called "Sei-don" by everyone.

My body had been tempered by hard labor in Hokkaido, so pulling handcarts stacked with heavy lumber all day long was not a great hardship. Not being able to go to night school, however, was difficult to endure. At that time, of course, no businesses would allow such a "selfish extravagance" to apprenticing young "greenhorns" such as I.

It was a time when, even if one worked from early morning to late at night, the most one could expect was to be adequately fed. When one's labor was not even compensated with what we think of today as "wages," to be allowed to go to night school would be a highly unusual consideration.

I wanted more than anything to attend night school, but when I thought of what that would mean to my sister, who seemed so intimidated by her circumstances, I could not bring myself to even mention it. I felt that if I showed even a trace of such feelings my sister would worry about how her husband, her father-in-law and her sister-in-law might react and work herself into a near breakdown again. To avoid placing that burden on my sister, I simply continued working every day with all my effort. I was unhappy, but there seemed to be no alternative.

Fulfilling a Dream, I Enter Night School

My brother-in-law became aware of my desire to go to night school. But, probably wanting to observe my behavior before allowing it, he did not say anything about it for quite some time. He first mentioned it one day six or seven months after I had arrived in Tokyo. Unexpectedly, he summoned me and said, "Sei-don, I think it's all right for you to begin preparing for night school." Since I had thought that night school would be impossible for a while, my joy at hearing this was beyond description—a great vista of opportunity suddenly opened out before me.

It was something I had looked forward to for such a long time, but when I actually received permission to do so I had no idea where to start. I did not know what types of schools existed nor where they were located, not to speak of necessary qualifications for admission or tuition costs. My brother-in-law and sister were of no help in those matters. Having no one to rely on, I began looking for a school in my own fumbling manner.

By chance, about a 30-minute walk from my brother-in-law's home, I was lucky to find a large, impressive-looking school. On the main gate to the school was a sign that read "Nippon University Preparatory School." Even at night many students could be seen entering and leaving. "There must be night classes here," I thought, and immediately went in for information. I found they offered exactly what I was looking for—night courses in engineering.

I quickly submitted an application and was soon called in for an interview. After asking many questions about my background, I was allowed to enter at the second year level without an examination. A school official said I should attend classes for a while, and if I found them too easy I could be advanced to the third year level. "What an accommodating school," I thought.

The dream I had held for so many years was becoming a reality and I thought my heart would burst with hope and aspiration. Going to school at night was not a hardship; I studied earnestly everyday.

Slowly, by increments, I came to know more about the school's circumstances, however, and with that my excitement quickly cooled. When I had enrolled I was told that I could advance from that school to Nippon University's College of Engineering, but I later discovered that even if I graduated from my present school I would not qualify to advance to another school. When I learned I would not be qualified to enter even a private university, not to mention a national university, my hopes shriveled in disappointment.

My dream was to study at a university and become a great architect. I later learned, moreover, that even if I graduated from my school I would not be qualified to take the examinations for certification as an architect. In order to be certified as an architect one had to pass a national examination. That examination was so difficult that only a few passed it. Having learned that the school in which I had enrolled did not have the accreditation that would allow its graduates to advance to higher schools or to be certified as architects, I quickly became very disillusioned.

I later learned that nearly all night schools were not accredited. In fact, even night school students attending technical institutes established by the government were not recognized as being qualified for certification as architects. Although students in general were held in great respect during this period, night school students were considered to be exceptions and were looked down upon as not being "real students." I was completely discouraged.

Then one day I learned by chance that there were only two evening technical schools in the entire country that were allowed to grant degrees and certifications equivalent to those of first-rate, government-established technical institutes. Graduates from those two schools qualified to advance to higher institutions or to take the examination for architects. I began searching desperately for those schools.

Fortunately, one of them was located at Honjo-Yokoami, not far from where I lived. It was called Hozen Technical School, a privately run technical school established by the Yasuda Hozen Company. It was at the time an exceptional school with a faculty of outstanding professors. I immediately took its entrance exam for the second year level, passed, and transferred to the school in April 1927.

Studying at Hozen Technical School

The first thing I noticed after transferring to Hozen Tech was the number of older persons enrolled. Among them were a number of elegant gentlemen with flourishing mustaches. I found myself studying side by side with persons such as the superintendent of the Umayabashi Branch of the Reconstruction Agency, which had been established by the national government after the great Kanto Earthquake of 1923, and the director of a project undertaken by a major architectural firm.

Approximately half of the students were married and responsible for growing families. Employed full time, they were attending school in order to acquire formal degrees. The other students were young people who commuted from their parents' homes. Although they attended night school, most of them obviously came from middle-class backgrounds—a poor student such as I was an obvious exception.

There were many well-recognized professors on the faculty, including a number who held doctorates in the sciences and engineering. Some held assistant professor positions at Tokyo Imperial University while concurrently teaching at our school. Among the teachers of English was a person who held a master's degree from Columbia University. It was, after all, a time of worldwide economic depression, when even graduates of the Imperial Universities could not find employment, and the teachers must have been attracted by the high salaries subsidized by the Yasuda Hozen Company. The Depression, which caused many hardships for me, also blessed me with excellent teachers. In that sense, it had a "silver lining" that brought much happiness for me.

When I entered Hozen Tech, military drills for students were emphasized in all regular day schools. Unsettling developments were occurring in China and no regular school could avoid such drills. Night schools were exempt from that requirement, but ours was the only one that set apart time for such drills. During the summer holidays we were called out to Susono, in the foothills of Mt. Fuji, to participate in two-week long joint exercises with the infantry of the Imperial Guards. We were instructed by five or six lieutenants from the reserves, under the command of a major in active service. I managed to get good evaluations for drill performances and when we went out for field maneuvers I was always made a platoon leader. At such times a long sword swung from my hip.

At Hozen Tech the courses I enjoyed most were "Legal Systems" and economics. "Legal Systems" was similar to what might presently be called "introduction to law," and was part of the core curriculum for the students. In that class, I actively responded to problems posed by the teacher and, prodded by further questions that drew us deeper into those problems, I often debated with the teacher. He seemed pleased with this and teased me by saying, "You're more suited to be a lawyer than an architect." He made me aware of my tendency to pursue matters to their logical end, and I resolved thereafter not to carry that tendency to excess.

As for the specialized classes, I felt least comfortable with my ability in mathematics. Because of its importance, during the summer holidays I enrolled in a "cram school" in the Kanda area of Tokyo and studied with all the effort I could muster. I also went to a specialized school for courses in calculus and engineering.

Classes at Hozen Tech started 30 minutes earlier than other night schools, so I was always pressed to rush through my work in the late afternoons. I was often late because of my work and many times I would have to grab whatever I could find for meals. At such times, I would buy a roasted sweet potato for 5 sen from a street vendor and eat it while running to school.

My sister seemed to be extremely concerned about my leaving for school while in the midst of a task and did not want further to upset my brother-in-law. So, whenever I was forced to leave without finishing a job, she would not set aside supper for me to eat when I returned from school. I was not particularly upset about that. Rather, when I considered my timid sister's situation, her position seemed to be so pitiful that I too shrank with concern.

The demands of heavy physical labor during the day, combined with my studies at night, resulted in insufficient sleep. Furthermore, because my meals were taken irregularly, I was often weak with exhaustion and fell into ill health. Once during drafting class I collapsed with anemia and had to be carried to the infirmary. That grew into a frequent occurrence. Never had I ever forced my body more than during this period, and it is a miracle that I did not come down with a major illness.

In 1929, the worldwide financial panic wreaked its havoc everywhere. My brother-in-law's business could not survive those conditions and finally reached a state of bankruptcy. My brother-in-law was the type of person who fully immersed himself in his work. There was no more honest person, but there was a side to him that seemed too naive for the world of business. He trusted everyone and even allowed people he didn't know very well to buy lumber on credit. He was driven into bankruptcy mainly because of accounts he could not collect on. Even I, who at that time knew nothing about business, sensed that my brother-in-law was too good natured. But of course I was in no position to give advice.

After my brother-in-law went bankrupt, I was left adrift with no one to rely on. Fortunately, I was hired by the Kihei Company, a lumber wholesaling firm located in the Fukagawa area of Tokyo. My main job was to unload imported American lumber brought to the docks on small sampan boats. In those days the standard import material from the United States were large pieces of lumber 20 inches wide, four inches thick and 20 feet long. It was my job to carry the lumber from the boats to a site about 100 feet away, where they were stacked high.

The work went far beyond the demands of normal heavy labor. I was confident about my physical strength, but the work was even more than I could take. Unloading raw lumber, filled with moisture, was such tough work that even my bones flared with pain. Soon after I started to work there I injured my chest. According to the doctor I consulted, I had contracted pleurisy. I was ordered to rest, so, for a while, I refrained from work and continued to see the doctor.

I did not even have the means for daily survival, so I could not expect to be able to pay for continued medical treatment. I had to stop seeing the doctor, even if it resulted in death. I did so partly out of desperation and frustration, but the fact was I had no alternative if I expected to eat .

I worked at whatever I could find in order to meet living expenses. I could no longer do heavy physical labor, but I took anything that did not overtax my body. There were times when I delivered newspapers and collected empty bottles to meet my needs. Fortunately, the illness began to heal and soon I was completely recovered.

Around this time I moved from Fukagawa to the Kanda area of Tokyo and rented a three mat (6' x 9') room on the second floor of a tailor shop. I was now completely on my own. In that narrow room I slept and awoke, prepared meals, and devoted myself to studying. Undiscouraged by my brother-in-law's bankruptcy or by my illness, I continued to attend school. No matter what happened, I could not abandon my dream of becoming a great architect.

An "Apprentice Architect"

After moving to Kanda, I continued to attend school and began working as an "apprentice architect." I did work for construction firms to help them apply for and receive building permits. I had never done such work before, but I had earlier had a number of opportunities to design homes, so the work was not hard.

I had put together my first full-scale architectural plan in 1927, the year I transferred from Nippon University's Preparatory School to Hozen Technical School. In the autumn of that year, with his business still flourishing because of the construction boom following the great earthquake of 1923, my brother-in-law had decided to build a new establishment in Honjo that would combine his home and the business facilities.

He left the design of the building entirely to me. The building was a two-story structure that included his business offices and lumber warehouse, his residence, and six rooms for rental. It was an unusually large structure for those times, which made complying with building codes and other regulations a major task. But my plans were approved, and construction was completed without incident.

The newly completed building for the Sakaguchi Company was in the traditional "Sukiya" style and was constructed entirely with *hinoki* (Japanese cypress), a highly prized wood. It was a splendid, eye-catching building that stood out in the Honjo area. I was delighted with this achievement and took great pride in it.

That project gave me the confidence to take on other projects. The following year, when I was asked to design a complex of three, three-story, Japanese-style "tenement flats," I accepted without hesitation. This project was likewise completed quickly and without problems.

Because of such experiences, soon after entering Hozen Technical School I sought opportunities to visit construction sites. In those days, students had to only show their identification cards issued by their school to be allowed to enter and freely observe almost any construction site. The year before I graduated from Hozen Tech, I observed various types of construction. I not only visited construction sites for small-scale wooden buildings, but also large ferro-concrete structures.

The latter half of the 1920s was a time when multi-storied, ferro-concrete buildings began to be built all over Tokyo. Whenever I had any free time, friends and I would visit construction sites. In particular, we went many times to the site of the Imperial Diet Building. We observed the details of its construction from the basement to its rooftops. Perched at the highest points of its rooftop, we often felt that our lives were in danger. At about that time, too, the Musashino Hall in the Shinjuku area was being built, and we were allowed to observe the construction in progress.

Because of such experiences, from about the time I moved to Kanda I was confident I could handle any small-scale wooden residences. I began taking work from construction firms referred to me by the school. I prepared whatever drawings and plans were needed to acquire building permits.

During this period, many construction firms, including some very big ones, were headed by builders who lacked architectural certification. Thus, when they were selected for a project, they came to the school to request help with everything from design work to permit application. The school would then pass on such jobs to poor students such as I.

Fortunately, my grades were good and school officials came to trust my work. Because I made no mistakes in the first few jobs I took, after a while all the jobs brought to the school were given to me. The result was that I had more than enough work. At times, I had to rush about frantically to keep up with everything. But we were in the midst of the Great Depression, and fees remained low. My life did not get any easier.

In those days, fees for such jobs were usually paid at the end of the month or several weeks after the work was done. Few contractors, if any, paid immediately. Even so, it was good that they paid at all, for often I was not able to collect the fees. I disliked having to go out to demand my fees and did not aggressively do so. There were many instances in which I simply let non-payment of fees pass.

It was during this time that Mr. Sasaki came to my aid. I don't recall exactly how I met Mr. Sasaki, but I remember that he often came over to my little room and we would talk about a wide variety of subjects until late in the evening. Once I mentioned a fee that I was not able to collect, and he immediately said, "For them to have a struggling student do their work and then not make payment is not right. I'll get it for you." He rushed out and collected the fee for me. After that incident, he often went to collect my fees and, because of his efforts, my situation greatly improved.

At that time, Sasaki must have been about 30. He never spoke to me about it, but I suspected that he was a communist engaged in some sort of underground activity. He truly was a kind person. He seemed to sympathize with my struggle to acquire an education and helped me in many ways. Whenever he came to visit he always brought roasted sweet potatoes or large rice-crackers. When he left he would always leave an encouraging word, saying, "Don't be discouraged! Keep working hard!" Even to this day, I cannot forget Mr. Sasaki.

Dreams of Going Overseas

After some time in Tokyo, I started dreaming of going abroad. I considered my prospects—even if I did become an outstanding architect, Japan did not hold great promise for my future. Without a single hopeful path before me, I could not endure the wretchedness of having to grope about in the darkness and uncertainty of those times in Japan. Besides, I was physically and mentally exhausted by my hardships, to which I saw no end. If escape from my misery was impossible in Japan, should I not look elsewhere? Even while not fully conscious of it, I began to pursue a dream of escaping from Japan.

Even without proper medical treatment I had recovered from my severe case of pleurisy. That had given me absolute confidence in my physical strength and stamina. From childhood my body had been tempered again and again in the bitter cold of Hokkaido. I did not even dream that I could be felled by some careless act. With that kind of physical strength, I thought, a man should be able to make a living overseas or anywhere else.

A poem written by the Buddhist priest Gasho remained etched in my mind: "To bury one's bones must one look only to a cemetery? Wherever one goes there are green hills."

In reality, however, my dreams were not so easily fulfilled. From the time I was about 17, I had read whatever books and articles I could find about emigrants who had built successful careers abroad. I had also heard various accounts directly from people who knew of such matters. Yet, I knew of no good leads to help me actualize my dream.

My first choice was really to go to America. The books I had read about America described a great, vast country based on the principles of liberty and equality, with equal opportunity for everyone. But from some years earlier, the United States had completely prohibited immigration from Japan, so to go to America was an impossible dream.

I believed, however, that a person could only engage one's opportunities if one actively went out to meet them. I searched everywhere—in Tokyo and outlying areas I went from building to building to inquire at companies that had overseas offices, but found nothing. In the worst case I was physically thrown out.

In the midst of the Depression, such opportunities seemed out of the question. Moreover, my background in architecture seemed completely useless in finding a position in the area of business and commerce.

One of the few possibilities for emigration was as an agricultural worker to the rubber plantations of Southeast Asia or the coffee and cotton plantations of South America. But my first-hand experience in the hardships of farming in Hokkaido ran so deep that I could not bring myself to make such a choice. Rather than experience such hardships again in the far reaches of some unknown country, I thought it was still better to remain with my dissatisfactions in Tokyo.

Another possibility was to emigrate to the Chinese mainland. At that time anyone could readily get a job working for the Southern Manchuria Railroad Company. Actually, several of my classmates had been hired and had left Japan. For some reason, however, I did not feel like going to China. While China was a foreign country, it somehow seemed to me to be an extension of Japan and I could not work up any enthusiasm about going there. It may sound odd, but I felt that if I were to go to a foreign country at all, it should be "what a foreign country should be."

A Faint Ray of Hope

With no one to consult, I continued on alone in my fruitless search. One day it occurred to me that I should raise my sights higher and discuss my hopes with my school's dean of academic affairs. Without delay I asked to meet with the dean, Prof. Jitsutaro Umehara. The professor kindly welcomed me in and intently listened to what I had to say. He replied, "What you say is quite true. In our present condition, Japan's future appears dark indeed. I also have some interest in this area, so let me see what I can find out about it." His words raised my spirits. I finally felt a faint ray of hope in the darkness.

Of course it was not as though everything was solved by my meeting with the dean. I continued to consider strategies for going overseas and, whenever I had some time, pursued every possible lead I could. My situation eventually came to the attention of Prof. Torakichi Hamano, emeritus director of the Tokyo Colonial Trade Language School.

I believe the language school was also sponsored by the Yasuda Hozen Company, and Professor Hamano had probably heard about me from Professor Umehara. Professor Hamano, who was over 80 years old, was the founder of the language school and for many years had provided practical foreign language training to middle school graduates.

I received a message one day that Professor Hamano wanted to meet me, so I immediately inquired about the professor's schedule and arranged to see him. When I met him, I found him extremely lively and high spirited. He immediately understood what I told him and asked many detailed questions. I was deeply moved by his understanding of my situation. I was especially happy about his strong words of encouragement: "Put all your efforts toward the realization of your goals. Without a doubt, good results will come about," he said. From within my body, an indescribable will to fight on seemed to surge forth, and I felt success abroad was no longer just a dream.

Soon, news of my desire to go overseas reached the ears of the president of Hozen Tech, Prof. Kakichi Tokuno. I was summoned to meet him. Professor Tokuno had previously been in charge of internal affairs for the Directorate General of Taiwan. He likewise gave me strong words of encouragement. When he said, "The school will not hold back its cooperation, so make a sincere and honest effort toward your goals," I was so grateful and happy that tears welled up in my eyes.

I had not even imagined when I consulted the dean in desperation that it would have produced such broad repercussions. It was truly fortunate that I had gone to Professor Umehara for advice. Everything that happened after that was because of his efforts. Both directly and indirectly he had exerted himself to help me. That I later succeeded in leaving Japan is because he, almost as a parent, had lent me his strength.

About this time, it happened that one of my classmates, Gun'ichi Uchimura, expressed his desire to go abroad and joined me in my efforts. He lived with his mother and older sister and, while working at a government office, attended Hozen Technical School.

I am not sure when and why he came to consider the possibility of a life overseas. Unlike me, Uchimura came from a samurai background and held a respectable and secure government position. Financially, he was much better off than I. But in the process of working with me he became very excited over the idea of leaving Japan. He likewise began to work toward his dream of building a successful life overseas for himself.

It is important to note that Gun'ichi was the eldest son of the Uchimura family. By custom, he should have carried the heavy burden of maintaining the continuity of the family line. Yet, his family agreed to his plans of going abroad and made no effort at all to stop him. For his mother it was no doubt a decision that required much courage and understanding.

Now my situation had completely changed. I was no longer alone. I had a good friend and had gained the support of many sympathetic persons who understood me well. I was very grateful and happy. My dream of success abroad was now much closer. The faint ray of hope that I had seen earlier now began to shine like a bright star of great possibilities and high expectations.

Looking to Peru

By this time, my plans to leave Japan began to grow more concrete. I determined that my destination would be Peru in South America. I studied the conditions of that country and gathered information to prepare for my departure from Japan.

I chose Peru for a number of reasons. Aside from the United

States, Peru had the next largest number of Japanese immigrants who had found success. Most of the Japanese who had crossed over to Peru had done so as agricultural workers, but later moved to urban areas to build successful commercial enterprises. In that sense, at that time the Peruvian Japanese community was even more advanced than Japanese immigrants in North America, who were still based mainly in agricultural activities. With my experiences in Hokkaido, I had no intention of going overseas to become involved in farm work. Peru seemed to be the ideal destination.

I was also lured to Peru by the "success story" of Shintaro Tominaga, an outstanding leader amongst the Japanese immigrants in Peru. Mr. Tominaga first gained success in construction activities and later expanded his interests to timber and lumbering. At that time, he was reported to be managing a large enterprise with over 200 employees. When I heard this, I felt that my architectural skills might be put to use in Peru, and my heart jumped with hope.

Among Mr. Tominaga's many achievements, the most impressive was his building of Peru's Presidential Palace in the early 1920s. I learned that the time allowed for the project was so short that even companies backed with large amounts of capital from England and the United States had hesitated to undertake it. Finally, Tominaga's company won the contract. When they heard the news, the Japanese in Peru spontaneously came forth to offer their assistance and approached the construction as a cohesive group. It happened that there were many carpenters, masons and others experienced in construction who had immigrated to Peru. The project was completed without incident by its deadline. Mr. Tominaga received a letter of commendation from the President and the project greatly enhanced the reputation of the Japanese in Peru.

This "success story" had been transmitted back to Japan. When I heard the story, I wanted very much to engage in such work overseas. Fortunately, through my connections with the Tokyo Colonial Trade Language School, I received a letter of introduction to Mr. Tominaga. My dreams grew more expansive, and I felt that if conditions allowed, it might be possible to work in my chosen field.

Just at this time, I received information about Tatsumi Yamada, who was to be sent by the Foreign Ministry to examine the condition of the Japanese in Central and South America. Before he left Japan in January 1930, Mr. Yamada had signed a short term contract with the language school to report back to them about the conditions in those countries as his trip progressed. I immediately went to the school to ask for a letter of introduction to Mr. Yamada. I hoped to be able to learn of conditions there in case I met him in Peru.

A Barely Legal Passport

The biggest obstacle to my plan was obtaining a passport. The government of Peru had already prohibited free immigration and the Japanese government had stopped issuing passports to that country. Only family members and employees of Japanese companies in Peru were still allowed entry. But with absolutely no ties to Peru, I did not meet either condition. I searched everywhere to find a loophole, but gaining a passport seemed impossible.

Again, it was Professor Umehara who made the impossible become possible. The professor made many trips to the Bureau of Public Safety, but to no avail. He then sought help from other sources and eventually obtained a passport for me under the pretext that I had been called over for employment by Mosaburo Ota, the Lima Branch manager of the (Japan) Overseas Development Corporation.

According to Professor Umehara, he had heard of Mr. Ota from Kiichi Oshima, then principal of the Hokkaido Settlers' School. Mr. Oshima had advised him, "Both Ota and Higashide are from Hokkaido, so Ota will probably allow it." On that basis, the professor prepared documents stating that I had been summoned by Mr. Ota and applied for the passport.

In form the application was not entirely illegal, but in content they were close to forgeries. When I think of it now, I shudder at the extreme recklessness of what was done. But, in any event, the passport was granted. Later, I met Mr. Ota in Peru and explained in detail what had transpired and offered him my fullest apologies. So it was that I received his permission "to be summoned for employment in Peru" after the fact.

Shortly after my passport was granted, an account of Uchimura's and my plans to go overseas appeared in a lengthy article in the *Jiji Shinpo,* a large Tokyo-based newspaper. Within a few days we received a huge stack of letters from people all over the country encouraging us to pursue our plans. Since the date of departure loomed before us and we were busy with preparations, I greatly regretted we could not answer each of those letters. Those warm words of encouragement from all over the country moved me deeply.

Now that I had finally arrived at this stage, I was filled with emotion and a great confidence surged forth from within me. The dream of escaping from Japan, which had once seemed so hopeless, was now becoming reality.

The newspaper item in the *Jiji Shinpo* had been written by Shuzo Ishida, a reporter assigned to the Bureau of Public Safety. Ishida was a graduate of Tokyo Colonial Trade Language School, a sister school of Hozen Technical School. He had found Professor Umehara's frequent appearances at the bureau very odd and had inquired about it. Ishida was moved by our story and waited for us to be granted our passports. Even before we left Japan, the article was sent to Peru and was reprinted by a local Japanese language newspaper. By the time we reached Lima it seemed all the Japanese in Peru knew about us.

Spanish Lessons at the Ninth Hour

It was toward the end of 1929 that I received my passport. I had been making detailed preparations for leaving after graduation from Hozen Technical School in March of the following year. As the date of departure gradually approached, however, I became acutely concerned with the problem of language. Although I had decided on Peru as my destination for some time, my work, commuting to night school, and being pressed with preparations for departure had left me no time to study Spanish. I was very anxious about entering a Spanish-speaking country without even knowing the rudiments of conversational Spanish, but I simply had no leeway to study the language at all.

I finally brought my concerns to Professor Umehara. Expecting to be turned down, I asked permission to attend a Spanish language course from January of the following year. The three months of the last trimester at our school were extremely important, for that was when we had to complete our "graduate designs." Fortunately, my grades had been good and I had never fallen below fourth in my class ranking. The school made a special exemption freeing me of the graduation requirement so I could attend Spanish language courses.

I was elated with this opportunity, yet I regretted having to abandon my "graduate design" in mid-stream. I had started to design a ferro-concrete museum building that outwardly resembled the Imperial Diet building. I had completed only its ground plan and part of its exterior design before I was forced to abandon the project.

From January 1930, I began exclusively to attend a language school to study Spanish. In fact, I became so involved with the language course work that I did not even attend the graduation ceremonies at Hozen Technical School. The school, however, still found it possible to rank me sixth in my class.

I entered the language school's intensive course in Spanish and attended classes in grammar and reading. To my disappointment, however, it offered no classes in Spanish conversation, the course which I considered to be the most important.

There were about 15 students in my classes. Among them were four or five who had confirmed plans for going abroad. Two of us were destined for Peru—Yoshiko Shioya and myself. Miss Shioya was about my age and planned to depart in March of that year to live with her uncle in Lima, from whom she had received quite detailed information about Peru. We happened to ride part of the way home from school via the same streetcar, so every evening I was able to hear a number of accounts about conditions in Peru from her.

Miss Shioya left for Peru one ship earlier than I did. Later, I learned that her uncle was Ichitaro Morimoto, a graduate of Doshisha University who had established himself as a leader in the Japanese community in Peru. Many years later, it happened that Mr. Morimoto was among those of us who were interned in the United States during WWII.

Farewell to My Motherland, Japan

After all the necessary documentation and procedures had been fulfilled, I had to face yet another major problem—it was the simple matter of the 150 yen fare for the passage to Peru. Professor Umehara knew I was a penniless student and had, from the beginning, consoled and encouraged me by saying, "Don't worry about the travel expenses. If it is only that, something can be done." But, when it actually came close to the departure date, it loomed as an overwhelming problem that I could not readily resolve.

For some time I had severely restricted my expenditures, trying to save as much money as I could. Still, after buying a cheap suit, a pair of shoes, and a few smaller items, I was in the impossible position of not even having 50 yen in cash. I was at a loss as to what to do.

Once again, Professor Umehara came to my aid. Saying that it was his parting gift, the professor gave me the extremely large sum of 100 yen. Without a doubt, such an amount was equal to about two months of his salary. Tears of gratitude came to my eyes. Later, I also received a total of 300 yen from our school and its alumni association as a traditional *o-senbetsu,* or "parting gift." Again and again, my heart overflowed with emotion at the goodwill and generosity directed to me by so many people. I vowed that for the rest of my life I would never forget such kindness. With their support, I was able to pay the steamship passage. I then had only to await the day of departure.

That day, April 7, 1930, finally arrived. At the pier along Yokohama Harbor about 250 of our classmates, carrying the school flag before them, came to send off Uchimura and me. Director Emeritus of Tokyo Colonial Trade Language School, Professor Hamano, along with Professor Umehara and other teachers from Hozen Technical School, my sister's family and our friends gave us a magnificent send-off. Many times, they dedicated to us rousing cheers of *"Banzai!"*

Eventually, the ship began to move away from the pier and streamers that I held together in a great sheaf began to break away, one by one. It seemed, as each of the tapes broke away, my motherland became a step further away. Tears rushed to my eyes. I felt as if something was striking at my breast. The people who had come to see us off slowly became smaller in the distance and I repeatedly called out, *"Sayonara! Sayonara!"* as tears choked off my voice. Overwhelming sadness filled me, for I knew that I might never again set foot in my motherland. In this manner, we embarked on our voyage to Peru.

Filled with wanderlust, 18-year-old Seiichi (seated) went to live with his older sister's family, the Sakaguchis, in Tokyo.

Chapter Three. My New World, Peru

First Steps in an Alien Land

Our passage by ship from Japan to Peru was extremely pleasant. Uchimura and I were aboard the *Heiyo Maru,* a newly built ship. Ours was her maiden voyage across the Pacific. It was a good time of year for sea travel, and the waves on the Pacific were smooth and gentle. Both of us were able to enjoy the voyage in high spirits. Our crossing took a month, but it seemed to pass in an instant. It was May 13, 1930 when the *Heiyo Maru* finally arrived at its destination of Callao in Peru.

From the ship, Peru appeared to be a bleak and desolate place. A vista of severe, dry desert terrain and stony mountains sprawled out endlessly before us. Where I had previously held that "wherever one goes there are green mountains," my immediate response now was to recall the couplet, "In another land ten thousand miles away, one becomes a desiccated mummy." I learned much later that many Indian mummies had actually been discovered in that particular coastal area. My intuition had thus not been simply a matter of casual observation. I felt that we had come to a very harsh place.

When the ship anchored in Callao harbor it was announced, "Everyone is to assemble on the upper deck." We hurriedly put our hand luggage in order and went out to the upper deck.

What happened next took us by surprise. A ship's officer went through the entire ship, from each of the passenger cabins to the ship's offices. One by one, he locked up everything until, finally, he even closed off the passageways. Then the anchor was lowered. It seemed very odd. "Why in the world are they doing that?" I thought. Then, I began to hear from different directions, "Be alert for thieves." Locking everything up was their way of preventing thieves from entering the ship's compartments. I thought to myself, "We have truly come to a fearsome place."

While we were caught up in the confusion of arrival, many people came on board to greet the passengers. In a blink of an eye, the upper deck filled with people. Along with those who had come to meet passengers, laborers came aboard to carry off the luggage. They jostled each other, competing to take up the luggage. I had no idea of their working procedures and was completely bewildered. But no one complained, and as I wondered if that was their way of unloading the ship a worker suddenly grabbed my luggage and went off somewhere.

I was simply dumbfounded. Not knowing what to do, Uchimura

and I simply stood there in the milling crowd. Just then, we made contact with Mr. Tatsumi Yamada, for whom I had received a letter of introduction from the Tokyo Colonial Trade Language School. He was in Peru on one part of an inspection tour of Central and South America and had come to greet us. He was accompanied by Mr. Takahashi, who managed the Kurotobi Company. This was, indeed, the proverbial "meeting of a Buddha while in one of the hells." I felt such a sense of relief that it seemed all my strength had left me. I could breathe freely again. It was such an intense occasion for me, and I was overwhelmed with gratitude for the kindness of those two.

Bribes and Thieves

The *Heiyo Maru* had dropped anchor quite some distance from the pier, so all of us had to board small sampan boats to get to the pier. After we landed we had to go through complicated entry procedures.

I can never forget my first experience of going through customs. While we were waiting in line to be processed through customs, a person nearby who had gone through the procedure before whispered to me, "There's a chance that small valuables might be taken by the agent, so when they open your luggage be sure to pay close attention."

"What a country I have come to," I thought.

The inspection was extremely thorough—even items we held in our pockets were examined. All new and unused items, including handkerchiefs, toothbrushes and bars of soap, were subject to customs. The officials extracted a very large duty from me. I had not expected such an inspection, so I had agreed to bring along gifts from people in Japan for their friends and relatives in Peru. Because of this I was assessed a huge sum of custom duties and took a great loss. More than half of my meager funds had disappeared.

Later I was told that if I had given the customs agent five or 10 soles, everything would have passed without comment—but it was too late. I began thinking that I had to reconsider the Japanese habit of unthinking honesty in such situations. Even so, I cocked my head and wondered what type of country I had come to where even a small bribe worked with custom officials.

It was something of a shock to be "baptized" in such matters of bribes and thieves immediately upon landing, but my later experiences confirmed what I had learned at the customs station. Specifically, the matter of thievery was beyond imagination. I was told that when walking about one must be alert to everything one had on him, from wallets and purses, hats, handbags and even to fountain pens pinned in shirt pockets. Anything with any precious metals in it had to be constantly watched.

From those first days in Peru, I never let down my defenses. Even so, I once had my hat stolen in Lima. In another instance, while walking in a crowded area, a fountain pen in my chest pocket was expertly lifted without my knowing. Someone had bumped into me, I later recalled, and in the next moment the fountain pen had disappeared. It had been a matter of exceptional skill.

Since such conditions prevailed, every shop owner worried about thieves. It was said that "half of the work of shop clerks is to watch for thieves." Later, when I would manage my own shop, I would experience the fierce aggressiveness of such thieves with hopeless disgust. The professional thieves were too skillful to be effectively dealt with. Even magicians would have been put to shame by them.

I was often advised by the old timers, "When you see a person, consider him to be a thief." For a new immigrant from Japan, it was beyond belief. While thieves existed in Japan, the two countries were beyond comparison. On that point, I felt proud that Japan was such a safe country.

Disappointment and Uncertainty Strike Early

While still overwhelmed and excited by our arrival in a new country, Uchimura and I were taken by Mr. Yamada and Mr. Takahashi to the home of Tatsujiro Kurotobi, the owner of the Kurotobi Company. He greeted us warmly and treated us as honored guests. But Mr. Kurotobi also informed me that Shintaro Tominaga, whom I had hoped would employ me in his construction business, had been killed in an accident at a construction site three or four years earlier. I was stunned by the news.

According to Mr. Kurotobi, Mr. Tominaga had operated four types of businesses: lumbering, construction, smelting and rubber manufacturing. At one time he had employed more than 250 people and his business interests grossed up to 2 million soles a year. After his death, however, his businesses fell into the hands of Europeans and, by the time of our arrival, only the rubber factory remained within his family's control.

I had hoped to find architectural work with Mr. Tominaga's company, so this information naturally came as an upsetting setback. The rubber factory that was left employed about 50 people to manufacture products ranging from small toys to inner tubes for automobile tires. Such work was so completely unrelated to my architectural training that I did not think it proper to even inquire about employment.

In a dark mood, I said farewell to Mr. Kurotobi and was taken to the Yamato-ya Hotel, which was operated by immigrants from Japan. It had been arranged for us to stay there while we got better acquainted with our new surroundings. Exhausted by our trip, but even more so from the shock of hearing about Mr. Tominaga, we faced a gloomy night.

With no other arrangements or prospects, we did not know what to do. The two of us spent the next several days at the hotel passing our time aimlessly. It was during that time that we met Kuninosuke Yamamoto, the owner of the *Peru Jiho,* a Japanese language newspaper. Mr. Yamamoto took us out and showed us the town.

Mr. Yamamoto was an extraordinary person who had been a professor at the business school of Aoyama Gakuen University in Tokyo and had been the director of the Japan Christian Youth Association for more than 20 years. In Peru, he was then the general manager of a company called the Peru Lettuce Farms as well as president of the *Peru Jiho* newspaper. Having learned of our situation, he invited us out to familiarize us with the conditions in Lima.

He took Uchimura and me to see the lumber plant formerly owned by Mr. Tominaga and the rubber factory that was being managed by Mr. Tominaga's brother-in-law. He also took us to several construction firms that were backed by Japanese capital and to several Japanese building contractors to inquire about work. But it was at the height of the worldwide economic depression and all of the companies were worried about the employees they already had—there was no possibility for them to hire new employees.

The waves of the Great Depression had also come to Peru. Employment related to architecture, which we had hoped for, seemed impossible to find no matter where we looked in Lima. So Uchimura accepted Mr. Kurotobi's kind offer of temporary employment and became a shop clerk at the Japanese grocery store run by the Kurotobi Company. For the next three weeks I spent my time at the hotel, adrift with no prospects at all.

To Canete to Find a Job

One day, as I was idling about the hotel, a man named Mr. Kamizono suddenly spoke to me. He was an immigrant from Kagoshima Prefecture who lived at the hotel and worked for the *Peru Jiho.* "If this situation continues you'll run into problems," he said.

"Do you have any money?"

Still accustomed to the indirect, polite nature of Japanese conversation, I thought at first his comments reflected a poor upbringing. But although Mr. Kamizono's words might be considered crude, he seemed to be genuinely concerned about my situation. Later I came to understand that the Japanese in Peru did not speak like people did in Japan, where language carefully recognizes higher or lower status.

"There's someone I know from Kumamoto Prefecture who has a contracting business in a place called Canete. He might have some work for you, so why don't you try it? I'll write a note for you," he offered. Those were words to be grateful for. Again reminded that even in hell a Buddha appears, I decided to rely on Mr. Kamizono's kindness. He immediately wrote a letter of introduction for me addressed to a Mr. Araki. I decided to go to Canete at once.

By luck, it happened that a Mr. Kenzo Watanabe, manager of the Watanabe Company in Canete, was in Lima on business. He had been staying at the hotel where I had been passing my days. I asked him to allow me to accompany him back to Canete and he readily agreed. For me, not knowing the language, that was truly a stroke of luck. I waited for Mr. Watanabe to complete his business before we departed for Canete.

When the day came to leave, we boarded our bus at about 10 in the morning and began our trip. The "bus" that we rode was actually a large truck with a simple arrangement of seats crudely hammered together on its flatbed in the back.

My first journey over the road to Canete was an unforgettable experience. The road cut through a desert that seemed to spread out endlessly. We then traversed over hills and mountains, and crossed through valleys that continued on and on. The bus continued on along the road, rattling noisily. There were many sections that could not truly be called a road. The dust and sand blown up by the bus made our whole bodies scratchy with grime.

The bus reached Canete at about 11 that night. Because it was so late, I was reluctant to visit Mr. Araki, but there was nothing else I could do. So with Mr. Watanabe showing the way, I went to see him. Having seen the substantial homes of Mr. Kurotobi, Mr. Tominaga and Mr. Yamamoto, the Araki home seemed unexpectedly simple. Rather than a residence, it seemed to be more like a warehouse.

That evening it happened that many people had gathered at the Araki home and a lively party was in progress. Mr. Watanabe introduced me to Mr. Araki. Bowing in respect, I handed over the letter of introduction written by Mr. Kamizono. I was invited to join the party and was introduced to Mr. Araki's younger brother, Sueo, and to the others present.

Being Told the "Facts of Life in Peru"

Among those I met at the party was a person named Shizuo Taura, who owned a bakery. He introduced himself to me as a graduate of Chinzei Middle School in Kumamoto Prefecture. Shaking my hand, he said, "You must be the architect written up in the *Peru Jiho*. You've certainly come to a fine place. We don't need engineers or anyone like that—everyone builds his own home here. Carpenter's squares and measuring devices are unnecessary. Just look at this house. The walls were built by piling up adobe and for the roof *totora* were simply lined up and mud smeared over it. Why in the world would you come to a place like this?"

He seemed to be quite inebriated, but even so I thought that he certainly was a person who bluntly said what he thought. I wondered if I was being insulted. But it was true that the Araki home was a simple, two-story adobe building. "Adobe" was mud that had been shaped and allowed to dry into a brick-like form. The "totora" used for roofing was what the Japanese called "gama," a reed that grows in marshes. The Canete area was hot and dry all year round, with no strong winds, so adobe structures were very appropriate. What Mr. Taura had said was completely true—I was overwhelmed into silence.

At the party, I also met a person named Mr. Kurihara, who ran an electric light company in the neighboring town of Imperial. He was introduced to me as "the president of the electric light company." Much impressed, I conveyed formal respects and bowed deeply. To be the president of an electric light company is indeed to have achieved great success. With much admiration I thought, "There certainly are some outstanding individuals among the immigrants here."

But sometime later I learned that Mr. Kurihara's "company" was not what I had thought it was. When I did visit the town of Imperial, it turned out to be more of a tiny country hamlet rather than a town. No matter where I looked, I could not find a building that resembled an electric light company. No wonder. Mr. Kurihara's electric light company was located in a small building that looked like a storage shack on the outskirts of the town. The building did house a real generator and an engine. It even had a generator operator, who was addressed as "Dirty Matsu."

The generator was an amazing thing. "Dirty Matsu" had apparently picked up an abandoned motor somewhere and had completely rewound the copper wiring in it so it ran as good as new. It was powered by a small engine similar to the type that farm families use.

I admired the simplicity of the system. The electricity was sent to town through two thin lines stretched out on electric poles that looked like flagpoles with fuzz on them. Of course the town could not be lit with only such rudimentary equipment, but it was better than nothing.

One 10-watt bulb hung from each electric pole. Even if many such bulbs were put up, it was not enough to light up the interiors of the shops, so all of them hung one or two gas lanterns from the ceiling. The lanterns gave off such brilliant light that they nearly blinded anyone who looked at them directly. It was comical, but at least Mr. Kurihara's electric light company was not merely a "ghost company."

The "Three Matsus" and "Oye, Viejo"

There were three well-known personages called "Three Matsu" in the Canete area. Each had family names beginning with "Matsu-," such as Matsubara and Matsui, but at some point they had come to be called "Dirty Matsu," "Drunken Matsu," and "Bragging Matsu." Those names had become so widely used that no one knew the men's real names.

"Dirty Matsu," the above-mentioned engineer, was always splattered with machine oil because he did not wash it off even when he was completely covered with black oil. The other two were exactly what their nicknames denoted. Although their nicknames were not at all complimentary, none of the "Three Matsus" apparently felt badly about it and would casually answer when addressed in that manner.

At first I was reluctant to use such names but did so gradually as I came to understand the temperament of the Japanese in Peru. I learned that by insisting on being formal and calling them by their real names, I was being distant and lacking in camaraderie. Within the Japanese community in Peru everyone was treated as if he were a family member and even derogatory names that normally would be unacceptable in Japan were taken as expressions of closeness.

In the case of the "Three Matsus" there was some sense of playfulness in their nicknames so there was some leeway for acceptance, but for a long time I could not accept the Peruvian custom of addressing people in terms of their physical defects. This custom was not particular to the Japanese community, but used generally in Peru. A person without an arm was called "manco" (armless); a blind person, "ciego" (blind man); a person with bad legs, "coho" (cripple); a person with little hair on his head, "coco" (bald); etc. Such persons were directly addressed by reference to their deficiencies. These expressions were not used in the conversations of cultured persons; but they were often heard in general conversation.

People often called out, "Oi, Coho," or "Oi, Viejo." "Viejo" conveys the sense of "doddering old man." It seemed cruel to address a person directly in this manner. The "oi" is correctly "oye," a Spanish verb that means "listen!" or "hey!" and is used to catch someone's attention. Since this happens to resemble the Japanese term "oi," which has an amazingly similar function and connotation, the Japanese in Peru commonly used such "pidgin" phrases as "Oi, Coho" and "Oi, Viejo" without hesitation.

I could not bring myself to use such terms. Yet, it was also true that when someone came to use such terms naturally, it was a sign that one had begun to blend in with life in Peru.

The Closely Linked Japanese Community

In time, I came to see that the Japanese in Peru shared other unique attitudes that could not be found in Japan. I was deeply impressed with the strong bond that linked the immigrants—they interacted with a closeness and intimacy that was even stronger than between brothers and sisters in Japan.

Undoubtedly, this was the result of their having shared many common experiences. They had all experienced long ocean voyages to reach the shores of an alien land. Knowing no one, they had often walked near the edge of survival before they were eventually able to build a secure base for their livelihood. Had they not drawn together, aided each other, and encouraged each other, they would not have survived. In doing so, a strong sense of connectedness was formed.

Since everyone was treated as family, everything in that immigrant society was handled openly and informally. They gladly welcomed even young newcomers like myself and offered to help whenever we encountered problems. Because of such kindness, even in the most difficult times I was never overcome with feelings of loneliness. As a person moving to an alien land thousands of miles away from home, I felt truly blessed.

In Peru, no matter whose home one visited, beer was served instead of other beverages. It was awkward for me, as I did not drink alcohol. In each home burlap bags containing about five dozen bottles of beer were piled up high.

Whenever a few persons gathered, beer was served and the gathering soon turned into a party. At times, arguments and scuffles broke out, but someone would almost always step between the opponents to reconcile them. Often, the opposing parties would start drinking together again with their differences completely forgotten. By the time they went home, earlier adversaries were frequently even closer friends than before. In this manner, even disagreements were turned into opportunities for individuals to remain close.

Mr. Taura, whom I had met at the Araki home during my first night in Canete, was well-known in the Canete area for his ability to enliven any party he attended. But each time he would inevitably get involved in an argument. When he reached that state, he might leap up on a table and smash a beer bottle on his rival's head or begin overturning tables. He would not stop until he brought everything to a crashing halt. But then someone would intervene to reconcile the disputants and a second phase of the party would begin.

After a while Mr. Taura and his opponent would be on good terms and by the time they went home would embrace heartily before parting. This was Mr. Taura's routine behavior at every party. His were fierce but simple battles which were not based on simmering resentments or ulterior motives.

There were, indeed, frequent "gatherings" within the Japanese community in Peru. There were casual occasions, when a few close neighbors gathered to have some beer, and also enormous gatherings, such as weddings, when friends and acquaintances from the entire region would party over several days and nights. In this way the immigrants deepened relationships, formed new friendships, maintained close bonds, and retained their identity as Japanese in Peru.

A Live-in "Working Guest"

Another interesting phenomenon within the Japanese community in Peru was the practice of many immigrant homes to accommodate people who could neither be called employees nor guests. These people generally were "drop outs" from the older immigrant community or newcomers from Japan. They went from one home to another and lived as "part of the family," helping without pay with anything that needed to be done for food and lodging.

Among them were, in the most essential Japanese sense, those who did no real work at all. In such cases, however, these individuals risked overstaying their welcome. Keeping an eye to the appropriate time, they would move on to other "opportunities." In the Japanese community in Peru, almost every household of some stability had one or two such persons who were "working guests."

It was accepted that I would live with the Araki family and work for their company. I thought I had been employed by the Araki Company, but the Arakis apparently thought they had simply taken on another working guest. Besides myself, there were three other working guests at the Araki Company. One was Mr. Araki's younger brother, Sueo, and the other two were Mr. Araki's nephews. They all lived there and helped with the family business without pay.

In the beginning I had expected that at an appropriate time I would be paid. No matter how many weeks passed, however, there was no indication of it. I had not imagined that I would not be paid at all, so I vaguely expected that I would be paid a lump sum when I left. That was an entirely misplaced expectation. The result, ultimately, was that I worked at the Araki Company for more than two years without any pay.

Although I never got paid, I was still grateful. I had been given a place to stay and was never restricted as to food and drink. Mr. Araki had actually taken me in and looked after me when I was simply "a stranger wandering along the roadside." In Peru at that time, in the midst of the Depression, even a grown man would not have been able to survive if he did not have special skills.

"Working guests" had to be very thankful that the Japanese community in Peru took them in and provided for their basic needs. Yet, while they were sustained in that way there also was no future for them. No matter how long they continued under such an arrangement, there was no possibility for them to accumulate a "nest egg" for the future in order to attain their independence. Those who became successful among the immigrants had been fully aware of such consequences and had refused easy support. They had deliberately selected the more difficult path of establishing a livelihood on their own.

The Earliest Japanese Immigrants

If "working guests" complained, they would have been seen as ungrateful and open to punishment from the gods, for the Japanese community that took them in was built upon the blood and tears of the earliest immigrants. Those first immigrants had absolutely nothing to rely on and paid with many sacrifices and many lives.

The first group of contract workers left Japan in 1899 to cross over to Peru. Their passage was paid for under contract by their employers on the condition that they work exclusively on the sugar plantations and in sugar refineries. According to those contracts, each immigrant would either work 10 hours a day for field work or 12 hours a day in the sugar mills. Their monthly salaries would be paid in Peruvian currency equivalent to 20 pounds 10 shillings in British currency. However, for the first 25 months, the emigration company that had contracted them would deduct eight shillings every month to guarantee that the contract would be honored and to start a reserve fund to cover travel expenses when they were ready to return to Japan.

Converted to the value of the Japanese yen at that time, the monthly salary was equivalent to approximately 25 yen. Food, of course, was an individual expense; so, if five yen a month was allowed for food, there would be 20 yen left. If that was saved, in four years one could accumulate 960 yen. If one subtracted the return fare of 100 yen, one still would have 860 yen in one's pocket. Every worker's goal was to acquire that hypothetical "860 yen," which was a tremendous sum of money in Japan at that time. If everything worked out as planned, it would be a dream come true.

In life, however, it seems things seldom turn out as planned. Those who signed up as immigrants were young men in excellent physical condition so it was not surprising that they did not even consider the possibility of incurring illnesses or injuries. That, however, was a serious mistake. While Peru is a land blessed with good climate, it also had hidden liabilities such as malaria and other diseases, including bubonic plague and typhus.

Soon after they entered the fields, the immigrants were beset with illnesses and it was typical that three to five of them died every day. Older immigrants said that if anyone came down with a high fever, a hole was immediately dug in the desert to prepare for burial. No one had even dreamed that within a year the first group to enter Peru would have 150 of their fellow voyagers buried in Peruvian soil.

In the most severe cases, within a year of arriving one-half of a group of immigrants would become "those who would not return." Peruvian employers and the emigration company in Japan had, it seems, foreseen this. The two parties had worked out agreements to reduce their respective losses. Not a cent was provided to the families of the immigrants who died from illnesses. For them, the death of the family's main bread winner simply meant a complete loss of livelihood. The anguish and despair of those early immigrants who died in an alien land with hopes unfulfilled was surely beyond words.

Those in the first group in 1899 and the second group in 1903 had signed contracts of four years. Those of the third group in 1906 signed contracts for six months, but those in this group had to pay their own travel expenses. This seems to have been a countermeasure taken by the employers and the emigration company to reduce their risks in the face of the unexpectedly high death rate among the immigrants.

At that time, it was not easy to raise the 100 yen needed for boat fare. Many of those in the third group had to sell their homes and farmlands in Japan to acquire the money for passage. They were lured by the emigration company's claims that stated, "By working two or three years in Peru, you can return in glory to your home village with large savings." But conditions in Peru had not changed between 1899 and 1906, so again many were added to the dust of that alien land. Understandably, many of the early immigrants came to detest the Japan-based emigration company.

Although the contract period for those in the third group was six months, if a person worked for the same employer continuously for four years, a special grant equivalent to 7.5 pounds in currency from the employer and 2.5 pounds from the Morioka Emigration Company was awarded as a bonus toward returning to Japan. That formula continued in force until 1909. After 1909, the contracts were set for one-year, and one-year contract immigrants continued to enter Peru until 1922, when the contract system was abolished. Non-contract "free immigrants" also traveled to Peru, but they were few in number.

A number of immigrants in the third contract group achieved great success in Peru. For example, Tatsujiro Kurotobi, who came to be almost a surrogate father for me; Sengoro Watanabe, the owner of the Watanabe company, to whom I was much obligated while in Canete; Tajiemon Nishii, (my sister-in-law's husband's father) who built the Nishii Irrigation Waterway); Chuzo Fujii, who established the Suetomi business group; and my wife's father, Kahei Yoshinaga, were members of that third group. They overcame unbelievably poor conditions to become inspirational "success stories."

Even among those who achieved success, however, there was not one who did not experience the loss of a relative or close friend. My wife's mother was no exception. She was a woman who through her own efforts had been able to survive a period when even the most rudimentary sanitary and medical facilities did not exist within the immigrant community. Even such a strong woman, however, lost her husband. Soon after she was married in Japan, she and her husband had crossed over to Peru with the dream of building a nest egg. Within a year after arriving, however, her husband came down with a fever and died, leaving her alone in an alien land. Fortunately, however, she later married Kahei Yoshinaga.

After WWII, the two returned to Japan where they lived for many years in serene retirement. In that sense, she might have been among the more fortunate. The Japanese community in Peru was built and sustained on the efforts of such predecessors. They provided the foundation which received later immigrants such as I as "working guests" and offered us warm hospitality.

Days as an All-purpose Worker

The Araki Company where I was "employed" in Canete ran a variety of operations. Its main business was importing lumber from North America, but it also ran a sawmill and at times contracted to build residences. It also had a plant for manufacturing *fideos* (vermicelli), a type of pasta, and operated a retail hardware store.

Because I needed to learn Spanish as quickly as possible, I was assigned to work at the hardware store, where I would have the most contact with the general Spanish-speaking public. However, when building activities increased I was sent out to do construction. When helpers were needed at the sawmill I was sent there. I also delivered fideos twice a week to small shops in the Canete area. I had quite literally become the Araki Company's all-purpose worker.

In those days in the Canete area there were 15 or 16 *haciendas,* gigantic farming complexes each thousands of acres in size. They were large enough to utilize airplanes to spray insecticides. Each hacienda by itself could support a small village with a few shops to carry daily necessities. It was to such shops that the Araki Company sold its vermicelli.

Other than a few Chinese and local Peruvians, almost all of those shops were run by Japanese immigrants, so I did not have to speak fluent Spanish when I delivered vermicelli. Because of this, I was assigned to deliver vermicelli to those shops and take orders twice a week.

A black man named Cario drove our truck. Since there was a driver, my presence might seem unnecessary, but Cario was illiterate and could not even write his name. Fortunately, just before I left Japan I had studied Spanish for three months and could manage to write out invoices, receipts and order slips. I could not converse in Spanish, but I was glad that I had studied some Spanish, even if only at the most rudimentary level.

Nothing is more inhibiting than being in a foreign country and not being able to speak its language. Among the tales of hardship related to me by earlier immigrants many involved language.

Compared to those who had come in the first group I was much better off; but, because of the language barrier, I still had many difficult experiences. Especially in my first two years there, I was looked askance by the people in Peru simply because my Spanish was inadequate.

A Film Negative is not "Burned" —Limitations within Languages

Among the tales of errors involving language were some rather comical situations. About three months after I reached Canete, I tried to have a blueprint made at the local engineering office. The drawing was a cross-sectional drawing I had made of the five-storied pagoda at Nikko, Japan as an assignment for my drawing class at Hozen Technical School. It measured about four feet long by two feet wide and had been highly praised for its craftsmanship even by my teacher. Having spent many painstaking days to complete it, I could not discard it and had brought it with me to Peru.

As a memento of my days at Hozen Tech, I wanted to make it into a blueprint. I mentioned the idea to Mr. Araki. Fortunately, he was acquainted with Mr. Ramos, the head of the Canete Engineering Bureau, and he immediately made a telephone call to Mr. Ramos to see if his office would make a blueprint.

The telephone call, however, became difficult. Having just arrived in Peru, it seemed to me that Mr. Araki's Spanish was fluent, but apparently it was not good enough to handle technical terms smoothly. He used the term "quemar" many times, apparently translating the idiomatic phrase, "to burn a film negative," directly and literally into Spanish.

Since in Spanish the verb "quemar" means "to sear" or "to burn," to ask to "quemar" a negative would mean "to burn" or "set fire to" a negative. It is not surprising that his message did not get across. Mr. Ramos finally said, "At any rate, come over to see me." Taking the drawing, Mr. Araki set out for the engineering office.

I did not accompany him, but Mr. Araki told me later that when Mr. Ramos saw the drawing he instantly understood what was wanted and they both had a good laugh about it. Mr. Ramos immediately had several copies of blueprints "burned" for us. And, having asked my permission, he also made several copies for himself. During those days copying fees would have been considerable, especially those the size of this large drawing, but Mr. Ramos did not ask for any payment at all.

Because of that incident, completely unintentionally, I had been "certified" by the director of the Canete Municipal Engineering Office and came to be addressed with the title of "ingeniero" (engineer). In Peru it is title of respect similar to "doctor" (for physicians and scholars) or "senorita" (for females of high social status). Because of this curious turn of events, I suddenly became a "success" and came to be "Ingeniero Higachidei," as my surname was pronounced in Spanish.

From "Engineer" to Unskilled Carpenter

Contrary to the title I had acquired, however, I abandoned my "engineering work" to become an unskilled carpenter. The Araki Company needed me to help build small residential structures it had contracted to do. The jobs, mainly for nearby farms, were more like odd jobs rather than real carpentry work. The work involved small jobs such as affixing doors or windows or putting together furniture. At times, however, we were kept busy enough. Mr. Araki's younger brother had been a "shrine carpenter" in Japan and had great confidence in his skills. But, as Mr. Taura had pointed out much earlier, there was no real work for a journeyman carpenter in our area.

I had graduated from an architectural course and was now being called an "engineer." Since my specialty was ferro-concrete structures, however, my skills were not needed. It would have been better if I had specialized in wooden structures, I thought. In Peru, if one wanted to engage in work dealing with ferro-concrete structures, one first had to be naturalized, be a graduate of a Peruvian technical school, and acquire a government-recognized license. In Peru, the certificate I had received in Japan was no more than a scrap of paper.

Because of such conditions, I focussed all of my efforts on becoming a skilled general carpenter. I learned to hit a nail accurately and became adept in the use of Western-styled planes and saws. Although I gave up "engineering" and became a simple carpenter, the title of "ingeniero" remained attached to my name. Much later I was asked by the police chief of Canete to design a new building for his department. The new police department was to be a ferro-concrete structure with a rather large holding area for prisoners. I went over to look at the proposed site and saw that it would be a major project.

I felt strongly that if details could be worked out, I should attempt it. I had no knowledge of designing a cell block, but it was the type of building I had always hoped to design. The timing, however, was wrong. At that time I was faced with a move to the city of Ica and was overwhelmed by the preparations. Regretfully, I had to refuse the commission. The functional requirements of the building demanded a great deal of research, and there were a number of difficult problems related to construction, so I decided that it could not be done as a casual, "part-time job."

Bouts of Malaria

One day, about three months after I arrived in Peru, I received a message that Uchimura, who had become a shop clerk for the Kurotobi Company in Lima, had fallen ill and was in a hospital. It happened just at a time when the Araki Company was in a very busy period, so I hesitated to ask for a leave. I forced myself to ask and, with four or five days granted, headed for Lima as soon as possible.

By the time I reached the hospital, Uchimura seemed to be in better condition than I had expected. I felt relieved, but a little exasperated. But then when I thought of Uchimura's feelings, alone in the hospital bed, I could not hold back my sympathy. I wanted to watch over his recovery 24 hours a day, as would be expected in Japan. But Peruvian hospital regulations allowed only two visits a day. Moreover, I could not be away from work for too long, so after three or four days I said farewell and returned to Canete. Uchimura soon recovered, but he could not regain his full strength. At the urging of his doctor he returned, alone, to Japan.

For immigrants, the well-being of their bodies was their most important "capital," for without one's health everything could become undone. This was often repeated to me in warning by the earlier immigrants. I had confidence in my physical stamina, but I was also careful about maintaining my health. No matter how hard one tried, however, afflictions and injuries could strike at any time.

Not long after settling in Canete, I contracted malaria; for about a year I suffered severe fevers. Malaria, which the local people called "terciana," is a contagious disease transmitted by mosquitoes. While it alone carries terrible physical consequences, what is more frightening are the various types of secondary illnesses it can cause. The only treatment for it was to have regularly scheduled injections of quinine, extremely painful injections into the muscular area of the buttocks. After the injections, the muscular area had to be carefully massaged or the muscles tended to harden. Eventually, it would become impossible to take further shots. Some of the older immigrants had buttocks marked with permanent bruises from such attempted injections.

At that time in Canete there was a Dr. Maki, who had been a military doctor in Japan. He had traveled to Peru as an attending physician to one of the earlier emigrant groups and had remained there. Although he was not certified to practice in Peru, he treated members of the Japanese immigrant community.

In order to open a medical practice in Peru it was necessary to graduate from a local university, undergo a period of internship, and pass the national medical examinations. Dr. Maki, not having gone through the procedure, could not openly conduct this practice. Yet, when I contracted malaria, there was no other treatment than to endure my daily bouts with fever and to have him administer quinine injections.

Mine was considered a milder case. Even so, every day at about 4 p.m., as if someone had pushed a button, I would suddenly feel a deep chill and begin shaking. Then a high fever of 42 to 44 degrees Centigrade would arise and, after a period of incoherence, I would fall asleep. This was repeated every day at the same time. It was, indeed, a very odd disease.

At its outset I was terribly upset by what happened every day. Later, I became accustomed to it and would go about my normal work every day until about 4 p.m. Just before the chills would begin, I would go to bed and cover myself with Japanese-style *futon* quilts. Then I would wait for the shivering to begin. While I was in a state of shaking, three people would straddle me to hold me down, but an unbelievable strength would surge forth from within me that was enough to topple them over. I went once a week to our uncertified doctor to receive the painful quinine shots.

My affliction continued for about a year. Then, apparently, I recovered and became immune, never again to contract malaria. That no secondary illnesses developed and that I contracted only a relatively light attack was, I think, because my body had been tempered with hard physical labor in Japan.

The Cerro Revolution and Attacks on Japanese Shops

Coincidentally, when I had gone to Lima to see Uchimura in the hospital, revolution erupted in Peru. The Leguia regime, which had held absolute control for 11 years, was about to be toppled.

The worldwide depression had severely impacted the Peruvian economy, and the populace expressed its dissatisfaction through violent incidents. Spurred on by such conditions, Lt. Sanchez-Cerro of Arequipa City began leading revolutionary forces and took over that city. Using Arequipa as its main base for controlling southern Peru, his revolutionary troops then moved northward and entered Lima.

When I arrived in Lima, the revolutionary troops were still battling government troops in the streets of the capital. Curious, I decided to walk unobtrusively through the city on my first evening in Lima. No curfew had been announced, but the streets were empty and all the shops were closed down. In the distance, I could hear shots being fired from the direction of the Santa Catalina military base. I started walking cautiously toward that direction.

In the area near the military base, revolutionary troops and government troops were fighting in the streets. I could not determine one side from the other. Suddenly, I became frightened and quickly began retracing my steps. I later heard that during the night several civilians had been killed by stray bullets and that among them was a Japanese immigrant named Okubo. Chills ran down my spine. I thought that even if I did have the experience of actually seeing that terrible action it was really a very stupid thing to do.

President Leguia had gained control of the government in 1919, and led a pro-Japan faction in Peru. So at that time, when his fate seemed like a lamp buffeted by strong wind, it was understandable for most Japanese in Peru to feel uneasy about the developments. Besides, regardless of Leguia's political leanings, they knew from experience that whenever there was a violent change of government, Japanese- and Chinese- owned shops would be attacked and looted by unhappy mobs. Asian storeowners began securing protective shutters over their shops. Unnerved and fearful, they awaited the outcome.

As expected, their premonitions were fulfilled. President Leguia was toppled by the revolution, and attacks began as soon as the revolutionary troops gained control of Lima. Although not on a major scale, Japanese-owned shops in Lima and other cities were ransacked.

One major reason for the attacks not escalating to more widespread violence was the quick preventive action undertaken by the Japanese minister in Lima. Minister Saburo Kurusu immediately went to the command headquarters of the revolutionary forces to speak with Gen. Sanchez-Cerro. He requested that such violence be stopped for the sake of law and order and common civility. At first,

General Cerro equivocated. It was reported that Kurusu then stated, "As long as troops are not sent out to prevent such mob attacks, the Japanese will resist even if they have to arm themselves for self protection." The lieutenant agreed to honor the request.

Troops were immediately sent out to maintain order and security within the city of Lima. Even with such measures, more than 20 shops owned by Japanese in Lima were broken into and looted. Shops owned by non-Japanese also were attacked, but more than half of those victimized were owned by Japanese. The memory of those attacks, specifically directed at Japanese-owned shops, constantly remained in a corner of my mind; it seemed to forebode an unhappy future for the Japanese in Peru.

Military Obligations Cross Overseas—"The Barrier Guard at Ataka"

About seven or eight months after I arrived in Peru, my life came to another major crossroads. It all began with the arrival of a letter from the Japanese Consulate General in Lima. Curious, I opened it and was stunned to find a summons demanding that I appear immediately at their offices.

Among the immigrants at that time, the Consulate General was an entity more awesome than even the Peruvian authorities. We had all been indoctrinated to absolute submission to the Chrysanthemum Insignia. Moreover, we had been told that the consulate grounds were endowed with extraterritorial rights which gave the Consul General complete police and judicial powers over Japanese subjects. Although I had done nothing wrong, I felt completely unnerved.

I examined my situation from various angles, but could not find any reason for being summoned. Still, I felt compelled to respond without delay and left the next morning for Lima. It took 10 hours by bus from Canete to Lima, so after arriving I stayed overnight at a hotel and went to the consulate the following morning.

Not knowing why I had been summoned, I apprehensively entered the consulate building. Just as I had heard, the people at the consulate displayed an air of authority and aloofness. I had my identity confirmed by a receptionist and was taken to the Consul General's office in the interior of the building.

Consul General Yodokawa Masaki had an even more severe demeanor than the other officials. When I entered, he looked up and said, "By order of the Imperial Government, we shall return you to Japan." For a moment I stood petrified. But I eventually regained control of myself and asked, "Why is such action being taken?"

The reason cited was "the crime of evading military service by absconding overseas." The charge was all-embracing. I was aware of Japan's laws concerning military service, and I had no way of refuting the charge.

While I was enrolled at Hozen Technical School I had been allowed a one-year deferment from military service. But I knew that as soon as I graduated I had to be examined for military service. Yet, while aware of my status, when my passport was granted I had graduated and left Japan without much concern over the matter.

I had inwardly been happy that I would not have to fulfill the military obligation. I did not want to become a soldier. I did not want to give up two years of my precious youth. Of course it was not because of that reason that I had decided to leave for Peru. I had merely thought that it was my good fortune to have been exempted from military service by emigrating to Peru. But it was not so simple. The obligation had crossed on the waves over thousands of miles of open sea to follow me to Peru.

I had evaded military service, the highest priority of all major obligations placed upon Japanese subjects. In this manner, a noose had been set by the Consul General. There seemed to be nothing more that I could do, and I began to prepare for the worst.

I knew that if I accepted the charge, I would not be able to face my teachers and classmates in Japan who had given me so much strength and support. If I was sent back to Japan bearing the onus of being a "draft-dodger," I felt I needed to express what I felt. I resolved to do so and decided to pour out my dissatisfaction to the Consul General. At this point, I no longer felt afraid of the Consul General or even the Japanese Minister to Peru.

"Mr. Consul," I began boldly as if in public debate, "in Japan, in the cities and in the countryside, everywhere, people are in such a condition that they do not know whether they will even have enough to eat. The Consul, I think, is already aware of this. Even if a person graduates from an Imperial University, I hear that his salary is only about 40 yen per month—and that is only if he is lucky enough to find employment. Last year, banks everywhere in Japan were faced with runs of withdrawals and they all closed their doors. I have also heard that bankruptcies have reached uncountable numbers. . . .

"As the son of a settler family in Hokkaido, I was raised in a poor family. I was barely able to struggle through school and it was through my own efforts that I was able to graduate. Upon graduation, with the help of school officials and teachers, the alumni association, friends and acquaintances and family members, I accumulated, as if wrung out from blood, funds sufficient for emigrating to Peru. I believe that in these times, even if it is only one less mouth to feed, that is to the benefit of our country. . . .

"Not much time has passed since I have come to Peru. If I am returned now, other than the onus of being a draftdodger, there is nothing I can bring to our motherland. It is that which fills me with regret. From daybreak of the day that I reach Japan again, I will work with all my heart to benefit her, so at this time may I not ask for a favorable resolution, at least, of this criminal charge of evading military service?"

When one reaches a certain emotional point, it seems, there is nothing that one cannot do. At times, becoming aroused, I pounded the table with my fist; at times, I asked for sympathetic understanding. I expressed my feelings, even to my own amazement.

The Consul General looked at me intently with his stern visage and silently listened to what I had to say. When I came to the end of my appeal, he calmly said, "It is alright. Something can be done. You needn't return to Japan, so do your best here in Peru."

I couldn't believe my own ears. I had not expected such an answer. "Is it really alright?" I asked. The Consul General nodded. It is a self-centered perceptual phenomenon, I am sure, but the Consul General, who until then had seemed to be a monstrous sort of person with an evil countenance, suddenly seemed to be a compassionate deity or a Buddha. Where I had seen a cold indifference, it seemed now that I could even detect a trace of a smile pass over his face.

Bowing profusely, I thanked the Consul General by repeatedly saying, "*Arigato gozaimasu.* I shall exert all my efforts so the Consul General's kind actions shall not be taken in vain." As I was about to exit his office, a matter of concern must have passed through his mind for he said, "If you want to return home to Japan, this is your chance. The passage will be free and when you reach Japan you will only be drafted into the military. You will not be charged with any particular offense."

Those were words said in kindness. The Consul General understood the harsh conditions of the immigrants in Peru, and he had undoubtedly made the remark out of concern for my welfare. I had no intention of returning to Japan, but his words, offered in kindness and concern, filled me with warmth and gratitude. As I left the Consulate building, I suddenly recalled a scene from the kabuki drama, *Kanjin-*

cho. In my heart, I placed my palms together to offer thanks to the "Barrier-guard" who had let me slip through.

In subsequent months the Consul General deflected orders from Tokyo calling for my arrest by responding that my whereabouts were unknown.

If I had been sent back to Japan at that time, I do not know what would have become of my life. It was just about the time of the "Manchurian Incident," so I very likely would have been sent to Manchuria. Whenever I heard reports of classmates and acquaintances dying in battle, I remembered Consul General Yodokawa with thoughts of gratitude.

Twenty-three years after the end of the Pacific War, I visited Japan and was startled to find that this draft incident, so many years earlier, had reached unexpected places. According to a nephew in Hokkaido, the local police received a report that the whereabouts of Seiichi Higashide was unknown. It seems they thought I had returned to Japan and was hiding from the authorities.

They searched my home village many times. In particular, at about the time I was due to report for military service, they repeatedly questioned those in neighboring homes. I was completely disgusted to learn they had persisted in their searches for three or four years. But since it was true that I had neglected one of the "three great obligations" of Japanese subjects, I was not in a position to protest very loudly. I had become a "non-citizen" and a felon.

The Revenge of the Calavera

One day, about two years after I went to Canete, we had loaded up our truck with vermicelli to go to the Lunahuana area to make deliveries as usual. However, on that day, instead of our usual black driver, the owner Mr. Araki took the steering wheel. Lunahuana was a small country town located in a deep gorge along the Canete River, about midway between the first rise of the Andes mountains and the seacoast. That area and on upstream to the high Andes was one of the few grape-growing areas of Peru and it was known for producing good wine and *pisco,* a strong alcoholic drink.

There were four or five other shops on the way to Lunahuana. In Lunahuana itself there were two shops owned by Japanese and three owned by local Peruvians. They were all regular customers of the Araki Company. We went from shop to shop to deliver the vermicelli and turned around at Lunahuana to make our return trip.

On one side of the road to Lunahuana was a steep cliff into which the road had been cut and on the other side was a steep gorge hundreds of feet deep. Since it was not paved and had no guard rails, great caution was needed when driving over what could barely be called a "road." Because of this, by the time we turned around at Lunahuana the sun was already beginning to slant westward.

That day, on the way back to Canete, I unexpectedly discovered some *calaveras*, ancient Incan skulls. I thought them to be very unusual and selected four of them—some with hair on the top and some with a full set of teeth—to take home. At that time, Mr. Araki did not say anything in particular about it. Later, however, it became a matter of major concern.

On the way back to Canete, five or six laborers who maintained the road asked for a lift so we let them ride in the flatbed of the truck. We reached a point where we had to pass over a steep rise before we entered the Canete plain. The truck rattled along, climbing up the incline. Just when we reached a point near its peak, the truck suddenly lost power and was about to stop. Mr. Araki thought he could coax it forward by shifting gears but could not get the gears to engage.

The truck slowly began to roll backwards. The laborers sensed the danger and they all began to leap off the flatbed. I also jumped out and tried to block a wheel with a large rock, but it was too late. The truck simply hopped over the rock and continued to roll backward, picking up speed.

Helpless, I wrapped my arms around myself and watched the truck descend. The laborers, while rubbing their bruises, also stared intently. Mr. Araki reacted splendidly. Never letting go of the steering wheel, he turned to face backward and guided the truck along its downward flight. Luckily, some distance below was a long fence along a parcel of pasture land on the mountain side of the road. Thick fence posts had been set several yards apart and was connected with wire to hold grazing animals. Mr. Araki steered the truck, intentionally crashing it into the fence.

Forty or 50 posts were pulled over to lean like fallen dominoes before the truck finally came to a halt. We all sighed with relief and clapped our hands excitedly. It had been a perilous situation. If the fence had not been there, Mr. Araki and the truck would have plummeted into the deep gorge.

The incident ended with that, but it had further repercussions after we returned home. Everyone agreed that the incident was caused by the revenge of the calaveras I had picked up. That evening we solemnly made offerings to the four calaveras to appease them and lighted candles in front of them before going to bed. Early the next morning, we bought incense and candles and made a special trip to their original location and carefully buried them. It was a major effort that took up the whole day. I personally thought we were behaving in a foolish manner, but everyone else thought it should be done; there was no choice but to agree.

Subsequently, I saw many calaveras and skeletons but I never again attempted to pick them up. Although I never saw one personally, it was said that there were also remains that became mummified through natural conditions. Such bones and remains were probably the results of wars among the Indians or battles between the Indians and the Spanish invaders.

At first, I looked at the Indian calaveras simply from the standpoint of curiosity, but then I came to think that if I died in Peru I also could become another calavera. Thereafter, I no longer could regard them so casually. As long as I stayed with the Araki Company, I at least did not have to worry about food and daily necessities. Yet, there was nothing to hope for beyond that. If anything happened to Mr. Araki, I had no assurance of what would become of me.

Given my circumstances, the risk that my own calavera would be cleansed in the sands of the desert was even greater than that of those Indians who had gone out to battle. I had also reached a point where I felt the time had come when I had to do something about my situation. I could see that it was urgent that I make a move in order that my own calavera not come to be bleached in the sands of Peru.

Incan ruins at Canete, Casablanca.

Chapter Four. Moving Toward Financial Independence

Becoming a Teacher at the Japanese School

In 1932, during my second year in Peru, I was unexpectedly recommended to a position at the Japanese elementary school in Canete. Choichi Otani, then the chairman of the Canete Japanese Education Committee, approached me with the offer. I hesitated briefly, as I had never thought of becoming a teacher.

Yet, I was aware that due to the Depression the Araki Company had more than enough workers. The Arakis were in a difficult position, and I knew I could not rely on their hospitality and goodwill forever. I considered the alternatives and saw that my situation did not offer much of a future. At least I would earn a modest salary as a teacher and it might lead to new opportunities. I resolved to become a teacher and gratefully accepted the offer.

At that time, young "intellectuals" who had emigrated from Japan often spent their first two or three years in Peru as teachers in Japanese elementary schools. Jobs were scarce in the midst of the Depression, and although such young men were educated, most could not speak adequate Spanish so there were few jobs available to them.

As a teacher, one held a respectable social position in the community. Thus, if at all possible, such newly arrived persons quickly took such positions. I had taken a "detour" of two years, but now finally fell into this often followed course.

San Vicente Japanese Elementary School was a very small school which in Japan would have been considered an isolated "annex" of a regular elementary school. It had approximately 30 students and three teachers, including myself.

Of the 30 or so Japanese elementary schools that had been established in Peru, most were that size or smaller. The only exception was the Japanese elementary school in Lima which had over 1,000 students and was the only such school in South America that had been designated an official overseas school by the Ministry of Education in Japan.

As could be expected of a school recognized by the Japanese Ministry of Education, the school in Lima had many outstanding teachers on its faculty who had graduated from normal schools in Japan. But the same could not be said for schools located in outlying areas. It would be an overstatement to say that anyone could become a teacher in those schools, but rural schools could not be very particular about the educational qualifications of their teachers. I, too, had been selected more because of my youth and vitality than my educational background or technical qualifications.

Although there were many teachers with rather dubious backgrounds at such local schools, in general they were splendid teachers. These "instant" teachers were often extremely effective in actual classroom work and contributed significantly toward the education of the immigrant children.

Parents supported the educational efforts. A major activity of the various local Japanese associations was the organization of "school committees" to finance and operate the schools. Even for a small school such as ours, it was not easy to pay salaries for three teachers and to maintain facilities. Not a penny of assistance came from outside the area. Parents with children were, of course, assessed for "school maintenance," but even those who had no direct ties with the school, such as single people and the elderly, were pressed to make compulsory "donations."

Baseball Fever in Canete

The principal of our school was an elderly teacher named Yasuda, a graduate of Waseda University in Tokyo. He had immigrated to Peru many years earlier and had become principal of the elementary school at Canete. Although he held the title of "principal," there was only a Peruvian-born woman and myself on staff, so he had to carry out educational duties as well as all the miscellaneous tasks related to the school.

Mr. Yasuda seemed very pleased when he greeted me. "I'm very glad that you have come to our school," he said. He was a very likeable and kindhearted person, but for some reason had never been married. Probably because of the loneliness of living alone he often played *hanafuda,* a Japanese card game, and was criticized by parents for that. "How can a teacher behave in such a manner?" they often said; but the principal would not give up the pleasure of his card games.

In Peru there were many single, older persons such as Mr. Yasuda. I sympathized for them, as I knew that if it was lonely to live alone in Japan it must be even more so in a foreign land. Later, Mr. Yasuda took an overdose of sleeping pills to end his life. That occurred not long after I left the school and I was truly saddened by it.

I felt concern for older immigrants such as Mr. Yasuda, but when I considered the immigrants' situation carefully, I also realized that the children who attended the school were in pitiful circumstances. Those children of immigrants were often denied opportunities for receiving an adequate education. Moreover, they had to work at a very early age to contribute to their families' livelihood or were left to manage all the household chores.

They had no organized recreational activities or amusements. At an age when children love to play among themselves, these children were not allowed even that freedom. In that sense, even the children of the settlers in Hokkaido were better off. We had been poor, but minimum standardized educational opportunities had been guaranteed and children were free to explore and develop their own special worlds.

Above all I wanted to do something for the immigrant children. Even if it was only for the time they spent in school, I at least wanted them to have some fun. So, as one possibility, I began teaching them how to play baseball, which I had learned during my early days in Hokkaido. It was a great success. Day by day the children became more like normal children and soon lively, happy voices echoed about the schoolyard.

Eventually, our school came to have an outstanding baseball team. Soon, schools in neighboring towns such as Imperial and San Luis followed suit and formed their own teams. Later, we began to play competitive games with them. The baseball fever that began with the elementary school children of Canete spread to the area's youth and adults—baseball became an extremely popular pastime in the Canete area.

Encouraged by this success, I introduced other sports and even organized athletic meets. I arranged for the girls to be taught not only sports but handicrafts and dancing. Fortunately, women graduates of the school cooperated to provide such guidance. With their efforts, these activities grew to enjoy great popularity. At last, laughter had returned to the children of Canete. Nothing could have made me happier. The families of the children were also happy about it. Mr. Yasuda smiled and remarked, "Since you have come, the children and their parents, too, have completely changed."

A "Facilitator"

When I began teaching, I left the Araki Company but again became a "working guest" in the home of Sengoro Watanabe. "We have a large house, so don't worry about it," he said. Accepting their hospitality, I went to live at the Watanabes' home.

Mr. Watanabe ran his own business; he was the adoptive father of Kenzo Watanabe, who had let me accompany him on my original trip from Lima to Canete. Kenzo was the nephew of Mrs. Watanabe. As their adopted son, who would continue the line of the Watanabe family, he worked as the manager of the Watanabe Company. Mrs. Watanabe had formerly been the head of the housekeeping staff of a large traditional Japanese inn in the Osaka area and was an extremely intelligent person who was always alert to the smallest details.

In their home were four or five young men, relatives who had been called over from Japan. They all had been through middle schools in Japan and had come over to Peru to become "working guests" cared for by the Watanabe family. There were also four or five young, *nisei* (second generation) girls who had been taken in as "trainees" so that they could acquire work skills and guidance in proper behavior.

Since I was then earning a salary, even if it was only a small amount, I offered to pay for my room and meals, but they refused completely. So during holidays and whenever work let up at the school I went over to their shop to help with the duties there. This was a natural "unspoken obligation" for being provided my room and board.

The shop was also an excellent classroom for learning conversational Spanish. I continued to study Spanish from textbooks, but I looked for free time and whenever possible went over to their shop to practice my Spanish.

Even if I was only a teacher at an elementary school, my life was filled with activities. Other than my teaching duties, I served as a sports coach for the children, oversaw other extracurricular activities, and was expected to provide their everyday moral guidance. Of course, I could not neglect my obligations to the Watanabes and had to deal with numerous miscellaneous problems faced by my students' parents and our neighbors. It seemed that I had been "promoted" from my position as an all-purpose worker for the Araki Company to become a school teacher and, simultaneously, had "opened practice" as a "facilitator" who was called on to handle a variety of community problems.

As a "facilitator," I responded to whatever request came to me. One day a request came to me, quite misguidedly, to conduct a land survey. Peru was then in the midst of a minor "cotton boom," and the heated competition to acquire lands for growing cotton had spread to the Japanese there.

It happened that the owner of a large hacienda had put some land in the broad Canete plains out to lease. Shozo Tachibana, originally from Shizuoka Prefecture in Japan, and Suketsune Kudo, who operated the "Kudo Colony" along the Amazon River, both got wind of the opportunity. Both already operated large farms and were extensively involved in cotton growing.

The rivalry between Mr. Tachibana and Mr. Kudo to acquire the leasehold lands progressed until it reached a loggerhead. Among the immigrants, whenever matters reached such a point nothing could happen until the Japanese Consul made a move. Finally, the consul intervened and both parties agreed to divide control of the lands.

Yet, even after that agreement was struck, it was not a simple matter to divide such a huge area of land equally. First, a survey was necessary. When they considered who could do it, they decided, "Oh yes, there's Higashide."

They had very casually reasoned, "if he's an architect, he should be able to do a survey." But I was not a land survey specialist, and I had no equipment to conduct such work. Still I was urged to "do whatever you can," and the responsibility was placed on my shoulders. As a "facilitator," I could not escape the assignment. With four or five assistants provided by Mr. Tachibana and Mr. Kudo, I somehow managed to survey the land and to divide it equitably. Fortunately, following that division, good relations were established between the two men and disagreements never again arose. Since the cotton boom continued for some time, I'm sure both parties made huge profits.

An Unbelievable Offer—A Turning Point in Peru

I worked for about a year as a "facilitator" and developed a reputation for good work. One day I received an unbelievable offer from Choichi Otani, president of the parent's association of the Japanese elementary school.

I had been invited to dinner at the Otani home and was seated at the dining table with members of the family when Mr. Otani suddenly said, "Higashide, would you consider taking over my businesses? There are no strings attached." At first, I didn't grasp quite what he meant and did not know what to say.

Mr. Otani explained the situation. The Otani Company consisted of a gift shop that handled luxury items, a barber shop, and a liquor store that had an attached bar. He would hand it all over to me for 25,000 Peruvian soles but would not require any down payment. "I was struck by your upbringing and personality, so I decided that it would be best to transfer my businesses to you," he said. He explained that as soon as he settled the details of transferring the businesses he planned to return to Japan.

This proposal, of course, was not a casual undertaking that I could handle in my spare time. Even if I devoted all my attention to it, the responsibility was so large that I didn't think I could manage it alone. I said, "That really is beyond my capabilities," and refused the offer. I felt badly about refusing Mr. Otani, who had singled me out with his trust. I thanked him for his kindness and consideration and took my leave.

Several days later, however, I was again invited to the Otani home. "Why won't you accept my offer?" he asked. Mr. Otani seemed convinced that he could place his trust in me. He stated that he wanted to leave his businesses with me badly enough as to be flexible about the conditions of the agreement. At that time 25,000 soles was a very large sum—but in terms of the scope of the businesses it was an exceptionally low price. I wanted to jump at it, but out of respect for Mr. Otani I could not accept his offer so casually.

Citing my lack of business experience and inadequate command of Spanish, I again refused. But Mr. Otani responded directly, "Spanish and business experience are not the problem. What is important is whether or not the businesses are run on a steady basis and in an honest manner. On these points, you qualify." I was grateful that he trusted me, yet I did not have full confidence that I could do it.

I was already feeling badly about refusing him when Mr. Otani further compounded the problem by even offering to find a bride for me. While I was in that state of indecision Mr. Otani made an alternate proposal. "Well, then, how about doing it jointly with Kato who works at our barber shop? Kato is quite a serious and straight-forward young man, so I'm sure he'll be a good right hand man for you."

The idea of joint ownership cast the matter in a completely different light. Mr. Kato was a young man about my age. He had graduated from a middle school in Fukushima Prefecture and had emigrated to Peru, where he found a job at Mr. Otani's barber shop. I felt that if the two of us worked together we might be able to accomplish the task.

Actually, what had worried me the most was not my lack of business experience or Spanish—I was concerned that I could not look after all three shops by myself. I knew if I tried to do so I would be tied down by those shops from early morning to late at night. The bar, in particular, was open until about midnight. Even if I let an employee manage it during the day so I could take naps, I knew my body would not hold up. If I lost my health, everything would be lost. More importantly, if that happened I would be letting Mr. Otani down. Based on such considerations, I had been reluctant to accept.

But now, on the condition that it be held in joint ownership with Kato, these concerns were lifted. I gratefully accepted Mr. Otani's offer. I resigned my teaching position at the San Vicente Japanese Elementary School after a year and a half to become co-owner of the Otani Company. It was June 1933, the beginning of my fourth full year after crossing over to Peru.

The Otani Business Philosophy

After we took over the Otani Company, Kato and I wholeheartedly put all of our efforts into our work. We worked every day, at times even forgetting to eat or sleep. We naturally wanted to increase profits, but we were motivated even more by the feeling that we could not forsake Mr. Otani's kindness and generosity. Mr. Otani had, with almost no conditions, handed over his hard-earned assets, diligently built up over many years, to two young wanderers. I knew what an extraordinary decision that was, and I vowed to myself that no matter what happened I would not let down his trust in me.

The shop specializing in luxury items was a rather unlikely one for a place like Canete. Its decor was quite different from other shops and its merchandise was mainly expensive, high-quality goods and gift items imported from Europe and the United States. I later came to appreciate Mr. Otani's rare business sense. He had seen the potential of handling expensive items, which other local shopkeepers had avoided. By doing so, he had built up a solid, upper class clientele with strong purchasing power. These customers were mainly American and British owners of the great haciendas and their families.

According to Mr. Otani, "Rather than having a shop always crowded with poor laborers, a shop where the wealthy might frequent even just occasionally would be more profitable." In Peru at that time, the differences between the wealthy and the poor were extreme. The wealthy snapped up unusual items without any concern over prices. To an untrained eye, Mr. Otani's gift shop would not have appeared to be successful, but it brought in surprisingly high profits. We came to realize this only after we took over the shop and were amazed at Mr. Otani's sharp business sense.

Mr. Otani 's business philosophy was reflected not only in the gift shop but also in his management of the liquor store. At first glance, the shop looked like a regular liquor store selling bottled liquor. The rear area of the shop, however, had been transformed into a rather smart lounge. As with the gift shop, most of the clientele of the lounge were owners of haciendas and their families.

The atmosphere of the lounge area behind the front counter of the liquor shop was such that average workers could not enter readily. Fine, high-quality wines and whiskeys were served. It was never crowded, but it never lacked customers.

Later, when I came to have my own business in the city of Ica, I found that the most effective business policies I could follow continued to be those based on Mr. Otani's business philosophy.

As for Mr. Otani's return to Japan, it seems that he had gone over to Manchuria and launched a huge enterprise there. Through the connections of an officer he knew, Mr. Otani had decided that the coming great opportunity was in Manchuria. He had, of course, taken over a substantial amount of capital, but I was more overwhelmed with admiration for his almost heroic decisiveness and splendid entrepreneurial spirit.

In a letter I received about a year after he left Peru, Mr. Otani wrote that he had acquired a large site in the heart of the city of Hsinching in Manchuria and was awaiting the completion of a multistoried building. In the relatively short time since his departure from Peru he had already achieved such a level of business activity. In his letter, he explained that the Southern Manchurian Railway Company had already signed a contract to lease the entire building. I was astounded. Later, communications between us were interrupted by the war, but I felt sure that with his abilities Mr. Otani would be able to pass through any difficulty encountered.

Finding a Marriage Partner in Peru

From about the time when I was a teacher, the question of marriage concerned me. I had often been urged to get married and I felt that sooner or later I would like to do so.

Within the Japanese community in Peru, however, marriage was not a simple matter. For a period after emigration had commenced, there were very few Japanese females in Peru, resulting in an imbalance of males and females of marriageable age. As with Mr. Yasuda, the school principal I had described earlier, there were many men who spent their entire lives alone. By the time I was ready to get married, conditions had changed some, but there were still more Japanese males than females in Peru.

Because of this situation, immigrants pursued many different plans to solve the problem of finding marriage partners. None, however, actually brought satisfactory results.

One strategy was to return to Japan, get married, and then bring one's spouse back to Peru. This was an ideal method, but it required at least enough money to pay for a round-trip ticket, so it clearly eliminated all but a very few exceptions.

Another alternative was to marry a local Peruvian. This might have been difficult for immigrants who knew very little Spanish, but there were ample possibilities for the nisei generation who had been born and raised in Peru. Yet, at least prior to the Pacific War, it was rare for a Japanese to marry a local Peruvian.

There were several factors deterring Japanese from marrying Peruvians. First, the Japanese community in Peru was self-contained and tightly closed, so young Japanese of marriageable age had almost no opportunities to get acquainted with Peruvians. Also, first-generation immigrants harbored a strong sense of discrimination. Their attitude was, "How can talented Japanese marry people of a third-rate country?" If their children considered marrying Peruvians in direct opposition to their parents, it meant they would have to completely cut themselves off from the Japanese community.

There was, of course, within that "third rate" country an upper class society. If marriage with someone from that stratum was contemplated, the proud first generation Japanese would have had no objections. But upper-class Peruvians had their own air of exclusivity, so even if Japanese young people had wanted to approach them, there would have been no way to do so. Ultimately, because of such circumstances, there seemed to be no possibilities for Japanese to marry Peruvians.

I did not feel that Japanese were superior, nor that Peruvians should be looked down upon as inferior. After I married and had children I came to see that I could not direct their marriage choices, but in my early days in Peru I felt that since my children were to be born in Peru and would live there I wanted them to fully enter Peruvian society. If any of them chose to marry a Peruvian, I would not have opposed it simply on the notion of race or nationality.

In one sense the exclusiveness and feelings of discrimination held by the Japanese in Peru contributed to their strong cohesiveness and played a large part in maintaining their "organically constituted" communal group. But, in another sense, it cut them off from Peruvian society, creating a separate "nation within a nation." I believe the anti-Japanese movement that later arose in Peru was related to that exclusiveness and sense of discrimination held by the Japanese immigrants.

An Image of the Ideal Bride and Reality

About the time I was married, there were a number of second generation Japanese Peruvians who were reaching marriageable age. In the Canete area, however, it seemed there were many more males than females. If this was so, I was indeed very fortunate to have made a good marriage.

Needless to say, I did not have the finances to return to Japan to seek a bride. Yet, I also had not assimilated enough into Peruvian society to be able to take a non-Japanese Peruvian bride. My only hope was to meet a nisei girl or a young girl who had come over from Japan. At that time, however, emigration from Japan had already been almost completely prohibited, so the latter possibility was almost nil.

Although the only hope for me was to marry a young nisei lady, I still had problems with that alternative. Realizing it might sound high-handed to say so, I still felt that the second generation young girls did not fit my idealized image of a bride. I felt I needed a person who would understand me and work with me, someone to whom I could reveal my innermost feelings. On the surface, I showed an air of confidence, but inwardly I felt an inexplicable loneliness. I wanted a partner who would understand this and support me in my endeavors.

If I ever met such a person, I thought, it would not matter at all if her countenance was not so beautiful, if there was some discrepancy in our ages, or if there was some blemish in her background. Among those born in Peru, however, there seemed to be no one who fit my ideal.

As was commonly discussed, the gap between the first and second generation Japanese was something broad and unbridgeable. Even if we were close in age, I was still a first generation immigrant and my bride would probably be a second generation Japanese raised in Peru, different from girls in Japan.

First, the nisei were generally not fluent in the Japanese language. They could make some sense of it when they heard it, but could not speak or write it correctly themselves. Moreover, they did not really understand Japanese society and culture in which the first generation had been born and raised. They had heard of such matters from parents and teachers, but that was at best indirect, learned information. If they did not have the type of instinctive understanding that is part of one's blood through long experience, how could they understand the particular turnings and involutions of the heart of someone like myself, a first generation male from Japan?

I felt that if it were possible, even if she were nisei, my ideal bride would be someone who had experienced life in Japan. Even if she had lived in Japan for only a short time, she would have a different outlook and understanding. At that time there already were children of established families in Peru who had gone to Japan to study and had returned to Peru. But the great majority of those who had studied in Japan were young men. It was a rare exception that a girl born in Peru would have experienced life in Japan.

My search for an ideal bride in Peru thus came up against various barriers. I was not particularly anxious about it, but the uneasy feeling that I might never meet the girl I had hoped for was constantly with me.

Angelica

The Japanese community in Canete seemed to be limited, but after some time I met a good number of immigrant families residing there. When I was at the Araki Company, I went out several times a week to the shops in the Canete area to deliver vermicelli and there I met a number of young second generation Japanese girls. Because of this, even after becoming an elementary school teacher, I had the opportunity to meet a number of young ladies at social gatherings. Of course those "social gatherings" were no more than formal community events and were not premised with the goal of possible matchmaking.

I knew, too, that with my small salary as an elementary school teacher marriage was still out of the question. There were two young ladies, however, to whom I was particularly attracted.

One of them was Angelica Shizuka, the oldest daughter of Kahei Yoshinaga, who owned a sundries store at the Arona hacienda on the outskirts of Canete. I first met her when I was still delivering vermicelli for the Araki Company. At that time she was 13 or 14 and was known in the Japanese community as "a very attractive and likeable young girl." Although still very young, she was capable of handling the daily operations of her father's shop by herself. She had a strong and sensible nature, and was very mature for her age.

Angelica's father was a diligent worker who dealt directly and honestly in his relationships with people; he did not drink or gamble. Her mother was an honest and very gentle woman. Both were very protective toward their three daughters. The Yoshinaga family had accepted as a matter of course the strict patterns of behavior practiced by the upper classes in Peru.

Their daughters were not allowed to leave their house without a chaperone. Much later, when I began inviting Angelica out on "dates," someone always accompanied us. When I visited their home we were not allowed to be alone in a room. I had already become somewhat familiar with Peruvian upper class behavior at that time, so I did not think it strange that we were accompanied on our dates by a chaperone. I really did not mind this arrangement. Rather, because the Japanese community often gossiped about any "improper" behavior between men and women, the Yoshinaga family's strict rules even enhanced my reputation of respectability.

Having been raised in a family which held such protective attitudes, Angelica did not socialize much with other young people. It was not surprising that she tended to be shy and introspective. She tended not to speak openly with anyone. When spoken to, she responded only with direct answers. Still, the young men of Canete devised various excuses to visit her. After I became a teacher at the elementary school, I did not have many opportunities to see her, but I continued to hear comments about her. I even heard remarks to the effect that she was "self-involved" and palangana (haughty).

Whether she was *palangana* or not, she was the object of great interest to marriage-conscious Japanese immigrants. From an early stage there were inquiries about marriage arrangements for Angelica. Some, I heard, even considered the lack of male heirs in the Yoshinaga family and proposed the intended groom be adopted by the Yoshinaga family. Her parents, however, found reasons to turn away all inquiries. I began to sense that her parents had other plans in mind.

An Overblown "Scandal"

Soon after I became a teacher, I became acquainted with another young lady, Masami Kuroiwa. She was the third daughter of Kizo Kuroiwa, who became the president of the parent's association of the school where I taught. After I took the position, there were many occasions when I needed to visit the Kuroiwa home and I became acquainted enough with the young lady so I could speak easily with her.

She had an older brother named Shigeyuki and three younger brothers who attended the elementary school. Shigeyuki, who was about my age, had immigrated to Peru when he was about 5 or 6. He returned to Japan to study, graduated from a middle school, then had returned to Peru. Masami also had two older sisters who had married and were living in Japan.

No matter when I visited the Kuroiwa home it seemed to be a lively and happy household. Near their home was a large open field which served as a good exercise area for the schoolchildren. Once or twice a week I took the children there to coach them in baseball or track and field sports. After the practices I always stopped at her home and was made to feel welcome. She was extremely kind and attentive to me as a teacher at a school from which she had graduated.

Different from Angelica, Masami was a very lighthearted and extroverted girl who talked about all sorts of things in a carefree way, often smiling and laughing. It happened that Miss Kuroiwa's mother and Miss Yoshinaga's mother were from the same prefecture in Japan and the two families were very close, almost like a blood relationship. The two girls were great friends and constantly visited each other's homes.

There may have even existed an unspoken understanding between the two families that Shigeyuki and Angelica would be married someday. About a year after I took over the Otani Company, however, discord arose between the two families over assumptions about that marriage. I heard rumors that I was the cause of the falling out between the two families. That struck me like a "lightning bolt out of the blue." I was dumbfounded.

The rumor circulated that Shigeyuki Kuroiwa had assumed he would marry Angelica, but I had entered the picture and become a "hindrance." Shigeyuki had confronted the Yoshinaga family and questioned how they could have allowed such a thing to happen.

The members of the Yoshinaga family, faced by such accusations, must have been at a loss for an answer. It was I, however, who was most astounded. Angelica and I had not even held hands, and, of course, we had never exchanged any flirtatious words. I could not understand how such a situation arose.

It was common for rumors of that sort to be passed around within the Japanese community in Peru. Even when I was a teacher, talk about Angelica and myself or Masami and myself were passed about everywhere.

I had been greatly embarrassed by such rumors. I had taken the position as a teacher only as an interim measure, but even so I firmly believed I should not bring disgrace to the school. I had been extremely careful not to cause unseemly rumors, but I could not control speculation within the community.

Since I was alone in Peru, with no family, no one in the community had to be concerned about consequences of telling false tales or complaining about me; I was an easy target for gossip. I could take being the butt of such talk, but I felt very strongly that it was unfair to the girls whose names were dragged into the rumors. It angered me, but there was nothing I could do to stop such cheap, baseless rumors.

Unexpected Marriage Discussions

Not long after Shigeyuki Kuroiwa confronted the Yoshinaga family with his dissatisfactions, I was paid an unexpected visit by Angelica's mother.

My work as co-owner of the Otani Company had fallen into a regular pattern, giving me some free time. I occasionally visited the Yoshinaga home and had been invited to stay for dinner. Since the Yoshinagas lived near San Vicente, where the Otani Company shops were located, it was not that I made special trips to their home. Rather, it was more a matter of casually dropping by to see them.

While I had gone many times to visit them, members of the Yoshinaga family had never come to visit me. When Mrs. Yoshinaga came to visit me, therefore, I wondered what had prompted her visit and became somewhat anxious. After the usual exchange of pleasantries, Mrs. Yoshinaga changed her demeanor and began speaking of the reason for her visit. It was, as I had expected, about Angelica.

According to Mrs. Yoshinaga, Angelica was in love with me. It had become painfully obvious even to the eyes of others, so Mrs. Yoshinaga had come in Angelica's place to find out what my feelings and intentions were. It was not that the topic was completely unexpected, but it was brought up so suddenly I did not know how to answer her.

It was truly a sudden development. I felt that I would get married sooner or later, but when I was asked so directly what my immediate intentions were I was at a loss for an answer. I tried to find a way around it by saying, "I am so completely taken up with the work of the Otani Company. . . ." but Mrs. Yoshinaga immediately answered, "If you truly accept it, we shall have Shizuka wait three years or even five years." She emphasized her point by deliberately using Angelica's Japanese name, Shizuka. She added, "Shizuka still has many things to learn and to be trained in."

Still unable to make a definite reply, I said, "At this moment I cannot say, but I shall give you an honest answer after considering the matter fully." The visit came to an end.

For the next four or five days this question, which had come to me so suddenly, consumed all of my thoughts. There was no question about Angelica's proper upbringing at home. She was a good-natured, healthy person who had a reputation for being diligent in her work—not to mention that she was very beautiful.

I thought, should I not rejoice that in this land under the Southern Cross there was a young lady who held such feelings for me? As for the problem of language, although she may not be completely fluent in Japanese I had heard that she often read Japanese magazines. If we were married, I was sure that it would work out. When I considered everything, the entire matter seemed to be too good to be true for a solitary young wanderer such as I. I do not know exactly when, but my heart had suddenly turned fully toward Angelica.

Several days later, I arranged with the Yoshinagas to visit Angelica. She appeared in a charming outfit and had put on light makeup. She was so beautiful that I could hardly recognize her as the girl I had seen so many times before. I immediately invited her out for a walk in a nearby park. Her parents were acutely aware of the significance of the occasion, and allowed us out this time without a chaperone, something rarely allowed even after a girl's engagement.

In the park I proposed to Angelica, "Let's get married and with all our efforts live out our lives together." I wanted to express my feelings fully to her. She seemed to be overjoyed with my words. In planning for our future, however, we still had many things to consider, so I asked that our understanding be kept between the two of us for a while.

In this manner, we became engaged to be married. There was no intermediary, as was traditional in Japanese wedding arrangements, nor did we exchange Western-style engagement rings. Angelica's parents seemed a little concerned about this, but nevertheless came to view us as being engaged.

Shigeyuki Kuroiwa, who had lost his expected marriage partner, later moved to Huanco in central Peru. Together with Hiroyuki Nagano, who had been the principal of the Japanese elementary school in the neighboring town of Imperial, the two began a large-scale commercial orange orchard. Shigeyuki's sister, Masami, returned to Japan where, I have heard, she entered into a happy marriage.

Angelica Attends School in Lima

Angelica was only 17 years old when we got engaged. I felt that it was still too early for marriage, so I asked her parents to send her to school in Lima.

Although I had clung to it for so long, I felt by this time that I had to completely abandon any hopes of doing architectural work. My future now had to be focussed fully on achieving success in my business activities. My dream for the future was now that the two of us would work together toward establishing a successful business.

Since I had very little formal business training, I hoped that my fiancee would acquire formal training in that area. I asked Angelica's parents to allow her to attend a business school in Lima for a period of four years. In four years she would be 21 and, I thought, by that time my own situation would be more solidly established.

But the idea of attending a school was not a simple matter. First, because Angelica had led a sheltered life we were concerned that she needed someone who could be trusted to look after her while she was in Lima. After considering it carefully, I decided to seek the help of Tatsujiro Kurotobi, who had been so kind to me when I first arrived in Peru.

Mr. Kurotobi quickly agreed and said, "It will be no problem for her to stay with us while attending school. But we have many young men in our shop, so let me find a more appropriate place for her to stay." What he then added was unexpected and more upsetting. "It won't do for her to go to a business school. You should send her to the homemaking school run by a Japanese. The course is only for two years. . . ."

For those born in the Meiji period, even after many years in a foreign land, a woman's place was set solidly and could not be changed. Yet, when considered, there seemed to be a certain logic to what Mr. Kurotobi said. I said, "We gratefully accept your kindness," and left everything for him to arrange.

Angelica moved to Lima and began commuting to a Japanese-operated homemaking school. Mr. Kurotobi looked around but could not find a more appropriate place for Angelica to live while she attended the school, so she continued to stay for a while at his home. In the Kurotobi home she was treated very specially as the person "who is to be young Higashide's bride."

From childhood, however, Angelica had been accustomed to work, so when the Kurotobi's employees dining tables were crowded, or when the maids and cooks were pressed with their work, she naturally tried to help. When she was caught doing so by the owner or other members of the Kurotobi family, she was scolded and told that she should not do such things.

The Kurotobis felt that Angelica should not go out of the family's residential area within the Kurotobi compound. Mr. Kurotobi was extremely concerned about this and finally decided that it was not appropriate for her to live in his business-residential compound. He arranged for her to live in the home of the principal of the Lima Japanese Elementary School, where he felt she could learn the social graces of an "upper status household."

Angelica was to commute to the homemaking school while living in the home of the principal of the large and prestigious school. But, as we learned, the home of such a leader is not necessarily a "splendid household." Angelica soon became upset by her life at that household and called Mrs. Kurotobi. She was brought back to live in the Kurotobi home. "There is nothing that I can learn from that household," she said. One cannot judge, it seems, the nature of people simply by their educational backgrounds or their official positions.

A Big Decision. Transition From Being a "Wanderer"

About a year after Angelica went to Lima, I was confronted with a big decision regarding my co-ownership of the Otani Company. When we had taken over the businesses, my cooperative arrangement with Kato had worked extremely well. After two years, however, we had both become familiar with the operations and our initial anxieties settled into a familiar routine. It was then that disagreements over the operations began to arise between us. The employees of the shops were caught up between our differing decisions and were often confused about what they should do.

I felt that such a situation was not good for either of us, and I decided that we should end our joint ownership agreement. With two years of experience in running the businesses, I was confident that I could manage them alone. On the other hand, I was also fully prepared to give up my share of control of the Otani Company. I made the proposal.

Whatever happened, I insisted that our dissolution of joint ownership had to be premised on complete repayment of our financial obligations to Mr. Otani. Thus, if I took over the company I would need a large sum of money. It happened that there was someone who was willing to advance me that capital so, emphasizing the condition that our debt to Mr. Otani be completely met, I made the proposal to Kato.

When approached with this proposal, Kato asked me to wait two or three days, apparently to arrange his own financial backing through his many acquaintances. He was much more fluent in Spanish than I and was quite adept at nurturing social relationships. Moreover, in Canete there were quite a few successful businessmen from Kato's home prefecture in Japan who were alumni of his middle school or close friends, so he quickly arranged funds for a buy out and proposed that he take over the business entirely.

The transaction was completed. I asked Fusauemon Murata, who was from Kato's home prefecture, to serve as agent and intermediary for Mr. Otani. Having cleared all of our obligations, I left the business.

It seemed to me that to abandon those shops, which Mr. Otani had left to us at an exceptionally low price, was to disappoint and fail him. It seemed to be a pitiful and unsatisfactory outcome and I felt very upset about it. Yet, my deepest gut feeling told me there was nothing else I could do.

My only consolation was that I had at least fulfilled my financial obligation to Mr. Otani. Having done so, with profits of 1,500 soles for two years of work, I moved forth to become a different type of wanderer.

Looking back, it seemed that I had taken a big loss. When viewed from a different perspective, the differences between Kato and myself could have been contrived as part of a self-serving scheme undertaken by Kato. There were many things that I could cite to confirm this, but there was no benefit in pursuing such thoughts. I vowed to cleanse my mind of such matters and sought to stride forth to face the vital decisions regarding our future.

Planning Our Future

After I left co-ownership of the Otani Company, I stayed for a time in the home of Angelica's father, Kahei Yoshinaga. There I began planning for a new start in business. The Yoshinaga family had sold their shop in the Arona hacienda to a Chinese family and had bought a shop not far from the Otani Company. Their shop handled items of daily necessity and also began manufacturing *somen,* a type of Japanese noodle. While helping at their shop, I explored possibilities for my future with Angelica.

My plans were based, first of all, on the premise that we had to leave Canete. I had concluded that the Canete area did not offer much hope for success. In that small town there were approximately 120 Japanese families, all alert for new business opportunities. Many types of businesses had already been tested, and there did not seem to be much room for carving out a place in the local business community. There were no indications that the area could expect any major developments in the future.

Although I had come to such a conclusion, I did not have enough capital or experience for us to move to Lima, where there were unlimited opportunities. After much thought I set my sights on the city of Ica, the governmental center for the province of Ica. I visited the city to see for myself the actual conditions there and the possibility of establishing a business there.

The city of Ica was a medium-sized urban center, located about 200 miles south of Canete. I spent about a month there getting to know the nature of the city and its outlying areas.

My assessment was that business possibilities were very good, but my lack of capital seemed to present an insurmountable barrier. It did not seem possible to establish myself in the central area of the city. Disappointed, I thought I had to abandon my hopes of opening a shop in the central area when, by a stroke of luck, a completely unexpected find came to my eyes.

In an area near the central plaza of the city, I came upon a hosiery shop which was being closed down. After I spoke with the Spanish owners of the shop, I began to feel there was a possibility that I could take over that shop. After some negotiations, we reached an agreement whereby I would pay the owners 500 soles for the rights to the shop and another 500 soles for their remaining inventory.

I felt certain I could take over the business, which I envisioned as a shop as specializing in Western goods and small accessories. It was a small shop, but I knew I could not handle everything by myself. I considered a number of alternatives, but decided that since I was already engaged to be married the best path might be to drop our earlier plans and get married immediately. I felt badly about disrupting Angelica's program at her school, but having decided to purchase the shop, I knew I had to be bold in confronting our circumstances. Angelica's parents agreed, and they approved our immediate marriage.

Angelica left the homemaking school. For the marriage ceremony, Mr. and Mrs. Kurotobi agreed to stand in place of my parents and our "intermediaries" were Mr. and Mrs. Kuninosuke Yamamoto, owners of the *Peru Jiho* Newspaper Company. Although we were not Christians, we had our wedding ceremony in a Protestant church.

After we exchanged our wedding vows, we had a somewhat

unusual non-alcoholic wedding reception. In Peru, alcohol seemed to be an integral part of life. But I could take very little alcohol, and decided not to serve alcohol at our wedding festivities. Moreover, I felt there were so many people in Peru who had ruined their health with alcohol that such a decision might focus some community attention on the need for moderation.

Our wedding celebration was a totally unique event in Peru. Whether one agreed with our decision or not, there was much interest in the event. It was reported in Peruvian newspapers and even in newspapers in Japan. Shortly after the ceremonies I received an unexpected letter of congratulations from a cousin, Eikichi Miyamoto, who was in charge of the educational division of the Japanese South Pacific Bureau. It seems he had read an article in a Japanese newspaper about our "non-alcoholic wedding" and was moved to send us his congratulations.

Angelica and I were married on March 7, 1935. We looked forward to building a new life in the city of Ica.

A non-alcoholic wedding, 1935.

Chapter Five. Approaching Storm Clouds

Starting Anew in Ica

Ica was the commercial, cultural and political center of Ica Province. Much larger than Canete, Ica felt somewhat like a "small Lima" set out in the countryside.

The surrounding farmlands were very different from the areas around Canete. Here, there were only two or three large haciendas which employed great numbers of people. Most of the families were relatively prosperous, small and middle scale independent farmers. Because of this, I had to operate our shop somewhat differently from the way we had run the Otani shops in Canete.

When we opened our shop, our greatest concern was finding a way to stretch our limited capital. If the shop had been in operation for a while, its track record might have allowed us some chance of receiving credit. But ours was a brand new business, and we had just arrived ourselves and lacked knowledge of local conditions.

In order to get through this situation, I sought various ways to secure credit from wholesalers or business loans from banks. I was determined, however, to avoid resorting to personal loans.

Our suppliers were mainly wholesalers in Lima. Mr. Kurotobi had very generously told me, "If there's anything you can use from the merchandise we have, take whatever you want." Unfortunately, the Kurotobi Company did not handle clothing or accessories, so we could not "borrow" any merchandise.

In the beginning, every wholesaler I went to told me that our transactions had to be "cash on delivery." They would not even agree to bill us monthly, as was the usual procedure. We had used up all of the nest egg we had acquired to purchase and open the shop. Having just opened the shop, our volume of business was less than what I had hoped for, so the first few months were truly difficult.

Our worrisome days continued until one day I stopped in, unannounced, at the Hayashi Company in Lima to ask if they would handle our trade. At the time, it was one of the few large wholesalers of clothing and accessories owned by a Japanese Peruvian. It was my first meeting with Mr. Heitaro Hayashi, owner of the Hayashi Company, but when I explained my situation he sympathized completely and said, "If you find our merchandise suitable, take whatever you want. I shall also try to find items suitable for your market."

I hesitantly asked, "Would it be acceptable to take the goods on credit?" Without even a flicker of his eyebrows he said, "Yes, of course. Please, take whatever you want. It will be completely acceptable if you pay in increments. Starting any type of business is difficult; I hope you'll work hard to make much profit and expand to a large scale." His gentle and friendly demeanor had not changed at all.

Mr. Hayashi had saved us from our desperate situation. I had already visited a number of wholesalers and most had refused me outright or would accept only cash transactions. When I heard Mr. Hayashi's words, I was so grateful that tears brimmed in my eyes. It meant we could survive our difficult situation. Even more so, however, I was deeply moved by his warm words of encouragement.

A True "Omi Merchant"

At our first meeting, Mr. Hayashi shared with me his experiences of hardship. To this day they remain with me as unforgettable lessons in business practices and attitudes.

The day after he arrived in Peru, Mr. Hayashi loaded a small trunk with merchandise—including cheap cosmetics, women's stockings, and underwear, handkerchiefs, etc.—and went out into the city to sell them. Not knowing any Spanish, Mr. Hayashi had prepared a small card on which he wrote, in Japanese syllabary characters, terms such as "buenos dias," "como esta usted" and "muchas gracias," the Spanish words for his merchandise, and the Spanish numbers, "unos" on up to ten. I admired his splendid spirit and self-confidence.

Mr. Hayashi said he went directly to the "red-light district" of the city and sold his merchandise to the women there. When the trunk was emptied, he immediately took the cash he had collected, bought more merchandise, and flew back to the district to continue his business with the women. After doing this for several days, the women came to look forward to his offerings and started placing orders for specific items with him. This was how the owner of the flourishing Hayashi Company began in Peru.

Hayashi had seen the possibilities in the red-light district, which then had nothing worthy of being called a "shop." He had chosen to deal, moreover, with persons who had ready cash, if only very small sums. His decision to start a street business was a splendid idea for it needed almost no capital.

I saw him as a true "incarnation" in Peru of those persons from Shiga Prefecture in Japan who had held to the proud, centuries-old business traditions that had been instilled in the "Omi Merchants."

Mr. Hayashi built up a business base in an unbelievably short period of time and, by the time I had arrived in Peru, had become one of the few large wholesalers who had many tens of thousands of Peruvian soles worth of merchandise in his warehouses.

Although he owned a large business operation, Mr. Hayashi did not behave in a haughty manner in the least. As with me, he met even unknown beginners with humility, demonstrated by a meticulous lowering of his head. Yet, he was also a person who had the courage to say, based on simple intuition, "It is acceptable to base our transaction on credit." I felt that this truly was what a merchant and businessman should be.

Mr. Hayashi's attitudes had been fully absorbed by others in the Hayashi Company. There was a young accountant in the company named Kishiro Hayashi, a nephew of Mr. Hayashi, who truly reflected Mr. Hayashi's attitudes. When I began to trade with the company, Kishiro was only about 18 years old. Already, however, he had been placed in the key position of handling all of the company's accounts.

Now one might expect to hear from an 18-year-old youth a resentful tone of voice or childish exuberances, but this young man was different. He showed an extremely humble attitude. Although he handled important work for the company, he did not once show any prideful emphasis on his position. I observed him with admiration; he was a splendid merchant heir to the attitudes and business practices of the company's owner.

Being in charge of the account books, Kishiro knew what my standing was with the Hayashi Company. I had indulged upon the goodwill of the company and had built up a sizeable credit balance. Whenever I went to their office I was afraid that something might be said about that balance. Yet, never once did Kishiro say anything that hinted of payment. Instead, he would always bow to me and say, "Please continue to favor us with purchases." It was I who was left at a quandary.

While feeling that it was improper, I continued to lean on Mr. Hayashi's goodwill and built up a large "accounts payable." Whenever I went to Lima to place orders I would put together some cash, resolved to "at least this once" pay the Hayashi Company. But there were very few firms that allowed me credit and, as I went about the city to look at merchandise, I inevitably made cash purchases. The money intended as payment to the Hayashi Company flew off in all directions. By the time I arrived at the Hayashi Company I could only lower my head in apology and, again, be allowed to order things on credit.

It was not surprising that my debt to the Hayashi Company continued to increase. There were many times when I owed them more than 10,000 soles. This situation continued for several years, but not once was I ever received at that company with a resentful face.

It is clear, however, that among wholesalers in Lima the Hayashi Company was an exception among exceptions. Other wholesalers might sometimes favor us by allowing a cash transaction, but more often they would not even allow us to buy in cash, telling us our volume was too low.

Change in Fortune—"Short Tempers are Forbidden in Business"

Although they were not wholesalers, I also encountered an interesting situation involving two very well-known shops in Lima. The Suetomi Company and the Ichikawa Company—both operated by Japanese nationals—had been conducting major advertising campaigns through newspapers and radio. Both shops had their own house-brand merchandise and promoted them aggressively through their advertising campaigns to the point where even young children in Lima knew the names of the two shops. I specifically recall that the Ichikawa Company advertised shirts, neckties, hats, etc., while the Suetomi Company advertised women's stockings and lingerie, high quality men's shirts, etc.

The two shops carried very high quality merchandise, and, because their blanket advertising reached every corner of the country, their sales were phenomenal. I really wanted to carry their merchandise because I knew it would attract customers. I approached the owners of the two shops to work out an arrangement, but both shops rejected my proposals. They both explained they were specialized retail shops. Furthermore, because they already had special contracts with outlets in Ica, they felt it would be improper for me to compete with those shops.

Although they had good reasons to reject me, I did not give up on the matter. Fortunately, I had acquaintances who worked for both shops, so I worked through them to reopen negotiations. We finally reached an agreement where I could obtain merchandise under certain conditions. The conditions required that I go to their retail shops to purchase merchandise in cash. They would sell me 12 items for the price of 10. It was, in effect, an offer of a 20 percent discount on their retail price. I would also be responsible for transporting the merchandise to Ica.

That, of course, is no way to do business. In principle, I should have refused such an offer as an insult. But I kept in mind the maxim, "In business shortsightedness is a forbidden luxury." If one thinks only of immediate profits one cannot even hope for large scale growth and development.

I knew that if the word got out that "they also have Suetomi and Ichikawa items" the status of our shop would be greatly enhanced. Bowing deeply, I said, "Thank you. May I continue to receive your kind consideration." I began taking in merchandise from the two shops on this discounted cash-and-carry basis.

Buying goods in cash from these two retail shops also gave me an advantage, however. Unlike buying from wholesalers, I could more fully control the choice and quantity of merchandise I purchased. Taking full advantage of that strong point, I carefully selected items I thought would sell well, based on design, color, sizes, price, etc. I consciously tried to avoid being left with unsold inventory or "remainders."

Among merchants in Peru, "remainders" were called hueso. The literal meaning of hueso is "bones," but in this context it had the connotation of being "picked over bones" or "leftovers." Saddled with much *hueso,* no merchant could expect to make much profit. When buying from wholesalers, however, there were always *hueso.* If any *hueso* appeared among the merchandise from the Ichikawa and Suetomi Companies, I would have to take a complete loss on them. But because I could be especially careful in selecting merchandise, items from those two shops produced no *hueso* at all.

Since there were shops in Ica with special contracts with Ichikawa and Suetomi, I was careful not to flaunt or push merchandise from those two companies. Yet, just carrying their merchandise definitely enhanced our business. Their merchandise brought me only a small margin of profit, but they also brought many customers into our shop. I came to understand fully that in business everyday pride and shortsightedness are forbidden luxuries.

An Amateur's "Financing Policy"

In business it is not only pride and shortsightedness that are forbidden "luxuries." Another very important point is to pay one's accounts without delay. By missing even one payment, one risks losing trust within the business community. It takes many months and even years to rebuild that trust. No matter how difficult a situation I was in, I always made it a point to repay bank loans, even if they were small sums, on time. After a while, I came to be trusted by the banks and, gradually, the banks came to listen and support my proposals, even when they were somewhat risky.

Business is an interesting thing. It is like being completely naked, yet being able to compete in a *sumo* wrestling match by borrowing someone else's loin cloth. While I did use bank loans, I was also able to stand in the competitive ring of business through use of promissory notes. When we first opened our shop it was difficult to establish transactions based on promissory notes, but I later made full use of those procedures.

In the early going I had more time on my hands than money, so when I did purchase merchandise via promissory notes I did not mind having to spend the time to carefully plan and make small, specific purchases.

For example, if I purchased merchandise worth 3,000 soles all at once, I would have to go through the procedure only once. Ninety days later, however, I would have to pay the full sum of 3,000 soles. But I took to breaking up such purchases so I would take in 1,000 soles worth of merchandise with a 90-day promissory note, then another 1,000 soles worth a month later, and finally another 1,000 soles worth after another month. By so doing, in a little more than two months I would have 3,000 soles worth of merchandise, but at the end of the third month would be required to pay only 1,000 soles.

It was not always possible to follow this practice, but whenever I could I would handle my purchases in this way. Besides making payments of bills manageable, the practice helped me to maintain a manageable inventory, and also allowed me to respond to changes in my customers' tastes.

At first we did not have much business volume, so I resold some of the merchandise acquired through the use of promissory notes to peddlers who worked at open markets and on the streets. Such business did not generate high profits, but they were cash transactions. I could use that income to purchase "bargains" or items sold at distress prices when they became available. With these first steps, my wife and I began to establish ourselves in the city of Ica.

Becoming a "Millionaire" is No Longer Just a Dream

In time, our shop began to establish itself. More and more customers entered our shop and we began to upgrade the quality and increase the variety of our merchandise. We began to sell good quality, luxury items for higher profits. When our retail sales began to flourish, wholesalers from other areas even began to send salesmen to us to promote their goods.

As the scale of our business grew, I began to shift our dealings gradually from the more inflexible Japanese-owned wholesalers to local Peruvian and other foreign-based wholesalers. Among the new business sources, I found companies owned by Jewish people particularly easy to work with. I had already heard of their business practices, but it was indeed true that they were stout-hearted businessmen. Once they came to trust you, they allowed a great deal of leeway in conducting business transactions. True to their reputation, they were superb businessmen in the best possible sense.

My reputation for trustworthiness steadily grew at the banks as well. I never missed a payment and deposited what we made in sales. At first I dealt with the Ica branch of the Bank of Italy, then the largest bank in Peru. Later, when business increased, I began dealing with the Popular Bank. Then, when the International Bank opened a branch in Ica, it happened that its first manager was an acquaintance from my days in Canete so I opened an account there. Eventually, I came to use these three banks. As our business flourished, the banks sent over officials to propose transactions and even were willing to consider some of my more risky initiatives.

With the backing of the banks and having received the full confidence of trading partners, our business grew so rapidly that even I was astounded. Four years after opening our first shop, we opened a branch location on one of the main streets in central Ica. The number of employees grew to 14 or 15 persons. Our retail sales flourished, but wholesaling also accounted for a large part of our business. We moved unexpectedly large quantities of merchandise, and with the larger quantities the discount rate offered to us became larger and the period allowed for promissory notes grew longer. Business became more and more easy to conduct.

While I placed full attention on the operations of our shop, I did not neglect efforts to win over public confidence in it. Whenever possible, I tried to publicize our growing success. My wife was especially effective in the area of public relations. She befriended wives of bank managers, wives of managers of large companies, and others who came into the shop. She made them aware of the flourishing success of the business. In the small business community of Ica, such information spread quickly and soon our shop was considered one of the major companies in Ica.

Good public relations inevitably will reap favorable results. In our case, such results came back by way of a number of specific offers for business affiliation. By 1941, some five years after opening our shop, major European companies such as Duncan Fox, Wessel Duval, Vargas, and others invited us to become their authorized retail outlet. Among such proposals were offers to make us their franchisees covering the entire area south of Lima to the city of Ica.

Soon, however, the Pacific War intervened and everything was reduced to nothing. Had the beginning of that war been delayed another two years I would have probably responded to those offers, which would eventually have proved disastrous for those fine European companies. In looking back, it is only in that business sense that I am grateful that the Pacific War began when it did.

As for that war, the approximately two years between the start of the war in Europe and the time when Japan became involved was a time of great prosperity for us. With war raging in Europe, imported products from that area—especially German products and products that used German-made materials—increased greatly in price. Believing that prices had not yet reached its ceiling, I gathered all the cash I could get and bought, bought, and bought again clothing and other products from Germany. With the full cooperation of the banks that I dealt with, I soon acquired an inventory worth many tens of thousands of soles. I was not sure whether it was a wise move, but I felt that the war would not end in one or two years.

My decision proved to be correct. The merchandise continued to increase in price. Retail prices for those items rose 200 to 300 percent. After a while it seemed best to sell. There were outrageous profits to be made, and our business developed in great leaps. Given the situation, it was no longer just a dream to think we could become millionaires.

President of the Japanese Association—A Dubious "Honor"

Our business success aside, I must move back in time to describe another aspect of our new life in Ica. In 1938, about three years after we had opened our shop in Ica, I was elected to the position of president of the Japanese Association of Ica.

The move came completely without warning. After all, we had been in Ica only briefly and had only two or three people there whom we could call "real friends." I had no ties to the association—and had not even become a formal member of that group. There were many others who had come to Ica much earlier than I who had established large, successful businesses. There was also a group of so-called "intellectual immigrants" who had come to Peru because of relationships with the emigration company or other major commercial enterprises.

Since that was the case, I thought, "Why should I, a young person of 30 years, be selected to take the responsibilities of the Ica Japanese Association? Moreover, is it proper, in a community that places so much importance on seniority, that this even be proposed?" I could not understand the situation.

Being selected president of the Ica Japanese Association was for me not a matter of honor but simply the imposition of unneeded and troublesome responsibilities. If I became president, I would have to spend a significant amount of time on the association's various problems and constantly go back and forth to Lima. First of all, the heavy burden of maintaining the local Japanese elementary school fell on my shoulders. If I had to bear such duties, I did not know what would happen to our little shop that was just then beginning to operate on a steady basis.

I later came to see that I had been maneuvered into the position by individuals who wanted to place those responsibilities on me. They had wanted to "do something" about our business success. A "young upstart" had suddenly come to Ica and, "without approval," had started a business. If I had failed, I would have been overlooked, but instead I was riding my first wave of success and had even opened a second shop.

I came to see that I had upset merchants with similar shops who had been in business from earlier years. One of those in the same type of business as ours, upset by the opening of our shop, stepped forward to lead the campaign to elect me. It was a typically Japanese move, formally expressed as goodwill, but was actually a "stab in the back."

The "manipulator" who had me elected as president of the Ica Japanese Association was a graduate of Tokyo Foreign Language University who had crossed over to Peru as a "director of emigration" for the emigration company and had later relocated to Ica to open a store carrying Western types of clothing. He was proud of being a university graduate who had "freely immigrated" to Peru and maintained almost no relationships with the general contract immigrant community.

Those who had come to Peru because of ties with big organizations such as the emigration company, Japanese government agencies, and so forth were called "free immigrants." There was constant, festering friction between them and the "contract labor immigrants." In day-to-day situations, they did not even speak to each other.

I had been made aware of the opposition existing between the two groups while still in Canete. I heard, until I thought calluses would form on my ears, about the resentments that the contract immigrants held against the intellectual immigrants. They felt the free immigrants took "too much pride in the 'Chrysanthemum Emblem' of the Japanese Consulate." The free immigrants, in turn, denigrated the contract emigrants.

I had been "set up" and forced into the "honorable" position of president of the Ica Japanese Association. I declined the position with strong words a number of times, but after a period of time had passed, I began to feel that if I refused so completely other problems would arise. Finally, restraining my feelings, I accepted the position.

The Question of Unrestricted Shop Openings

Although I was obviously uneasy about accepting the position of president of the association, I felt that I should execute the many miscellaneous tasks that came to me without complaint. If it had been an association that simply promoted goodwill and cooperation among its membership, my duties would have been more manageable, but the association actually functioned as an authoritative body that handled the legislative, administrative and judicial needs of the Japanese residents of Ica. The problems and questions brought to it were endless, and I often had to set aside attending to our shop to attend to these many duties.

I would have easily fallen into the trap the "manipulators" had set for me had my wife not been so willing and able to take on the burden of managing our shop. Because of her, I was able to handle the added responsibilities.

After I had become inured to the miscellaneous and routine tasks expected of the president of the association, I was suddenly confronted by an absurd situation: "A person is attempting to open a business without proper approvals. You must do something about it." When I heard the phrase, "without approvals," I thought it referred to the party's neglect of legal requirements. After I heard the matter out in detail, however, I found that it was not because approvals had not been received from the municipal agencies of Ica. The "problem" referred to the party's lack of approval from the Ica Japanese Association.

My immediate thought was that the Japanese Association had no authority to approve or disapprove business operations. Since the involvement of the association had been brought up, however, I began examining the association's by-laws. To my astonishment, I found a ponderously worded "ordinance" stipulating that new businesses had to receive "recognition by the association."

The by-laws of the association were written in a legalistic manner resembling ordinances for a major city. It contained many fine sounding regulations, one after the other. For the Japanese in Ica, these association by-laws carried more authority than the municipal ordinances of Ica or even the constitution of Peru. As president of the association, I could not let the complaint go unattended. Reluctantly, I finally made a move.

The problem had arisen when a brother-in-law of a certain "Mr. Matayoshi," a member of the association, had moved to Ica from northern Peru and was about to open a restaurant similar to one in the vicinity owned by a certain "Mr. Fussbudget," a recognized leader within the Japanese community. The matter was greatly exacerbated by the fact that the newcomer had already received approvals from municipal agencies and had reached the final stages of preparation to open the restaurant when the complainant had become aware of the situation. He had then initiated what could only be called a poor move in the face of difficult to change circumstances.

Whether I wanted to or not, I was drawn into the problem. In principle, I felt it was absurd for the Japanese Association to presume to have the authority to regulate the operation of businesses. Yet, I also could not understand how "Mr. Matayoshi," who was fully aware of the situation in the Japanese community, had allowed such a situation to arise in the first place.

When he became aware of the situation, "Mr. Fussbudget" would come to me almost daily to demand that the association ban the activities of his potential competitor. "Mr. Matayoshi" would also come to me, saying, "My brother-in-law is still not a member of the association. And, after all, the Japanese Association is basically only a social group. Can't you do something about this matter?"

Matayoshi appealed to my ethical sense with typically Japanese expressions couched in ambiguity so that they could not be pinned down either as a strict procedural appeal or as a plea for sympathy. I did not want to be caught up in such confusion forever, so I decided to set forth to find an equitable settlement.

"A Decision Can Only Come from the Japanese Consul"

In summary, my decision stated: "Mr. Matayoshi and his brother-in-law would apologize to the Japanese Association and vow not to engage in unfair competition with those in the same type of business."

Knowing my decision would not satisfy "Mr. Fussbudget," I began to explain my decision. Maintaining a controlled tone of voice, I turned to the representative of the complainant and began, "Mr. Yamamoto, the preparations of starting the business are almost completed. They have already received approvals from the municipal agencies. With their public statement that they will not engage in unfair competition, can we not come to an agreement? Even if there are the by-laws of the Japanese Association, this is, after all, Peru. Legally, the association's by-laws have no binding force. If it had not been a Japanese but a native Peruvian who had opened the business, what could have been done? Even if such a shop had been opened right next door, no complaints could have been made. Could you not take this into consideration?"

Hoping not to provoke them, I expressed my decision very carefully. My youth and inexperience, however, betrayed my true feelings. The complainants were outraged. They said I had "slandered" the by-laws of the Japanese Association and had capitulated to the authority of "this third-rate country, Peru." They accused me, the president of the association, of treasonous behavior. Rather than resolving the affair, the matter had become even more confused.

Of course, if my simple reasoning had been accepted from the outset, such an absurd problem would not have arisen. But the complainant held to the restricted view that "such a business cannot at all be allowed in the vicinity." No matter what I proposed, however reasonable, it was useless.

A general meeting of the association was immediately called. When the affairs of the association reached that level of disagreement, it was certain that there could be only one solution. As expected, by an almost unanimous vote, it was decided that the problem be taken to the Japanese Consulate in Lima.

In such a situation, it was customary for the president and vice president of the association to go to Lima. In this instance, however, I refused to go. It was decided that Dr. Wakabayashi, a dentist who was then serving as vice president, would make the trip along another person. He reluctantly agreed to go to Lima as a representative of the association president.

The next day, a representative of the Japanese Consul and a

secretary made a special trip to Ica. It was unfortunate, I thought, that members of the consulate had to get involved in such matters. When they reached Ica it was already dark, but a general meeting was immediately convened and they began hearing statements from both parties. The proceedings were drawn out over two hours until, finally, a decision was announced. Remarkably, or perhaps not, the consulate representatives rendered the following decision: "Mr. Matayoshi" was to submit a written apology containing a pledge that his party would not engage in unfair competition.

I had grown so disgusted with the matter that I could not even bring myself to attend that meeting. When I heard the results I could only say to myself, "It does, after all, have to be a decision made by the Consulate. . . ."

This conclusion was something everyone had expected from the beginning. I had been forced to expend my time in completely useless "legwork." Although I did not say it, I wanted to say to the complainant, "If you had enough time to go about complaining, why couldn't you have used the time to plan new business strategies to bring down your competitors?" Such were my true feelings.

Because of such incidents, my one-year term of office quickly passed. When the time came time for elections, I breathed a sigh of relief. That, however, proved to be a misguided moment. I found that I was to be "further honored" by being retained as president.

The situation was completely unreasonable. No matter how many times I refused, the manipulating faction would not listen. It was obvious, however, that their position was taken with malicious intent. I had put away the association by-laws expecting that I would no longer have any need for it, but I again pulled it out and read it from cover to cover. It contained many detailed articles about "approvals for new businesses" and so forth, but did not contain one word about the term of office of its president or the "retention" of an incumbent. I strongly felt that one year was more than enough to offer as sacrifice of my time, but I was again unwillingly maneuvered into office for another year.

At a regular general meeting held soon after I was "retained," however, I made an uncharacteristically strong appeal to the general membership. As a result, an amendment to the by-laws was passed to the effect that the term of office of the president would be one year and that extensions of that period would not be recognized. It required a major effort on my part to accomplish this, but had I not made such a move I could only expect more "honors" would come to me from the manipulating group. Finally, I felt, I had been able to strike back at them.

Bazar Bienvenida

I had not consciously attempted to socialize only with Japanese persons or only with Peruvians. As president of the Japanese Association, I had many occasions to meet with members of the Japanese community, which I had not previously had. Becoming president of the association also widened my social relationships with the non-Japanese community as well.

For my business, I had worked hard to earn the patronage of the local middle and upper classes from the Peruvian population at-large. We had named our shop "Bienvenida," purposely selecting a Spanish name rather than a Japanese name. We carried mainly high quality, "designer" items. Spanish was my wife's first language, so language was not a problem. Furthermore, Angelica was beautiful, gracious and had an affable personality that gained us a regular clientele of upper-class customers. They often came into our shop with a personal greeting for her, "Angelica, como esta . . ." Day by day, our shop continued to do a flourishing business.

I was not much bounded by traditional ways of thinking about business. No matter what others said, I was always willing to try anything I thought would help our business. Once when I considered launching a large-scale advertising campaign there were those who said, "If you try such a thing, you'll never cover your costs." But I felt it was worth trying and opened the campaign.

We advertised in the newspapers and on radio, and even came to use the two movie houses in Ica. During the intermission between films we used slides to introduce new merchandise or to publicize special sales events. For radio, we produced rather stylish "modern" commercial jingles and had them broadcast at regular intervals throughout the day.

It is true that in the beginning most of the added profits brought in by the campaign went to pay advertising fees; we were not sure if the effort was worthwhile. But there was also a steady increase in intangible results. After a while there was no one, even 3 and 4 year olds, who was not familiar with our name, "Bazar Bienvenida."

It astonished me that the name of our shop became known even in the city of Huancayo, on the other side of the Andes. A person named Suwa living in the city of Ica received a letter from a friend in Huancayo. The friend mentioned that the radio broadcasts from Ica were quite sophisticated and that he often listened to musical programs. He then added that the Bazar Bienvenida of Ica often advertised on those programs and asked, "What country does its capital come from? It advertises so often that it seems to own the radio station. . ."

When the name of a shop becomes well known, its owner becomes known as well and his social position rises. In Peru there was discrimination according to social class but, unlike the United States, there was no strong tradition of discrimination based on race. With economic success, the Caucasian community also came to respect and trust us. Eventually, I became acquainted with leaders in Peruvian society such as the provincial governor, the police chief, owners of great haciendas, doctors, lawyers, and others. Their wives, moreover, began to frequent our shop. That was extremely beneficial for our business and our sales steadily increased.

Our public relations efforts even extended to my personal activities. I took into consideration effects on our business and social status and, since I did not dislike the activity, joined the Ica Rifle Club. The club was an exclusive social group of "shooting aficionados." Members included the governor of the province, leaders in business and politics, and many other professionals. I made many friends at the club and many became part of our regular clientele.

The club not only benefitted our business but also offered splendid opportunities for relaxation and fellowship. I have many pleasant memories associated with it, but one that remains vivid even today is a birthday celebration for Juan Dongo, the provincial governor.

The party was held at a restaurant on the outskirts of Ica. Many prominent people were present and I, as usual, was the only Japanese. The affair began pleasantly and, after drinks had been circulated, some of the guests began to offer performances of their special talents. Although the governor was usually dignified and restrained, on this occasion he chose to join the talent show. He picked up a coal bin and began drumming on it and, having removed his outer apparel, gave a full and heartfelt performance of dance and singing. For that short time, the governor had become a typically exuberant and carefree citizen of Peru. I took a great liking to that not often seen facet of our provincial governor.

Governor Dongo was also a provisional commander in the Peruvian army. At that time he was not married and from time to time he invited a lady friend from Lima to visit. When she came to Ica the governor often brought her to our shop and bought her gifts. About two years after I became acquainted with the governor the two were joyfully joined in marriage.

Wanting to express our gratitude for their kindnesses and patronage of our shop I sent them a rather expensive wedding gift. I did not particularly intend it, but our gift was noticed even among the other splendid gifts. (In Peru, unlike Japan, wedding gifts are unwrapped and displayed for guests to see.) The wedding couple both seemed very pleased with the gift and I was touched that each separately made a point to come to me to warmly and formally express their thanks.

I was also friendly with Captain Zapata, the head of the Ica Municipal Police Department. The department offices happened to be located directly across from our shop so I often ran into him. The provincial police chief also stopped by at the shop from time to time to pass friendly moments discussing local developments. He was much in favor of the Axis alliance of nations and had much praise for Japan. He was proud that the Peruvian army was equipped with arms from Japan. Indeed, the Peruvian army at that time was armed, from pistols up to tanks, with equipment imprinted with the "chrysanthemum emblem."

At this time, we welcomed three children: Elsa Yukiko, our eldest daughter, Carlos Shuichi, our eldest son, and Irma Setsuko, our second daughter. Our home was completely transformed to become filled with busy activities. Every one of us was also in good health; our happiness was at an apex.

Disquieting Developments and Their Underpinnings

In the late 1930s, whatever official position the civilian government may have assumed, a significant faction within the leadership of the Peruvian military leaned toward the Axis nations and increasingly showed signs of distancing themselves from the United States. A similar phenomenon was also occurring in Chile and Argentina. The U.S. government reacted to this and used various tactics to pressure South American countries. It even sent out FBI agents into the civilian population to promote pro-American and anti-Axis public opinion.

In 1939, outrageous rumors began flying about, and disquieting developments were reported from various parts of Peru. Completely unsubstantiated reports that the Japanese in Peru had organized a "fifth column," that they had secretly built a military base, that they had landed large shipments of arms and ammunition somewhere in South America, etc., came to be rumored as if completely true. In passage from mouth to mouth, such rumors were even further distorted and exaggerated.

We also began to hear of the harassment of Japanese or "spiteful actions" taken against their businesses. In Lima, where a great many Japanese lived, Japanese economic advances were often commented on and I had heard that subtle friction arose with the non-Japanese community.

In Peru, few ever complained about immigrants starting businesses and becoming successful. The country could boast of large enterprises backed by foreign capital. It was not unusual, therefore, that Japanese immigrants and Japanese capital did likewise. Why, then, did the Japanese become a target for opposition?

One reason was the anti-Japanese attitude created by the U.S. government in the background. For another, there was within Peru an unnoticed stratum that was ready to respond to such stimulation. A basic fact was that the Japanese were the most recent immigrant group in Peru. It was less than 40 years since the first immigrant ship had docked in Callao. Yet, in that time the hard-working immigrants had fully set down roots in many areas of Peru and had started small businesses. In that short span of time they had improved their condition so that it rivaled those of earlier immigrant nationalities.

The quick economic advances of the Japanese was one problem. Of course, this in itself did not bring about major disruptions in the development of Peruvian society as a whole—but if one views a society as an organic entity, the rapid growth of even a small segment could create reactions in other areas.

Another point to consider is the fact that many of the immigrants had begun to move toward the central area that had Lima as its focal point. If the rapid economic advances of the Japanese had been dispersed in all areas of the country, it might not have been perceived as excessive. Concentrated in one area, however, its influence grew geometrically. Moreover, the Japanese community had a unique exclusiveness and cohesiveness. The concentrated energy of so many Japanese living in proximity made it unlikely that they would make efforts to assimilate with Peruvian society as a whole. In that sense, the Japanese economic advances created a number of danger points that gave rise to friction with other developments within the larger, non-Japanese Peruvian society.

More significantly, the economic advances of the Japanese immigrants threatened a highly volatile segment of Peruvian society. The Japanese mainly owned small shops in urban areas; they had found that by concentrating on small, neighborhood businesses a path opened out toward financial stability. In the beginning, of course, that was almost the only way that immigrant families could move upwards toward security. In the urban areas, however, a business structure had already been established long before the Japanese began taking over small shops. The competition created by Japanese businesses naturally created a few problems. From the standpoint of the older, established businesses the Japanese were seen as newcomers and unwanted intruders in the business community.

Among those who had to adjust to the Japanese shop owners, the most seriously affected were Peruvian owners of small, unstable businesses. The majority of them were also "beginning merchants" who had worked themselves up from the lower strata of Peruvian society. In that sense, they were different from the typically carefree and exuberant Peruvian "everyman." They were sharp and shrewd novice merchants who placed full attention on their businesses. The Japanese economic advances touched a sensitive spot among those of that stratum and brought forth a poisonous resentment. It was that group, indeed, that could be most readily co-opted by the anti-Japanese efforts of the U.S. government.

The Japanese Provide a "Trigger" for Anti-Japanese Riots

As a director representing Southern Peru in the Federation of Japanese Associations I had access to formal reports made to the board of directors and also heard informal reports from other directors. According to those reports, the incident that ultimately triggered the smoldering tinder box of anti-Japanese sentiments was an ugly factional struggle that arose within the Japanese Barber's Trade Association in Lima.

In 1939, the number of barber shops in Lima had reached a saturation point. It was clear that if the situation continued some shops would be forced to close. Reacting to this, Keiji Higa, the president of the barber's association, sought to have some of the shops shut down. He solicited the support of Hisashi Hayasaka. Hayasaka, an employee at the Japanese Consulate, was viewed in the community as being insolent and high-handed. Ingratiating themselves with officials at the municipal offices, the two succeeded in having an unconditional order to cease business issued to a number of Higa's business rivals.

Then, another faction was formed within the barber's association to oppose Higa and his supporters. The rival faction was led by Tokijiro Furuya, who had connections with powerful figures in the Peruvian government. Furuya was an old friend of those barbers who had received the orders to cease business. He even had been a "guarantor" of their *tanomoshi-ko,* a type of traditional Japanese "savings club." Furuya immediately retained an influential attorney who forced the city officials to rescind their orders.

Furuya also exposed the manipulations of the Higa faction that had resulted in such drastic and unfair actions and publicly denounced Higa. As president of the trade association, Higa in turn expelled Furuya from the association on the basis of Furuya's "disruption of the rules and regulations of the association." Not one to give up so easily, however, Furuya filed suit against Higa and the controversy moved to the courts.

If the affair had remained at that, it would have been a simple matter of disagreement within the barber's association. But in the narrow, tightly knit Japanese community, that was not to be:

At that time, Furuya also headed the Peruvian branch of the Shizuoka Prefectural Overseas Corporation. In that capacity he had received the request of the Japanese Red Cross Association to conduct fundraising activities on its behalf in Peru. The Japanese Consul, Mr. Shun Sato, then issued a "consulate order" to have that relationship severed and responsibility for Red Cross activities to be transferred to the consulate. With that action, it became clear that Furuya would also have to cope with the opposition of the consulate. It was apparent that the Consulate had chosen to back Higa.

The Japanese people were extremely compliant toward "higher authorities," so once the consulate made a move, everyone naturally followed. The Central Japanese Association in Lima, which had already become like a semi-official organ of the Japanese government, immediately sided with the consulate and the barber's association. Its president, Tadao Taniguchi, ordered Furuya expelled from the Central Japanese Association.

The two Japanese language newspapers, the *Lima Nippo* and the *Lima Jiho,* also sided with the consulate, so Furuya found himself under almost complete attack by leaders of the Japanese community.

Having inflated the affair to such a degree, the Consulate could no longer stand quietly by and simply observe the situation. As Higa's actions were being investigated, and his trial itself was still underway, the consul ordered that Furuya be sent back to Japan. No matter how unreasonable, the words of the consul were taken by the Japanese community as absolute. The Central Japanese Association fully supported the consul's decision and even offered to help expedite it.

On December 25, 1939, the consul issued an order for Furuya's arrest. On that day a person named Akio Banno, who had been retained by the Central Japanese Association, kept surveillance on Furuya from early morning and several times came close to taking him into "custody." He was unsuccessful, however, so he decided to wait for nightfall to try again.

The entire absurd issue grew even worse. Led by Hayasaka, the "adviser" to the barbers' association, a group of about 20 to 30 men surrounded Furuya's home. A "commando group" climbed over the outer walls of the Furuya compound, moved through a rear garden, and entered the home. They forcefully "arrested" Furuya, his wife, and two others. Marta Acosta, a Peruvian woman who happened to be at Furuya's home at the time, was also assaulted and seriously injured.

Having finally "arrested" Furuya, Hayasaka and Higa brutally assaulted Furuya in the automobile while on their way to the Japanese Consulate. It was reported that Furuya's appearance had been completely altered by the attack. The blood-stained Furuya was detained at the consulate that night. Early the next morning, he was transported to Callao harbor, where the Nippon Yusen Company's *Ginyo-maru* was anchored. The Peruvian customs official on duty at first refused to allow Furuya to board the ship because he had no passport, but Hayasaka took the officer aside and, after some "negotiations," gained an approval.

That was not, however, the end of the matter. That morning a Peruvian acquaintance happened to visit the Furuya home and was astounded to learn what had occurred the previous night. He quickly reported the incident to an "influential person" who immediately went to the *Ginyo-maru* and, through his connections, was able to have Furuya taken off the ship.

When Hayasaka learned of this, he did not back off. He proceeded immediately to charge Furuya with "subversive activities." He obtained extradition orders from the Lima Provincial Offices, "rearrested" Furuya, and again placed him in confinement aboard the *Ginyo-maru.*

It had turned into a complete free-for-all. Those from Furuya's side contacted Lima's provincial governor and had him rescind Furuya's extradition order. With the governor himself standing at the bow, they headed out on a police patrol boat to retake Furuya. They furiously pursued the *Ginyo-maru* as it was about to leave the harbor. Using the threat of activating the Peruvian battleship, *Grau,* which was anchored nearby, they ordered the *Ginyo-maru* to drop anchor. By a hair's breadth, Furuya was rescued.

A Tragic Finale

The astonishing event was like something one might see in an action adventure film. Still, the entire bizarre episode was but a prelude to the catastrophe which was to follow.

Marta Acosta died from the injuries she had suffered when she was assaulted by Hayasaka's group at the Furuya home. With her death, the incident suddenly escalated into unexpected dimensions.

It happened that Mrs. Acosta was related to the owner of a tabloid newspaper in Lima; thus the incident was not to be left to rest. Vindictive, anti-Japanese articles came to fill that newspaper on an almost daily basis. Other newspapers quickly followed and also began to carry defamatory articles. In general, the articles were completely baseless, fabricated accounts of "secret activities of the Japanese fifth column," reports of Japanese smuggling in large shipments of weapons through the northern port of Chimbote, or articles urging the boycott of Japanese-owned shops. As nonsensical as the reports may have been, they steadily influenced the Peruvian readership. It was not a matter that could be so easily laughed off.

The fact that a Peruvian woman had died after being beaten by Japanese assailants severely provoked the Peruvian populace. A menacing mood flowed through the city and the Japanese community grew apprehensive. It was then that catastrophe struck. On May 13, 1940, students at the Guadalupe Middle School in Lima staged an anti-Japanese demonstration. Holding placards with anti-Japanese slogans, the students marched through the city. Soon, onlookers joined the march and the demonstration grew.

After onlookers started joining the student marchers, some began to throw stones at Japanese-owned shops. This soon escalated to full-scale violence. While shouting anti-Japanese slogans, the mob broke into shops, looted their merchandise, and utterly vandalized facilities. Some shop owners had been notified of developments and had quickly lowered their street shutters, but the mob even used trucks to ram down the shutters to enter and loot those stores.

The violence spread from Lima to Callao and to other outlying areas. It also flared up in provincial cities. Not only shops, but even homes of individual Japanese were attacked. The fury of the mob was such that there were reports of windows and even flooring planks of homes being torn out and taken away.

Although the looting continued in broad daylight, the police made no move to make arrests or even to restrain the mob. The Japanese Consulate had received urgent reports of the developments and had contacted the Peruvian Foreign Ministry to request police protection of Japanese nationals and their property. Still, the police made no move. Violence and looting continued through the evening of the following day, when it was finally brought under control. Rather, it would be more accurate to say that the destruction was so complete that there were no targets left, so the violence had ended of itself. With the exception of a few shops in the central area of Lima, almost all Japanese-owned shops in the city were destroyed.

Although he was also victimized, the case of Shuei Nishihira had a mixed blessing. In the late afternoon of the 13th, when the mob neared the vicinity of his shop, Mr. Nishihira placed members of his family in the care of his landlord who lived nearby. Nishihira stayed back to protect his shop by himself. At about eight o'clock that evening, when the mob tore down the door to his shop and rushed in, he quickly escaped with his life through a back entrance. For several hours wild shouting of slogans and general mayhem continued, but, finally, in the early morning hours quiet returned.

At daybreak, Nishihira returned to the shop to find that his merchandise and the furnishings in the attached family living quarters had been looted; in the shop, shelves and counters had been destroyed. But, in that strictly Roman Catholic country, the image of Christ that had been placed on a wall had not been touched. "Can it be?" he thought, as he removed the image to look into a small niche behind the image. There he found, untouched, important documents, watches and rolls of currency that he had placed there, stuffed into stockings. He had received the "protection of the Christ image."

Mr. Nishihira's case, however, was a remarkable exception. The great majority of victims were not so blessed. They had fled their homes with only the clothes on their backs and with only desperate efforts had escaped with their lives. On the 15th, when order finally began to be restored, those who had taken refuge in the Lima Japanese Elementary School slowly began to return to their homes in groups of three or four. Some of the victims of this disaster had no homes to return to and had to remain at the school. These people had lost everything; they were left with no food or place to sleep.

Later, according to a survey conducted by the Japanese Consulate, 620 households reported losses due to the rioting. Of that number, about 500 were immigrants from Okinawa Prefecture. The losses totalled $6 million in U.S. dollar value at that time. For some 54 households, consisting of 316 persons, losses from that incident were so devastating that they were unable to recover. They were repatriated to Japan on July 14, 1940, aboard the Nippon Yusen Company's *Heiyo-maru*.

After violence broke out in Lima, I began to receive reports of developments there and was astounded. There were no guarantees that something similar might not occur in Ica. I immediately notified the municipal police department. Throughout that night, with its police chief whom I had come to know personally, we began to patrol the homes and shops of the Japanese in Ica. At the rear of a municipally owned market area, someone threw a stone that smashed through the window of our patrol car. Other than that incident, however, there were no major problems in Ica. I breathed out a sigh of relief.

Punishment from Heaven. The Peruvian Earthquake

The nightmarish violence had come to an end. For a time, however, the Japanese community did not recover from its shock. Japanese-owned shops had been attacked before, but this incident presented something entirely different. In Peru, whenever revolutionary activities turned violent, Japanese-owned shops had repeatedly been victimized. But this was the first time when only Japanese-owned shops were singled out as targets of attack. Previously, whenever mob violence had arisen, shops owned by Chinese, Italians and others were all victimized.

When violence erupted this time, Chinese shop owners posted reproductions of the Chinese flag on the exterior of their shops to indicate that they were not Japanese. Knowing that the violence was strictly aimed at Japanese residents, they took the "high position" of simply observing developments.

Because of these actions, there was a current of suspicion within the Japanese community that the Chinese residents had participated in inciting the violence. The Chinese were often business rivals of Japanese. Also, because Japan at that time was invading the Chinese mainland, there were strong anti-Japanese sentiments among the Chinese in Peru. While there was no proof to substantiate such speculation, it was not implausible that something of that nature had occurred.

Some people within the Japanese community began to directly and fully reflect on the causes of the violence, and issued heartfelt sentiments calling for a fundamental change in the attitudes and behavior of the Japanese community. Nevertheless, we had to continue our lives under the resentful eyes of the broader Peruvian community. Whenever one stepped out of the Japanese community, insulting epithets would be hurled at our faces. We could only endure such a situation with bone-felt painfulness. Now, every Japanese in Peru, without exception, feared that anti-Japanese violence might again flare up at any time. Our days passed, filled with anxiety and feelings of isolation.

Following the riots, even young children would casually shout at us, "Chino macaco." "Chino" means "Chinese," and "macaco" was used to indicate a "slave." Much earlier, the term had been used to demean the Chinese who had arrived in Peru during the 19th century as "semi-slaves" from the Portuguese colony of Macao. They were sold to Peruvian mine operators and owners of large haciendas. From that earlier time, when Peruvians could not differentiate between Chinese and Japanese, the term had been used toward Asians in general. With the sense of "damned Asian slaves," it had also been readily applied to Japanese immigrants.

"Chino macaco" was a crude term used by the uneducated. But, after the riots, it served to indicate how widely racism had grown to be accepted. Such epithets were heaped upon us daily, but there was nothing we could do. At that time, all we could do was humble ourselves in order to survive.

Then, 11 days after the riots began, an event took place to rescue us from our situation—a great earthquake struck Peru. It may seem odd to call an earthquake a "saving event," but this is what happened. Many of those who had participated in the riots were devout Roman Catholics. Removed from scientific explanations, they took the earthquake as an expression of anger on the part of their Lord for their violent behavior. They began to repent.

When the earth itself shook, people rushed out to open ground. Many women knelt down, placed their palms together, and prayed to their Lord. Those who had not participated in the looting pleaded, "I did not do anything wrong against the Japanese." One can only imagine what disturbed the hearts of those who had actually participated in the violence. It was, it seemed, a true "punishment from Heaven."

After the earthquake, it was reported that people returned things they had taken from Japanese homes. I even heard a crude and humorless joke: "The earthquake was brought about by Hirohito."

The earthquake had been fortuitous. It helped to diffuse anti-Japanese sentiments within the general Peruvian community. That did not mean, of course, that everything had returned to the earlier status quo, but it was true that it had ameliorated anti-Japanese sentiments.

(Left) Happier days in Ica: Seiichi with Irma, Carlos and Elsa, 1941.

(Below) The family's first store in Ica, the Bienvenida, 1935.

Chapter Six. Fierce Winds of Oppression

The Fateful Pacific War Arrives

During the year preceding the riots in Lima, problems frequently arose among the Japanese themselves. As in the case involving the Lima barbers' association, these problems were usually caused by business competition. Over a period of years the Central Japanese Association had come to view this as a major problem and with the encouragement of the Japanese Consulate had sought ways to ameliorate the situation.

As a director representing southern Peru in that organization, I often attended its meetings and had the opportunity to learn about conditions in Japanese communities in Lima and other areas of the country.

Among the often disturbing reports were not only accounts of fierce competition among the Japanese residents, but also incidents that confirmed the growing stream of anti-Japanese sentiment throughout Peru. I was aware that U.S.-Japan relations had entered an unstable phase and instinctively felt that the propagation of such rumors was part of an intentional strategy devised by the U.S. government. Not being able to prove such a claim, however, I did not speak of it openly.

Still, I feared that if such a situation continued, the pro-Japanese factions within the Peruvian government and military would steadily lose influence and the pro-U.S. factions would become dominant.

In 1939, I still did not feel that such anti-Japanese measures taken by those in the U.S. bureaucracy had been instigated with any definite expectation of a full-scale war between the U.S. and Japan. But by 1940, when the Japanese, German and Italian military alliance was formed, it seemed probable that such a war would occur.

From about that time, I began to listen carefully to shortwave broadcasts from Japan to South America. The reports were not encouraging. Yet, because they continued for about a year with no major incidents, the radio report on December 7, 1941 was astounding. "Can this really be happening?" I thought. But it was an indisputable fact. Japan was at war against the United States!

When I heard over the shortwave radio that Japan had declared war, I grew tense and uneasy. Japanese nationals in Peru, which was under the "umbrella" of U.S. protection and influence, could be affected at any time, yet we would be in no position to complain. We had to be prepared for anything, I thought. The memories of the anti-Japanese riots of the previous year remained vivid with us. Now the need to prepare for potentially greater disasters seemed tragic beyond words.

At that time, other than the usual busy activities of the year-end period, the Ica Japanese Association had been taken up by its yearly elections and installation of officers. I had been elected president for 1942 and had just taken over the duties of that office. I felt it very unlucky that this pivotal development had come at precisely the time I took office, but it was not a time to complain. I immediately sent out a notice to the more than 60 members of the association, announcing a special general meeting. At that meeting I proposed that the Ica Japanese Association be dissolved and that the Japanese elementary school that it operated be closed. Given our situation, the proposal was accepted by everyone without objections.

Before that final meeting was adjourned, those who attended cautioned each other to recognize the seriousness of the situation. Everyone needed to behave prudently, cancel all large gatherings, and meet any and all developments with a cool and rational attitude. It was with much sadness that we turned homeward. In a single night we had become "enemy aliens" placed in a situation in which we no longer could expect to receive the protection of the Japanese government.

The Blacklist
Although I was prepared for sudden developments, the days that followed were calm and uneventful. Our business continued to do well, and officers from the police headquarters located across from our shop continued to stop by for friendly conversations. They had heard of the Japanese military victories at the start of the war and joined us in welcoming such news. But, in the background, matters were steadily changing.

One day, those changes suddenly and unexpectedly came to light. It was December 24, 1941. On that unforgettable day, two major Peruvian newspapers, *El Commercio* and *La Prensa,* published a *lista negra,* a "blacklist" of approximately 30 "dangerous Axis nationals" residing in Peru. Of the 30, approximately 10 were Japanese.

Shivers passed through me. "Can this really be true?" I thought. My name was included in the list. We learned that the list had been leaked to reporters by a local U.S. agency. Although it had no connection with the Peruvian government, that did not alleviate our concerns.

Why was my name on the list? I could not understand. I had only been in Peru for about a decade, and what I had accomplished was quite insignificant. Our business was flourishing, but there were many others who had attained grander business successes who were not on the list. If not that, I thought perhaps it was because I had been president of the Ica Japanese Association for two terms. But, upon closer examination, the other Japanese on the list did not share such a background.

I could not think of other reasons. I had not committed any crimes. I had not participated in any propaganda activities for the Japanese government and, of course, had not engaged in espionage or underground activities. I could not understand what criteria had been used to compile the list.

Later, the newspapers published similar lists several more times and names of Axis nationals associated with major enterprises began to appear. Comparing the subsequent lists with the first, it could be seen that the initial list was different in nature. At the time I was not fully aware of this point, but when I consider it now it seems clear that rather than being influential persons or leaders within their respective communities, those on the first list were Axis nationals who had involved themselves deeply with the local Peruvian establishment.

When looked at from that perspective, I can see many reasons for my being included in the list. Whether it was fortunate or not, from the time I took over the Otani Company in Canete I had gradually widened my sphere of acquaintances to include those in the non-Japanese Peruvian society at large. Because my name was difficult to pronounce, they simply addressed me as "Ingeniero" and accepted me into their social groups.

For business purposes, too, I had felt it necessary to have connections with those in upper levels of Peruvian society and had made conscious moves in that direction. Because of this, I had formed social relationships with prominent figures in political and business circles and with leaders in law enforcement agencies.

My participation in such social activities was purely for business and social reasons, but U.S. agents may have perceived my behavior differently. The U.S. had been concerned about the existence of a sizeable group of individuals within the national Peruvian leadership who were pro-Japanese. Although I was not close to anyone in the national Peruvian leadership, I did have a number of acquaintances at the provincial level of leadership. It may have been that those in

U.S. intelligence agencies had seen my activities within the larger Peruvian society, even at the provincial level, as having more "dangerous motives" than simple business and social relationships.

A Quick Change to Become an "Employed Manager"

Whatever the reason, the reality remained that I had been placed on a blacklist. I felt pessimistic as I pondered our future. Yet I also could not help feeling, with a certain grim pride, that at the age of 32, I had gained enough notoriety to be included on a U.S. blacklist. It seems that the chief of the Ica municipal police also viewed the list in that light. Waving the newspaper, he rushed into our shop. Extending his hand to me, he said, "Congratulations, congratulations!"

But it was not a situation we could take lightly. At least as it related to our shop, everything seemed hopeless. My being on the blacklist meant that anyone who traded with me would surely be seen as suspect. I could not expect anyone to do business with us. It was only a matter of time, it seemed, before we would be pushed to bankruptcy. I had been prepared for unfortunate developments, but I had never dreamed I would be among the first to be stricken with such misfortune.

The evening when the list appeared was a sleepless one. It is said that desperation leads one to foolish thoughts, but this was surely a matter that needed full consideration.

A plan eventually came to mind. I decided that we should immediately terminate our business licenses and close our shop. We would then reapply for business permits in my wife's name and start up as a new shop. Although she was of Japanese ancestry, my wife was born in Peru and was a full-fledged Peruvian citizen so there would be no problems if the business were in her name.

By a lucky coincidence, we had registered our marriage in Japan but not in Peru. In Peru, my wife was legally still single. According to Peruvian law we were completely unrelated.

Under those conditions, I felt that such a plan might work. Even if it failed, I thought it was at least worth trying. I immediately notified the appropriate agencies, terminated the licenses, and closed our shop. To the general public it seemed that I had gone into isolation because of the blacklist.

My wife, however, applied for business licenses under the name of Angelica Yoshinaga and we prepared to open a new shop. After about 10 days the approvals came forth and the new shop was opened. We changed everything—from its name to its account books. We took every precaution so no connections could be made with the earlier business. I felt it was a fine response to our situation. In this way, I became my wife's "shop manager."

Disquieting Tides

Having thus responded to our first difficult situation, we tried to appear as calm as possible and quietly continued our lives. But, disquieting tides rose up to touch us in differing ways and with differing force.

One day, soon after the beginning of 1942, the chief of detectives from the nearby police headquarters stopped by as usual in the morning and began enthusiastically discussing developments in the war. When the conversation reached a lull, he casually said, "I'm sure you have a driver's license. If you have it with you, could I take a look at it? There's something I want to be sure about."

There was nothing especially different about his appearance or behavior and I had nothing to be suspicious about so I handed over the license. He flipped it over front and back several times and examined it intently. Then he said, "I'm sorry, I'll have to borrow this for a while. Actually, we have an order from Lima Police Headquarters to send the license to them immediately. I don't think they'll keep it long. When it's returned, I will personally bring it over to you."

This was, of course, a very smoothly handled order to remain within the local area. I had been placed under travel restrictions. As soon as the chief of detectives left the shop I called a number of community leaders to inquire if something similar had occurred to them. None, however, had even heard of such an incident. The matter was related to the blacklist, I concluded, as only I had been targeted. It was a seemingly small matter, but it filled me with anxiety.

Days passed, and I remained bothered by that incident. Then new and more serious political developments suddenly came upon us. On January 24, 1942, the government of Peru severed diplomatic ties with Japan and immediately began to deport leaders in the Japanese community.

Soon, disturbing reports began to arrive from Lima. We heard that Japanese diplomats in Peru had been confined to a hotel in Chosica, and that the president of the Central Japanese Association, the owners of Japanese language newspapers, the principal of the Lima Japanese school, and other leaders of the Japanese community in the capital had been arrested and detained at a school called Leoncio Prado.

Finally, a great storm had begun to wreak its damage on the community. The storm that began in the capital soon found its way to the smaller cities in the provinces. Whenever matters pertained to the Japanese community in Ica, it had become a matter of course that the police first came to speak with me. This occasion was no different. They came to me and asked, "Who is the president of the Japanese Association this year?" I took into strict consideration the time of dissolution of the association and answered, "At the time the war began the association was dissolved. It no longer exists."

"Well, then, who was the president last year?" they asked. Given the situation, it was no time to feign ignorance. I replied truthfully, "The president for the term last year was a person named Yamashiro. After the elections in November, I became its president. . ."

Even if we were in the provinces, I had also been president of the Japanese association for two earlier terms and my name was on the blacklist; I began to feel that I would eventually be repatriated to Japan. I felt there was no way to escape my fate and resolved to endure whatever came.

Later, deportation orders were issued to presidents of Japanese associations in every part of Peru; they were to be repatriated to Japan with treatment similar to that given to the diplomatic corps. In Ica, to my surprise, it was not I but Mr. Yamashiro who received that order.

At that time, Mr. Yamashiro and his children operated a large restaurant. They immediately closed it down and, within a week, were sent off by former members of the association. The entire Yamashiro family left for Lima. In Lima, however, the government's arrangements for ships did not move expeditiously and no matter how long they waited the exchange ships did not arrive. Leaving Mr. Yamashiro in Lima, the other members of his family returned to Ica. The matter ended with Mr. Yamashiro returning alone to Japan on the second exchange ship that left Callao harbor on June 15, 1942.

Because of my response to the police, Mr. Yamashiro had been sent back to Japan, and I could not bring myself to face members of his family. If I had not mentioned Mr. Yamashiro's name, I thought, or if I had not immediately had the association dissolved at the declaration of war, I as current president of the association would have been the one sent back to Japan. But such reflections were all after the fact. At Mr. Yamashiro's expense, I was to remain for a time longer in Peru.

Deportation Orders

That reprieve continued for only a short time. About the middle of March 1942, I was also served deportation orders. The first exchange ship still had not departed. The chief of the Ica police came to our shop and said, "Mr. Higashide, we just had a communication from the central office in Lima ordering you to appear there." It could only be bad news, I knew, but at that stage when diplomatic ties with Japan had already been severed it would have served no purpose to make any desperate struggle. I immediately made preparations and left for Lima, alone.

I spent the night at a hotel and early the next morning reported to the Lima Police Headquarters as ordered. I thought I might be detained on the spot, so I entered with much anxiety. To my surprise, the person who met me was extremely polite. That well-bred officer, who at a glance could be seen to have a high position, very calmly explained the situation to me. It was as I expected; I was to be deported.

The officer maintained his kind and gracious attitude, so I felt secure in asking him a few questions. He answered each of them fully and carefully, then added, "The first exchange ship, which will carry mainly diplomats and those with government connections, will leave soon. Your group will probably leave on the second ship. We do not know when that will be, but we shall inform you when it is confirmed. We will do all we can so that you will have at least a week's prior notice. It has already been decided that each person will be allowed to take $300, so there is nothing I can do about that. But there are no limitations on anything else you might wish to take aboard. You are allowed to take whatever you wish."

Having made that remark, the officer fell silent. After a while he continued, "It is truly unfortunate, but this also is the demand of the government of the United States. As you know, we are not in a position to take opposing measures. I ask that you understand that point."

Taking great care to express myself formally, I bowed to him and took leave of the officer. When I went out into the streets of Lima I began buying whatever I could find and thought might be necessary to prepare to return to Japan. Because it would not be possible to take much cash, I bought jewelry and items made of precious metals.

After I had made some purchases, I decided to visit the home of a friend to learn of current developments in Lima. I had expected that because a second group of deportation orders had been issued a great number of persons would be in a situation similar to mine, but I was informed that after the diplomats and community leaders had been detained, there had been no mention of a second group of deportees.

When I returned to Ica and inquired with others in the community, I found that the situation was the same there. It seemed that I was the only one to be summoned. Had I simply been passed over in the first group? Or was the second group made up only of the approximately 10 Japanese named on the first blacklist?

Whatever the case may have been, the deportation order had been issued and I did not have a moment to waste. I decided I would return to Japan alone and leave my wife and children in Peru. At the time, I felt certain Japan would win the war, so I did not believe we would be separated permanently from each other. After the war ended, I thought, I would return to Peru and be reunited with them.

While I was involved with preparations, I learned that the first exchange ship had left on April 14, 1942. "Well," I thought, "we will be next." About the same time, however, we received a report that another shipload of repatriates had been detained in Lima and that they were awaiting the next ship. I had no idea what the true situation was. I had been prepared to receive orders to board ship at any time, but that did not come even after an extended period. Then, two months after the first ship left, it was reported that the second exchange ship left port on June 15, 1942.

When I heard the report, I felt that by some good luck I might not be repatriated. Perhaps my deportation order was lost in the confusion. But I could not be too optimistic or secure with only such thoughts. About that time, information was passed about that the entire Japanese population in the United States was being moved inland from coastal areas. Rumors also flew about that the Japanese in Peru would all be removed to inland mountain areas. We even heard that all Japanese in Peru would be sent to the United States.

A Tour of Peru

At that point, international political developments left little hope for a favorable resolution. Anything could happen, and whatever happened would have to be accepted. It was not a time when one could calmly go about one's business—it seemed pointless to do anything. If that were so, I thought, why not leave the running of the shop to our employees and take a tour of Peru? I realized I had still not toured Peru; it would be sad to leave without doing so. Given the apparently hopeless situation, I began to think along such lines and decided to do something about it.

But since I was bound by orders to remain in the local area, it would be difficult to accomplish such a "pleasurable diversion." I decided to consult with the Ica provincial governor, Commandant Juan Dongo. Governor Dongo received me with great sympathy and kindness. "I am truly sorry about your situation," he said. "Japan is not at war with Peru, yet you have been placed in such a situation. Peru, however, is in a weak position and cannot oppose the United States."

He immediately wrote a letter of introduction for me to the Arequipa chief of police, Mr. Teran, who had jurisdiction over southern Peru. Elated, I expressed my appreciation and returned home. At the small gathering to celebrate my departure on the trip, the governor warned me, "We are in such volatile times; be careful about everything."

I knew that my behavior at such a time was somewhat outrageous. But it would be an unburdened, carefree trip by myself. I was still quite young, so I quickly put aside concerns about my decision. I felt I would be deported from Peru in any case—even if minor incidents occurred I need not be too concerned. I quickly made preparations and set out on a tour of southern Peru.

My first destination was Arequipa to meet Mr. Teran. There was no highway to Arequipa at that time, and it would take several days to reach Arequipa by automobile. If I did travel in that way, my journey would take a number of months, so I decided to make the trip by air. There were no regular flights from Ica, but I learned there was a flight from Lima to Arequipa and decided to use that route.

I boarded a simple, propellor-driven Faucett airplane—a small, almost toy-like plane that could carry five or six passengers. Soon after I opened our shop in Ica, I contracted intestinal typhus and needed to be transported immediately to a hospital in Lima. We had contracted a Faucett to take me to Lima. I suddenly recalled that incident and, for a while, was quite moved with remembrances.

Those airplanes were truly wonderful machines. When we boarded, the noise was so great that if we did not put cotton balls in our ears our eardrums would have been damaged. But we had a definite sense of flying in the sky. It was a great difference from the modern jets of today, which seem to have become only a means for moving "cargo." The Faucett plane that picked me up in Ica had only four passengers. It gently took us upward, and I felt like an eagle floating in the blue sky.

Our plane landed at Nazca airport to refuel. Although it was called an "airport," it was marked only by a small, reed-thatched structure standing in the middle of the desert. There was not even a trace of people. The pilot pulled out a drum of gasoline from the small building, began refueling the plane, and we were soon in flight again.

Nazca had been the center of a civilization that flourished for several hundred years, from about 100 B.C. It has now become world famous, but at that time no one was interested in it. The gigantic designs over the desert are now looked upon with wonder, but they had not yet been recognized as humanly designed figures. I had the opportunity of flying over them twice, but was not even aware of them.

The plane headed from Nazca to Puerto de Lomas on the Pacific seacoast, where we again needed to refuel. The coastline close to Puerto de Lomas was magnificent, and the pilot deliberately brought us down along the coast to show us the beautiful scenery. In the calm ocean waters we could clearly see large fish moving serenely about.

The airport at Puerto de Lomas was different from the one at Nazca. It was a small gravel field rather than in a sandy desert. The area was originally covered with desert sand, but winds had blown everything away to expose a lower layer of gravel. Our Faucett bounced up and down a number of times as we landed on the gravel runway. Refueling was quickly accomplished.

The airport was located on a rise just inland from the shore. To take off, planes had to head down a slope directly toward the sea. Our plane began to move downward to pick up speed; then, just as the ocean's edge came up to us, we lifted up to float into the sky. It was such a perilous and thrilling take-off that we all felt a chilling tingle at the instant before the plane rose upward.

It was a direct flight from there to Arequipa. As could be expected of a provincial capital, Arequipa was a rather large city. In contrast to Nazca and Puerto de Lomas, the Arequipa airport was quite impressive; it had a number of large buildings and people bustled about. As soon as we disembarked I took a cab to a hotel in the city.

The "Kindness" of Anti-Japanese Police Chief, Mr. Teran

After I got settled in a hotel and rested a while, I went out into the town. We had a number of trading partners in that city whom I had planned to visit. Although we traded with those companies, I had never met their owners, so I thought I would simply pay a few formal "courtesy calls." Wherever I went, however, I was warmly welcomed and many times heard the remark, "It is amazing that in such times you would make a trip to a place such as this."

On my second day in Arequipa, a totally unexpected pleasure came to me. My wife, who was then carrying our fourth child and was noticeably pregnant, suddenly appeared in Arequipa. Although she had earlier decided not to make the trip because of her pregnancy, she had come to join me. "After all," she said, "we didn't even have a honeymoon. . . ." Because she was a Peruvian citizen, she did not have to go through special procedures to leave Ica.

She was, however, somewhat fatigued by trip, combined with "altitude sickness." We decided to spend the day resting at the hotel. Arequipa is located approximately 8,000 feet above sea level and it was common for those who came from other areas to suffer from altitude sickness. One's body quickly recovers after one has adjusted to the altitude, so it was not a matter of great concern. By the next morning, my wife was fully recovered and back to her normal self.

I thought of taking her out to see the sights in the city, but since we did not know the area and because I was under "travel restrictions," I decided that it was best to first receive travel clearances from Mr. Teran at the Arequipa police headquarters. Without Mr. Teran's approval, I would not be able to travel through southern Peru.

Taking along the letter of introduction written for me by the governor of Ica, I went over to Mr. Teran's office. He read through the letter, then turned to me and said, "Because of current conditions, it would be better for you to give up your trip."

I could not determine whether his words were said in kindness or were motivated by malice. He continued, "Since I am an old friend of Commandant Dongo, I shall of course give my approvals if you insist. With your current status, however, it is dangerous for you to continue. It might be misunderstood and we cannot even guarantee that no bodily harm will come to you. I recommend that you give up your trip. Arequipa is my home area and is completely safe and secure. Why don't you spend a leisurely time here?"

What he said was true. If I insisted on going on as planned, I might be misunderstood by others and that could lead to severe consequences. I accepted Mr. Teran's warning and decided to cancel the remainder of my trip. I replied to that effect and took my leave.

Later, I described the interview to a number of local acquaintances in Arequipa. Among the local Japanese, it seemed, Mr. Teran had an established reputation. Everyone said the same thing, "With that one the main thing is to have something to grease his palms. If you don't do so, nothing goes well."

I had not been aware of that reputation and I realized what I had done was careless. But the matter could not be undone. There were still a number of places in southern Peru that I wanted to visit, but as the classics from China teach us, "A gentleman does not tempt danger." I decided to return to Ica.

We made our return trip on the same small aircraft. With my wife, we retraced the same route in the opposite direction. When the plane came to the area above the Nazca refueling site, we were startled to see the gasoline storage building had been toppled over. Gasoline drums were scattered about out in the open. After we landed, we found that the small adobe building had completely collapsed.

Even the stoical pilot, who was not the type to let small occurrences disturb him, seemed to be amazed. Looking out with concern over the desert that spread forth emptily, he said, "It must have been a large earthquake. I wonder where the center was?"

I immediately grew concerned about our family members and employees in Ica. Were the children safe? Had the shops been damaged? It was truly fortunate that we had cut our trip short and had decided to return early. "This also is a result of Mr. Teran's 'kindness,'" I thought. I felt like "thanking" that stern and proud police chief; his actions had truly been a blessing in disguise.

From the conditions in Nazca, we were prepared for the worst. Our fears were confirmed when we found that considerable damage had occurred in Ica. Everyone in the family was safe, however, and the shop had been only slightly damaged. The center of the earthquake had been in the Nazca area. Our children and employees had expected that our trip would take more than a month, so when they were surprised to see us back after only about a week. They were overjoyed and made a big fuss over us.

The Rough Tactics of the New National Police Superintendent

Shortly after we met in Arequipa, Mr. Teran was promoted to become the National Police Superintendent in Lima. Both in name and in reality, he had become a very powerful national figure who now controlled all police activity in Peru.

The Japanese in Arequipa believed he was extremely anti-Japanese. The impression I had from our meeting was that he was the type of person who would not be held back if he had an "axe to grind." It was well that I had taken along a letter of introduction from the governor of Ica. Had I not done so, I believe I would have been severely rebuked.

Since such a person now exercised power in the capital, we could expect outrageous and fearful developments. The Japanese, in their vulnerable position, faced a steadily worsening situation that ranged from simple police harassment, to improper detainment, and to forced deportation. The unjust and violent measures that began in the latter half of 1942, which resulted in mass arrests of Japanese and deportation to the United States, were all carried out under the direction of the new National Police Superintendent.

The memoirs of John K. Emerson, who was stationed at the American Consulate in Lima during the war, describes the following incident involving Mr. Teran. Mr. Emerson had gone to speak with Mr. Teran about the Japanese who were to be deported to the United States. When Mr. Teran demanded, "Where are our prisoners?" Mr. Emerson replied, "They all were not on our list of deportees so they were released." Mr. Teran flew into a rage and shouted, "Who ordered their release?"

That incident occurred about four or five months after I met him in Arequipa. At that time, Peruvian authorities were beginning to make random arrests of Japanese. Whether they were on the U.S. list of deportees or not, individuals were taken into custody without questioning. When those on the deportation list went into hiding or used bribes to avoid arrests, the police simply picked up anyone at random as substitutes. They were interested only in the number arrested and not in correct identities.

At one point, there were about 300 Japanese arrested in that random manner. Of these, however, many were released. On January 7, 1943, 168 detainees were sent by truck from Lima to the northern town of Talara. I would venture a guess that it was Mr. Emerson who released the other 130 or so persons. The 168 people who were sent to Talara were later deported to the United States to spend the war years in detention camps.

That one incident illustrates how Mr. Teran's anti-Japanese measures were carried out in an extremely undisciplined manner. Such tactics later spread out to the provinces and dark shadows fell over us.

In Ica, however, because the provincial governor and many of the leaders in the municipal and provincial police departments were pro-Japanese, the methods used were relatively more civil and sympathetic than in other provinces. On that point, we were blessed. For my part, I did not once experience any unpleasant encounters. If someone like Mr. Teran had been the provincial governor or a high officer in the police department, I don't know what our fate would have been.

Increasing Oppression of Japanese by the Peruvian Government

The Peruvian government increased its pressure on the Japanese community on a daily basis. By the latter half of 1942, with the exception of small shops run by couples or family members, all Japanese-owned businesses were black listed and ordered to close. They were to stop taking in merchandise and, when their inventories were sold out, they were to close their doors.

From that time, a government auditor, called an "interventor," came every day to the shops. He would confirm the daily sales and, leaving a prescribed amount for the owner's living expenses, took the remaining proceeds, claiming that such funds were "frozen."

It was merely a euphemistic form of confiscation of income and assets. At that point, not only merchandise, but even daily living expenses became difficult to handle. Fortunately, our shop was already under the ownership of a "Peruvian citizen" and we did not meet that fate. Almost all of the larger shops, however, were harassed into closing their doors or were sold for unthinkably low prices. Most of the shops that were put up for sale passed into the hands of Chinese merchants, our earlier business rivals.

The Japanese community in Peru underwent a major upheaval. The majority of those who had previously held higher economic and social status were pressed into conditions close to bankruptcy and fell to lower status within the community. On the other hand, owners of small, family run shops who had been exempt from the order saw their clientele and profits increase as a result of the demise of their larger competitors.

The "second major period" of establishment of the Japanese community in Peru was mainly carried forth by those who aggressively acquired capital at this time and later made great business and social advances after the end of the war. Of course, there were some who had been successful before the war who managed to pass through those difficulties. In general, however, the foundations of the Japanese community in Peru were overturned during the war years.

As Japanese-owned businesses were ordered to close, Japanese were being forcibly evicted from the area around the northern naval base of Chimbote, from the Oroya mining district, and from areas such as Chacra Cerro and Puenta Piedra. At first, the Peruvian government had decided that all Japanese adult males in those areas would be deported to the United States, but transportation could not be arranged and the forced expulsion policy was decided upon.

The Japanese engaged in much speculation among themselves as to why these areas were being targeted. Ultimately, however, it seemed the only possible reason was the completely baseless rumors that circulated throughout Peru. Even in Ica, some distance away, we heard rumors that several hundred infantry rifles were hidden in a storehouse owned by a Japanese importing firm called the Seo Company. We also heard that the Japanese army had plans to land in those northern areas. It seemed that the Peruvian government took those rumors as true and moved to evict Japanese from those areas.

In order to enforce the expulsion order, the governor of Ancash Province went out himself, snapping a bullwhip, to force out local Japanese. According to the governor, the forced expulsions were "precautionary measures necessary to prevent resident Japanese from taking actions beneficial to the enemy."

According to Kotaro Kanashiro, who was in Chimbote at that time, the Japanese were first ordered to gather at a designated place. Because air passage could not be arranged, their deportation was then cancelled. They were told, "Disappear from this area within three days," and were forced to disperse by police officers carrying pistols. Mr. Kanashiro immediately went home and sold whatever he could within three days. Undaunted, he said, "Well, what of it? When the war ends we'll come back and make a hundred times more." He chartered a bus, loaded family members and friends aboard, raised a Japanese flag over the bus, and went off to Lima.

At that time approximately 150 were forced out of Chimbote. Whatever the destiny of those like Mr. Kanashiro who went out to Lima, those who moved to the Huaraz region met a tragic fate. The great majority could not adjust to the unfavorable environment at Huaraz and many were overcome with fatal illnesses.

During the last weeks of 1942, following the forced expulsions at Chimbote, there occurred what was commonly called "the people's uniform incident." In Japan, everyone was wearing "people's uniforms," so a tailor in Lima began using khaki-colored cloth to make "people's uniforms." At first glance, these garments seemed to be military uniforms. This fashion became very popular among the Japanese in Peru, and many people went to tailor shops to have them made.

This came even to the attention of the F.B.I. "They're making military uniforms," it was reported. Immediately, those working in the tailor shops and everyone who had placed orders were arrested and deported to the United States on military aircraft. One felt compassion for them, but when one imagined Japanese residents of Peru dressed in "people's uniforms" boarding military aircraft it seemed somewhat comical. Exactly as the rumors had purported, the Japanese "people's army" of Peru was making a move.

But, apart from the absurdity of the incident, even those who escaped arrest were frightened immensely. This was because almost all the Japanese in Peru had expected that eventually they would order a "people's uniform." Even I, who can now write these words, escaped that disaster by only a hair's breadth. If circumstances had developed differently, I could very well have been one of those marched aboard those military aircraft.

When those "people's uniforms" had become popular, I went out to Lima on a business trip. While I was there, I bought some khaki material, but did not have enough time to go to a tailor shop. I decided to leave the matter for a more convenient time and took the material back with me to Ica. That was precisely when the mass arrests occurred. If I had just a bit more time in Lima, I would have been one of those who had "made that honored move of the Japanese people's army" of Peru.

Is There Law or Justice? The Peak of Oppression

From the end of 1942 through the beginning of 1943, Peru began to show symptoms of major social upheaval. Because of the war, the Peruvian economy had come to almost a complete halt. In urban areas, we began to see groups of unemployed men loitering about.

Peru's biggest export item at that time was cotton. Japan, which had been the second largest importer of Peruvian cotton next to the United States, had suddenly been eliminated as a trading partner. Exports to Europe had already reached a low point because of the earlier start of the war in Europe.

It was not surprising that the start of the Pacific War brought much confusion to the Peruvian economy. That economic confusion was eventually reflected in various aspects of politics and society in Peru and everywhere symptoms of instability could be seen.

The resident Japanese were easy targets amidst that confusion and were targeted as scapegoats. Feelings against the Japanese ran extremely high. Whether it was relocation or deportation, the methods used to carry them out grew completely undisciplined. People on the deportation lists were arrested without their identifications being confirmed. It was common for families not to know of arrests, and for persons to be held at undisclosed locations. In extreme cases, people were arrested off the street without questioning and were placed on ships for deportation.

Even the 168 persons described earlier who were transported to Talara and later deported to the United States had no information about their destination. Rumors flew among them that they would be taken to an inland, mountainous area of Peru, where they would be massacred. Matters were so confused by that time, it would not have been strange if that had actually happened. The procedures and discipline of the Peruvian authorities had deteriorated to that point.

I heard later that the individuals transported to Talara had been placed on uncovered military trucks in the midst of the heat of January (in the southern hemisphere summer and winter are reversed). They were hauled for long hours like simple freight under the blazing desert sun.

By this time, repatriations to Japan had completely stopped and resident Japanese were all being sent to relocation camps in the United States. American authorities apparently intended to transfer all "enemy aliens" residing in South America to the United States for the purpose of exchange, if necessary, for Americans held in Japan. From the latter half of 1942 through the beginning of 1943, deportation ships bound for the United States left many times from Peru.

One could be arrested without a word of warning and taken to the inner courtyard of the Lima Police Headquarters, where heads were counted and, with no questions or notification of destination, one would be placed on deportation ships. It was wartime and one could see that arrangements for deportation ships might not be met or that such ships might enter port without prior notice. But to go out to arrest any persons simply to meet quotas once the ship was anchored was simply without reason or justice. Because of this, a large number of persons not on the U.S. lists of deportees were nevertheless sent to the United States.

People sought to resist such blatant injustices through any means possible. Some sought to avoid deportation by offering bribes, some paid "substitutes" to take their places, and, in larger cities, some covered their tracks and joined the ranks of "whereabouts unknown."

I was supposed to leave Callao harbor at the end of February 1943, but I, too, outwitted the authorities to escape that fate.

Bravo! A True Daughter of Japan

On February 22, an acquaintance in Lima placed a long distance telephone call to us. Based on reliable information, he said, "Early this morning a number of plain clothes detectives left Lima toward the southern area. Please be careful." Thanks to that phone call I was able, by a hair's breadth, to slip out of the hands of the authorities and to hide myself successfully.

By that time, all telephones in Japanese homes and shops had been confiscated. Our house, however, was an exception. When we opened our new shop under my wife's name, we had also transferred our telephone account to her name. At our shop we still had the use of our telephone as before.

After receiving the telephone report, I flew out of the shop to pass the information on to a number of friends. I then hurried home. I had intended to stay quietly in our home to observe developments, but when I came back to the shop a detective was already there awaiting my return.

I rushed into the shop, but was quickly made aware of the situation by my wife's eye movements. I instantly became a "customer" and moved about the shop looking at items. With an unconcerned look, I casually left the shop. From a distance, I observed what happened at the shop. Eventually, the detective became impatient and left. I quickly entered our living quarters and kept out of sight.

According to my wife, the detective had warned, "I'll be back." I hid myself inside of our house and remained as quiet as possible. My wife calmly said she would continue to say, "He hasn't returned!"

After a while, the detective did return. Without any trace of nervousness, my wife said, "He still hasn't returned." The detective again went off somewhere. He repeated this a number of times, always asking, "Has he come back?" My wife, showing splendid courage, continued to say, "No, he still hasn't returned."

The detective became very impatient. He eventually said, loudly, "If your husband does not come back by sunset, I will take you into custody and send you to Lima. You had better start making preparations for that. Do you understand?" He no doubt felt he could frighten her enough to reveal my whereabouts, but my wife would not budge. "He still has not returned. Please wait a while," she said and deliberately picked up our three-month-old second son, Arturo, to appeal to the detective's sympathy.

Hidden within our living quarters, I could overhear the threats, but I was sure the detective was bluffing. Even if Peru could be said to be an "uncivilized country," they would never arrest my wife in my place. But in those severely deteriorated social conditions, it was not unthinkable. When the detective left, I said to my wife, "If they actually attempt to take you into custody, I shall give myself up."

My wife, however, remained absolutely calm and said, "No, I shall go. I don't expect they will place a woman with a three-month-old child in confinement with a group of men. At least, not as a 'substitute.' At worst, I will be taken to Lima. If I were to be deported, even the North Americans would not know what to do with me."

She spoke with such magnificent courage. I had heard about the wives of Japanese warriors who, when they had reached a resolution, became even more calm and objective than their spouses. Here, it was true that my wife had achieved such a state. Terms such as the "way of the warriors" or "true daughter of Japan" could be expected to be meaningless to her, but this "true daughter of Japan" who had been born in Peru superbly met those qualifications. She immediately filled a suitcase with clothing and other necessities. Thus, prepared to leave whenever necessary, she awaited the outcome.

Night came, shrouding everything in complete darkness. The detective came back to the shop and repeated several times, "We can't wait. We must leave soon." But after a number of hours he did not seem to make a move. Whenever the detective showed himself in the shop, I could only place my palms together to pray that the deities and Buddha would protect us.

The night passed anxiously by. Even the children knew that anything could happen and kept close to their mother that night, awaiting the consequences.

Later, a clock rang 11 times. The detective returned yet again. Confirming that I had not returned, he stared at my wife and children and at her hasty preparations for departure. Then, without a word, he left the shop. We waited, but he did not come back. His absence, however, only made us more anxious. When he did return, I thought, it would be the final move. I would certainly be taken into custody. My imagination was filled with pessimism. "He's probably busy arranging transportation to Lima," I thought.

An hour had creeped by when someone entered the shop. "Senorita, everyone has left. It is all right!" It was the chief of the Ica police from across the street. I was so relieved that all my strength suddenly left me and my eyes brimmed with tears. The long night had finally ended. My wife had held on and had carried us through.

I later learned from the police chief that he had seen me slip into our living quarters and was aware of my whereabouts. But he had taken the attitude, "This is not under our jurisdiction," and had simply observed what was going on. When I heard this I was grateful that I had befriended those in the general Peruvian community.

Earlier that day, I had notified my friend, Yogoro Ishizu, and a young man named Suwa, about the telephone report from Lima, but they had not been able to hide themselves in time. They had been arrested by the detective and were held at the provincial police headquarters. The detective had been assigned to arrest the three of us and transfer us to Lima. With the other two already in custody, it seems that he had searched everywhere for me until shortly before they departed for Lima. Because I had "disappeared," Ishizu and Suwa had to spend the entire day in confinement. I felt badly about that. Yet, because of the goodwill and cooperation of those around me, I had been able to pass through that crisis.

I was very lucky that the detective from Lima did not know how I looked. I had been "saved" mainly because the arrest had been left to a detective under the direct control of the National Police Superintendent, Mr. Teran. If the arrest had been assigned to the Ica provincial police or to the Ica municipal police it would have been accomplished immediately. Whatever the case, I had been greatly favored.

I could not expect, however, that such good fortune would continue forever. At any time, strict orders could come down to the Ica provincial and municipal police offices. If that happened, no matter how well acquainted I was with their leaders, I could not expect them to endanger their own positions and livelihoods to protect me. I had become a marked man, "wanted" by the central police. If I wanted to "escape," I needed to make a major and decisive move.

Last picnic at Huacachina, 1944.

Chapter Seven. The Pitiful "Japanese People's Army of Peru"

Life Underground

Although we had survived the "arrest incident" in February 1943, I still faced a grave situation. Circumstances had reached a stage where my only alternative was to go completely into hiding. When I considered places where I could hide myself, however, I needed to keep in mind my family and shops. Because of them, I did not want to go too far away. Ultimately, I decided to go into hiding in my own home.

I know it sounds odd, but I had thought it through and had made definite plans. I would excavate a place under the floor of a room in our living quarters. Whenever necessary, I could hide myself there. With great secrecy, I took up the floor planks and dug out an underground cubicle measuring about six feet on each side. I furnished it with a simple bed, a small desk and a shortwave radio.

I was prepared to remain in hiding for short periods of time. Secretly, I also devised a way of connecting the antenna of my shortwave radio via underground wires to an antenna at a neighboring school. I stored some emergency food, made arrangements for containment of bodily wastes, and completely camouflaged the entry to the underground "room."

When my preparations were ready, I suddenly "disappeared." Quite literally, I went "underground" in my own home. The only ones aware of my location were members of my family and our live-in employees. I considered allowing my situation to be known to a few close friends and neighbors, but, remembering a Japanese maxim that "the first step in deceiving an enemy is taken among allies," I decided to take complete caution.

My wife told everyone who asked, "Ever since that attempted arrest, I don't know where my husband went." We carefully repeated the instructions to our children. The children had vivid recollections of the evening of February 22, so whenever they were asked, "Where is your father?" they always answered, "We don't know." Eventually, everyone in the community came to believe that I had disappeared.

I did not stay in the underground cubicle all of the time, but it was still difficult not being able to take a step outside our premises. I kept abreast of developments by listening every day to shortwave broadcasts from Japan and reading every word of the newspaper, *El*

Commercio.

I did not have much to occupy my time, so every day I made detailed comparisons of the U.S. reports of war developments published in the *El Commercio* and the shortwave reports that came in from Japan. In that way I devised my own analysis of what was happening.

In the beginning, I did not even dream Japan would be defeated, but from my daily analyses of reports I could eventually see developments turning against Japan. For example, I came to see through Japanese reports when they used such terms as "the expected decisive battle" or "a decisive advance." It was the same for reports from the European front. It was clear that every day brought the Axis powers closer to defeat .

With the war going in its favor, I began to believe that the United States would no longer persist in arresting someone such as I in an outlying provincial area of Peru. But, having managed to escape detection thus far, I decided to endure my situation a while longer.

Even while I remained "underground," our business continued to grow steadily. In fact, rather than steady progress it would be more accurate to say that it made great advances. Our customers knew I had "disappeared," so they came to the shops and spoke to my wife with regret and sympathy.

The banks were also aware of my wife's situation and did not begrudge their continued cooperation. We had already shifted most of our wholesale suppliers to non-Japanese companies, so the government's policy of closing Japanese-owned businesses did not seriously affect us. On the contrary, a number of wholesalers began to deliver merchandise without invoices to retail shops still in business. Those wholesalers were greatly appreciated by the Japanese merchants still in business and, as their reputation spread throughout the Japanese community, their clientele increased markedly.

During that period of confusion, my wife managed the business splendidly. She gained the complete confidence of banks and trading partners; our storerooms and warehouse came to be filled with merchandise. Ironically, in that period when the real owner was hidden away, it became even easier to do business. Profits rose as never before. If not for the war, the situation clearly would have been an economic heaven for us.

We continued in this manner for six months. During that time there were many incidents that aroused our precautions and we were haunted by the thought, "Can this be it?" In general, however, these were mostly minor incidents, such as reports that someone was looking for me or that a telephone call had come from someone we did not know. Still, they caused much anxiety for the entire household.

There being no major difficulties for some time, however, I began to feel that it might be safe to "reappear." It had been six months since the last "deportation ship" had left. I had not heard of another ship leaving and had not heard of any new oppressive actions against Japanese. It had been many months since I last heard of a Japanese being arrested and detained. Furthermore, an Allied victory was assured, so I felt that American authorities would not push for the arrest of persons such as I at that point.

Concluding that the crisis had passed, I decided to show myself to the outside community. Thus, as suddenly as I had disappeared, I again reappeared in Ica. I did not make a big deal of it, but I was very happy to be able to move about in the community once again. I was even more grateful for the warm greetings that everyone had for me. They all expressed their happiness for my well being. "Were you safe and in good health, after all? This is good; this is good." Inevitably, they all asked, "Where did you go?" But I avoided answering the question by saying vaguely, "Well, there were many things. . . ."

A Sudden Arrest

For several months our lives continued without incident. The war was still on, so some uneasiness remained in the back of my mind. In general, however, I did not pay particular heed and began to conduct myself in a more open manner, not much different than the time before the war. But, one day, I was suddenly reminded of the fact that Japan was still at war. I can never forget . . . it was January 6, 1944.

It was a Sunday, and we had taken the family out for a picnic at Lake Huacachina. Lake Huacachina was a small expanse of water located at the lowest point of a basin that looked like an ancient volcanic crater. It was known for its cold, green waters that had some salt and sulfur content. Above its waters rose exquisite sand dunes, where people enjoyed a form of sand skiing. It was a wonderful, peaceful Sunday. We had leisurely spent the entire day there and returned home late that evening.

We had just sat down at the table for a late supper when it began. There was a knock on the front door. Previously, if it was not a special pattern of knocks, we would not have opened the door until I entered the underground cubicle. But we had enjoyed many months of an open and peaceful life, so we had forgotten those precautions. One of our employees, Victor, opened the door without hesitation. It was a fatal mistake.

Instantly, five men entered our home and one said, "We are from Lima Police Headquarters. Seiichi Higashide is under arrest." There was no opportunity to feign ignorance. Among the five was a detective from the Ica police office who knew me well. As I had been concerned about earlier, the central police headquarters in Lima had requested the cooperation of the Ica provincial police.

All avenues had been cut off. I was to be taken immediately to the Ica police headquarters. It is said that even rats in desperate circumstances fight back; I also needed to put up some resistance. "I will not hide or try to escape, so please wait outside," I said calmly. "We are having our supper." We finished our meal in a proper way and, after a change of clothing, I went out.

Soon, details of the situation became clear. A deportation ship was about to enter Callao, so it had been decided to arrest major figures who still had not been deported. While it is debatable whether or not I was a major figure, the fact was I was the only person arrested in the province of Ica this time. Four detectives had been sent from Lima to arrest me. Perhaps, I thought, I was a major figure after all.

Accompanied by the five detectives, I was taken to the local police headquarters. I was startled to learn that my friend, the pro-Axis police chief, was not there. It was unthinkable that he would leave without telling us, but he was gone. "He must have been temporarily diverted from the arrest with some assignment," I thought. I was certain that if the police chief had been there, this would not have occurred. I lamented my bad luck, but there was nothing I could do.

That night I was detained in the holding area at the police headquarters. My family thought I would be sent immediately to Lima, so they all came to the headquarters. When they learned I was to leave the next morning, they went home for the night. After an uneasy night, at first light I was told, "It's time to go."

I was taken outside to a filthy, dilapidated old police "paddy wagon." Although I had been arrested, I did not think I was a criminal; I refused to ride in that paddy wagon. It would have been too humiliating. I insisted, "I'll hire a taxi and appear at the police headquarters in Lima."

The detectives must have understood my position. They quickly agreed and said, "Well, then we'll have someone accompany you. But be sure that you appear at Lima Police Headquarters by 5 p.m."

I hired a taxi and, accompanied by a detective armed with a pistol, left Ica police headquarters. I wanted to say farewell to my family, so

I first directed the driver to our shop. I got off and entered to say my final farewells to my family. Much earlier I had given them detailed instructions on how to handle the family's affairs and the business, so there were no especially pressing instructions I needed to give them. But I knew this could very well be the last time I would see them and I was filled with a multitude of emotions.

Passage to Lima

Shortly after 9 a.m. I again got into the taxi. I looked out at our employees who had gathered nearby. Many had worked diligently for us over many years and my heart filled with sadness when I thought this might be the last time I would see them. I had hoped to eventually help each of them start his own small shop, but now we had come to this and I could do nothing for them. Our employees stood looking intently at me; they did not say a word but I could see tears in their eyes.

I could see my wife holding back her tears. She was in her last month of pregnancy with our fifth child. She brought the children over and stood by me silently. The four children sniffled, but they set their lips firmly to keep from weeping. When I said, "I'll be back soon," no one answered.

The taxi began to move. Suddenly, a young nisei employee, Victor Narita, rushed up to the taxi and grasped my hand through the open window while running beside the moving taxi. His face was contorted with emotion, and he began to cry unabashedly. The tears I had been holding back finally came streaming from my eyes. The taxi picked up speed and the figures of those standing in front of our shop grew smaller and smaller. They kept waving and called back over and over, "Adios, sayonara...." I leaned out of the window until I could no longer see them.

Oh, it had been a painful parting. What would happen to them? What if I never saw them again in this life? The only thing that consoled me was the fact that my wife's parents had agreed to move in with us. But with conditions in Peru, I could not be certain that even that would continue. If my father-in-law were arrested, it was possible that the family would have to be dispersed. At that moment, as never before, a deep feeling of hatred for war arose in me. No matter what reason could be given, I thought, wars were sinful and evil. Wars must be eliminated from our world. I set my lips with determination as these strong thoughts came over me.

The taxi eventually passed through the outskirts of Ica and

entered the desert. I slowly regained control of myself. It was done. No matter how much I lamented my situation there was nothing more I could do. Whatever happened from now could only be endured. I forced myself to return to civility and began talking to the detective who had been sitting silently next to me. I needed something to take my mind off of the situation. From an earlier time I had had a passing acquaintance with the detective, so we were able to find common areas of interest. Despite my situation, the long trip to Lima was not boring.

It was about three o'clock when we entered Lima. The detective agreed that we didn't have to go to police headquarters until five o'clock, so I decided to stop to say farewell to two or three friends. Between visits I had the driver stop at a photo studio. I had suddenly remembered that I had never taken a decent photograph, so, as a last memento, I had a portrait taken and arranged to have prints sent to my family in Ica.

I stopped at the Kurotobi Company, whose owner, Tatsujiro Kurotobi, had been so kind when I first arrived in Peru. Mr. Kurotobi had been detained soon after the outbreak of the war and had been repatriated to Japan on the first exchange ship. His oldest son Isamu had taken over the business, but, about a year earlier, had been deported to the United States. The business had been left in the hands of a manager, Mr. Yokota.

After the Kurotobis were deported, Mr. Yokota had also come to take on the large task of representing the resident Japanese in Peru. In every type of matter he acted as an intermediary between the Japanese community and the Spanish Consulate. It was time-consuming and exhausting work.

In early 1942, after Peru severed diplomatic relations with Japan, all direct contact between the two countries were cut off. Contact with those in Japan was possible only through the Spanish Consulate in Lima, which forwarded messages to Madrid, where they were passed on to Japanese diplomats. With the Japanese Consulate closed, Mr. Yokota had become an unofficial "acting Japanese Consul." I informed Mr. Yokota of my situation and said farewell.

At the Kurotobi Company I was introduced to Rokuichi Kudo, who owned a large trading company on the main thoroughfare in central Lima. We would come to share a common fate together for many years. When he learned that I had been arrested and was about to be taken to the police headquarters he said, "That's terrible. But, then, it may be that I, too..." I was just about to leave the Kurotobi Company and he, too, rushed out and disappeared somewhere.

I later learned Mr. Kudo had taken the information to several friends to warn them to go into immediate hiding. He then hurried home to inform his family and to go into hiding himself, but it was too late. When he arrived home, detectives were already waiting to arrest him. The next morning he was brought into the cell block where I was being detained.

Disgusting, Smelly Meals

Wearing a fine suit, I arrived at police headquarters at exactly 5 p.m. as ordered. I calmly confronted the investigating officer who had come over to take me in. I made it a point to look directly at him. I vividly recall that it was the investigating officer, rather than I who was being questioned, who avoided eye contact. After he confirmed my identity he said, "You will be held here for a while."

No matter how many times I asked for reasons and the nature of my offense, he would not answer me. Without any explanation, I was taken by a guard and was pushed into a cell.

The facility was wretched beyond imagination. The cell block was a three-story concrete building. The first floor was for murderers and thieves, the third floor held "political subversives," and the second floor was "reserved" for Japanese deportees. My cell was a concrete box about six feet wide and about 10 feet deep. The entry, facing a walkway, had a movable framework of iron bars. During the day, the gate-like framework of iron bars was raised and we could go out onto the walkway and into other cells. At night, however, the bars were lowered and locked. If we had to eliminate bodily wastes we were told to do it "wherever you want" in our cells.

It was completely disgusting. The wastes that accumulated during the night were hosed out with water every morning, but because this had been repeated over many years the stench had permeated the concrete and remained permanently. When I was pushed into the cell my first reaction was to that powerful smell.

It was somewhat bearable during the day, but at night after the iron bars were lowered one could smell the stench of urine everywhere. By early morning, the stinging ammonia fumes were so strong that one could barely breathe or open one's eyes.

The prison meals were beyond belief. When it was time for meals each prisoner was given a large empty tin can; someone then came over and slopped out an unrecognizable mixture into the cans. We were expected to eat that. The indescribable odor of the mixture brought me to the point of vomiting. I was brought to feel even a strange admiration at the accuracy and aptness of the commonly used Japanese term, "a smelly meal." In the cell block there was no menu. Everyday—in the morning, at noon and in the evening—the "mixture" was ladled out.

The Japanese detainees, however, were blessed. We could not escape the stench of the cell block, but we did not have to eat the prison meals. Through the kindness of an unknown benefactor, o-bento boxed meals were brought in for us three times a day from a nearby Japanese restaurant. Someone had made continuing inquiries about the number of Japanese detainees in the cell block and had arranged to have meals sent in to us. Later, of course, I arranged to pay the restaurant for my meals, but I was touched and grateful for the warm concern of those in the Japanese community.

Days passed. I knew I would be placed on a ship and sent somewhere, but I had not been told when that would happen nor what my destination would be. I expected I would most probably be sent to the United States. Beyond that, no matter how much I considered the possibilities, I could not be sure what to expect.

After about a week of prison life my family unexpectedly came to Lima. As a "special consideration," the Japanese detainees in Lima were allowed to meet family members twice a day—once in the morning and again in the afternoon—in an inner courtyard of the police headquarters.

My wife and children suddenly appeared there. According to my wife, she had received reliable information that I would be sent to the United States in the near future, so she had hurriedly hired a taxi and had come to Lima with the children. My wife arranged to stay at a friend's home in Lima and came with the children twice every day to visit and to bring in things that they knew I liked. Even as we visited, however, we knew that I would be deported, so we could not raise ourselves to a happy mood.

Departure in the Middle of the Night—A Rising Anger

Without warning, on the morning of January 18, three or four days after my family began visiting me, we were told that we would board ship that day.

That happened to be my birthday, so my family planned to have a quiet birthday party in the courtyard of the police headquarters. My wife and children who had come to the courtyard all greeted me with "Happy Birthday!" but my situation had changed so abruptly it was not a time for congratulations. My wife quickly rushed out to buy clothing and personal items I would need when I boarded the ship. During the afternoon visiting hours she brought in two large trunks packed with those items.

Toward evening we were made to assemble in the courtyard with our luggage. With deliberate movements, an officer took out a boarding list and began calling out names. For some reason, however, my name and that of a young man named Furuya from Arequipa were not on the list. "Incredible luck," I thought. "I'm saved." The officer seemed to accept that we had been detained by mistake and did not move to take any high-handed actions. I was grateful that good luck had again come to me even at such a desperate moment.

To the others who were about to be sent off to the ship I did not show any emotion, but I was overjoyed. I began helping them with their luggage. Eventually, tarpaulin covered military trucks carrying the deportees left police headquarters. Only a stillness remained.

I arranged that the two trunks be returned to my wife. Furuya and I were taken back to our now empty and lonely tier of cells. My wife was greatly relieved by this turn of events and returned to her temporary living quarters. Again, we had passed through a crisis. But it was to be only a brief reprise. While I rested my spirit-drained body, the metal gate crashed upward and a guard entered. "We're taking you to Callao, so come out immediately." Our luck had not held. The person who made the list had made a simple error and skipped our names. It was a cruel error. Both my wife and I now faced anxious moments.

Having returned the two trunks with my clothing and personal items to my wife, I had to get in touch with her immediately. I wrote a short note and, passing it over with some bills, asked a guard to deliver it to my wife as quickly as possible. Fortunately, the guard was an honest person and my wife got the note. The family had been in the middle of their evening meal, but my wife immediately called a taxi and, with the trunks, started out for the harbor with our four children.

Meanwhile, Furuya and I were placed on a truck and taken to Callao; at the docks we joined the others who had left earlier. Did my wife get my message? Would the trunks come safely to my hands? Would I see my wife and children before boarding? Concerns overflowed, one into the other. I received no word. It came time to board the ship.

Surrounded by American soldiers carrying rifles with fixed bayonets, we were lined up four abreast and marched over to the gangway to board. M.P.'s were on all sides of us and it was clear that elaborate precautions had been taken. It was then that I truly came to understand that I was a "prisoner of war." The ship was a small freighter that had been hastily militarized with the placement of a number of cannons on it.

When we were all on board the ship, we were made to strip naked and everything that we had brought on board was examined. Then, an officer appeared and began a long and detailed explanation in Spanish of the rules and regulations we were to follow. He ordered complete compliance and repeated that any infractions would be met with severe punishment. It was quite a long presentation, but no one made a sound; not even a cough or a shuffle came through the intent silence. Eventually, his speech ended. As ordered, we went down into the hold of the ship and were locked in.

About this time, my wife arrived in Callao. She recalls that when she reached the pier the ship was still there but that there was no sign of the deportees. She desperately wanted to get the trunks to me, so she entrusted them to someone nearby who appeared to be an American soldier. She pleaded that he bring back some receipt or proof that I had received them.

She waited on the pier for hours, but nothing came back. She waited with the children until about midnight, but no confirmation came. In the meantime, the ship left the pier and moved out to sea. She finally turned back hopelessly toward her temporary lodgings in Lima.

The ship lurched heavily and slowly began to move. Locked within its hold, I suddenly became very angry. I had earlier felt a deep hatred toward wars, but now I grew angry at the cowardliness of the Peruvian government. If Peru had been a direct enemy of Japan, I would have understood my situation. Peru had severed diplomatic ties with Japan, but it was still a third party to the dispute. Even if it had been pressured by the United States, what country with any pride and independence would have said, "Yes. We shall comply," and hand over innocent people? If it were only those with Japanese citizenship, a case might have been made. But the Peruvian government had given in to American pressure even to the point of deporting naturalized citizens and Peruvian citizens who had been born there.

In a civilized and respectable country, if one were there with proper approvals, it could be expected that even tourists would be given legal protections. If that could not be guaranteed, I thought, then no protest could be made when Peru was called "an uncivilized, third-rate country." I had always protested when I heard Peru called "a third-rate country" or an "uncivilized country," but now I felt justified in using such terms myself.

Americans in the United States also were not blameless. From the time I was a child I had read many books about America. I had felt that America was an ideal country that should be taken as a model for the whole world. Why, then, had that country moved to take such unacceptable measures? Where was the spirit of individual rights and justice that had filled the Declaration of Independence and the U.S. Constitution? If I termed Peru, even provisionally, a "third rate country," was not America, in this instance, no different?

Even if under emergency wartime conditions, was America not in violation of individual rights? This was not, I felt, only a matter of international law, it was a broader issue of human rights. Of course, undeniably, the Axis nations perpetrated similar outrages. Yet, I felt, could I not hope that America alone would not do so?

Temporary Detainment by the U.S. Military

We were not allowed to even step out of the hold of the ship. We had no way even to confirm the position of the sun or stars, so we had no way of determining where the ship was heading. We assumed that it was heading northward toward the United States, but we had no way of confirming it. Then, three days after we began our journey, the ship suddenly slowed and eventually stopped.

It was too soon, even on a direct route, to have reached the United States. Had something happened? In the hold of the ship speculation ran rampant. The ship did not move for a long time. Then, from somewhere, a touch of raw, warm air began entering the hold. In two or three hours the hold became unbearably warm. It must be Panama! I felt sure we were in Panama.

Later, the steel door was opened and we were ordered to disembark. Holding our hands up to shade our eyes, we climbed onto the deck. I took in a deep breath of fresh air. The air was warm but was nevertheless a refreshing respite from the stale air breathed by so many people in the hold of the ship. It was truly delicious, I thought. I looked out in all directions. Our surroundings were clearly in a tropical area. I was sure it was Panama.

Before we disembarked, we were given our luggage. The two trunks, which I had just about given up on, had been brought on board as my wife had hoped. We were told to carry our own luggage and I was immediately caught short. It would be impossible for me to carry those two cumbersome, oversized trunks for a long period.

I considered abandoning one of them. But, praying that our destination was not far away, I placed one on my shoulder, grasped the other with my free hand, and staggered forward. Luckily, we were directed to large military trucks not too far away. I got on a truck with a sigh of relief. Swaying back and forth with the movements of the truck, we were taken somewhere.

The trucks came to a stop in front of what seemed to be temporary barracks in an area reserved for American military forces in Panama. We had not been told where we were, but, in any case, there were several temporary barracks and in each we could see rows of 14 or 15 cots. As soon as the trucks stopped, we were lined up in formation in front of the barracks. We received a detailed explanation of rules and regulations and a strict warning about unacceptable behavior.

Speaking fluent Spanish, the officer before us explained the daily schedule. Finally, he repeated twice that there must be complete compliance with orders and that any infractions would be severely· punished. As was the case after boarding the ship, we listened with absolute attention and were again reminded that we were prisoners of war. We were given small, numbered badges and allowed to break formation. We were to enter the barracks and find our cots according to the numbers on the badges.

This was how we began our life at the temporary detention camp in Panama. In our shipload of deportees there were a number of people of German ancestry. There were a total of 29 Japanese; of these five or six were naturalized Peruvians and one or two were nisei who had been born in Peru.

It was clear that our group was different from the earlier Japanese deportee groups. Previously, groups of 150 or 200 persons had been detained for one or two days and immediately sent out. In our case, even when the Peruvian authorities knew the arrival date of the ship, it had taken more than two weeks to round up 29 persons. Thus, in our group there were no substitutes or persons with mistaken identities. Everyone was a major figure. Thus, as could be expected, there were many older people. I was the youngest in our group.

A Military Life for the Detainees

Because the camp in Panama was under the jurisdiction of the American military, everything in our lives was handled in a military manner. Just like soldiers, we arose at 5 a.m., got into our clothes, fixed our beds, washed up, and ran out to the formation area. At 5:30

a.m., together with the soldiers stationed there, we participated in the exercises that included the raising of the American flag, saluting the flag, reciting of the "Pledge of Allegiance," listening to the officer's instructions, etc. We were required to do everything the soldiers did. We would arrive at the assembly area in pitch darkness. By the time we returned to the barracks, there would be a touch of light in the sky.

Breakfast was at 6 a.m. We then went out to our assignments. We wore used military boots and work fatigues. We were each issued large sickles or hatchets. Our assignment was to clear out underbrush. For many years I had handled only a pen or abacus in my work, so our forced assignment was truly hard and painful labor. Moreover, since the great majority of those in our group were older, it was pitiful to see them strain at their work. Everyone acquired many large blisters and when those broke and settled, new blisters again grew back over those barely healed blisters.

Every day, two M.P.s carrying bayoneted rifles yelled and ordered us about as we cleared the underbrush. At day's end, the "Japanese people's army" that returned to the barracks was a pitiful sight. Dragging along in ill-fitting boots and hitching up overly large work uniforms, we plodded back to the barracks. I wished that the F.B.I. chief, who often spoke of the "Japanese fifth column," could see this sad sight. With the heavy labor, however, my arms returned to the knotty muscularity of my early years when I had worked in lumberyards.

After the day's labor, everyone was exhausted. After supper we would sit about in low spirits, silently watching the searchlights that beamed out from surrounding mountains and interlaced in the sky like a spider's web.

The searchlights were used to detect enemy planes that might enter the canal zone. At times, when a small plane got caught like a fly in a searchlight beam, all the other searchlights turned to focus on it. Then, from the mountains on all sides, artillery and machine guns spat out flames. There was a fearsome noise. When we became accustomed to our routine in the camp, however, no one even reacted when that happened.

Everyone was physically and spiritually exhausted. I tried to divert them by being overly exuberant, making silly jokes, and trying to provoke their laughter. But even if they laughed briefly, by the time we went to our cots we were again wrapped in heavy silence. In this way, a day would pass and, again, a dull sun tinged yellower than a lantern and as large as a wash tub would rise in the sky without any glint of renewal. We then willed our stomachs with a bland breakfast and went out to our assignment.

If the food had been better morale might have been different, but the meals were simple and tasteless so that even after a day of heavy physical labor we could not work up much of an appetite. Sauerkraut, spinach, beets, red beans, mashed potatoes and sausages appeared regularly on our plates. Everything was something that had been taken out of a can. The soft, American type of white bread was different from what we were used to in Peru.

We had no cause to complain about the amount of food served or its nutritional value, however. We were served the same food as the soldiers stationed there. We were not singled out for unfair treatment, but the older, traditional Japanese could not readily adapt to the American meals.

Everyone was starved for fresh vegetables. I'm sure the American soldiers there felt the same. One day I devised a little plan and crawled under the flooring of a building to a food storage room. I stole three or four large onions. I divided them up with everyone at our next meal. Normally, one would not notice slices of round onions but for us at the time they seemed so delicious. Everyone was delighted with them and ate them savoring each precious bite.

An Encounter with Sentei Yagi

Among the deportees sent to Panama were many who were looked upon as "senior advisors" by the Japanese community in Peru. Among them were Ichitaro Morimoto (the uncle of Miss Shioya whom I had met at the language school in Tokyo) and Dr. Genji Nimura. One I shall never forget is Sentei Yagi.

If my memory does not fail me, Mr. Yagi had been a member of the first graduating class of Waseda University in Tokyo and was about 60 years old when I met him. He was a naturalized citizen of Peru and was considered to be a senior leader in the Japanese community. Every night after supper it was Mr. Yagi's custom to walk up and down the passageways of our restricted camp area. He always focussed his eyes slightly downward and seemed to be deep in thought. One day, I felt like joining him so I stepped over quickly and said, "Mr. Yagi, would you mind if I walk with you?" He gave me a small smile and nodded, "Yes, it is all right." I strolled along beside him and we began to speak of many matters.

From that time, walks with Mr. Yagi became part of my daily schedule. After supper, Mr. Yagi would invariably invite me by saying, "Higashide, *vamos* (let's go)." I was grateful one day when he said, "When I walk with you my feelings brighten up."

One evening as we strolled along Mr. Yagi said, "Higashide, what do you think will happen with this war?" I hesitated for a while and then answered with carefully selected words. Although there were only 29 of us, I did not want to create any disturbances in our little "Japanese village." Yet, I felt it was wrong to say anything I did not really believe.

"I don't think Japan will lose the war," I said, "but it may be difficult for her to have a complete victory. More and more, it seems that it will be a long war and the world. . ."

"Do you really think so?" he interrupted. "I think it is hopeless. Japan has entered a bad war. I feel that she should enter into peace negotiations right now."

"But, Mr. Yagi. . ." I answered and unexpectedly found myself in the position of taking the side of those who vigorously supported Japan's actions. "Japan did not enter the war recklessly. Isn't it true that after a long period of endurance and caution and careful examination of conditions, they took that step because they felt that they could cope with it? What Japan has done is not an accident or a blunder."

I was aware that there were increasing signs of Japan's defeat. At the time, however, German U-boats were even then in the Caribbean creating havoc, so I felt that my statement had some basis of support.

"Yes, that is so," Mr. Yagi replied. "Japan also has the experiences of the Sino-Japanese War and the Russo-Japanese War. But in this case the historical situation and all other conditions are completely different. Japan has taken on the United States, the largest industrialized country in the world. Just by looking around you here, I think you can see what that means. Their military supplies and everything else, from general provisions such as clothing, food and so forth, are not what Japan can match. America is a great country with a fearsome amount of materials and advanced technology. It probably controls half the wealth of the world. Japan has chosen to go to war against the wrong country."

Mr. Yagi spoke rapidly, but every point he made was correct. I could not reply and fell into silence.

Mr. Yagi and the Early Contract Immigrants

My relationship with Mr. Yagi continued over a long period. He had been a pioneer among the Japanese in Peru. Settling in Lurin, on the outskirts of Lima, he had opened a general store and a hotel, and had become involved in cotton growing. While maintaining wide business interests, he had gone out to examine the mountain areas and the head waters of the Amazon in Peru. Because he had such experiences, we never lacked topics for discussion.

Among the many accounts I heard from Mr. Yagi, one that left a vivid impression was an episode that reveals the desperate situation of the early contract emigrants. From about 1909, contract emigrants had been sent out to provincial areas to work on cotton farms and sugar cane plantations. Most could not bear the harsh working conditions and inhumane treatment they received, so, in groups of three or four, they attempted to escape to Lima. More than a few had to go for days without food or were caught by pursuers, beaten and returned. When such "escapees" reached Lurin, Mr. Yagi would take them into his home and provide them with food and clothes. If they were sick, he took them by horseback to the Chorillos Hospital in the suburbs of Lima. He found jobs for those who were still healthy. For those who died in his home, he would take care of funeral arrangements.

Such conditions persisted for many years. Mr. Yagi decided to establish a facility that would provide temporary shelter and assistance to such escapees. He undertook a trip to major areas where Japanese resided to solicit funds for such a facility. Everywhere people donated one or two soles from their meager funds. He recalled that he went to Canete to ask for donations and while there he went out to its suburbs to see the immigrant cemetery.

He was startled to find two corpses there. Nearby, there were small *vela de sevo* (candles) burning with lonely, flickering flames. He asked immigrants who happened to be there, "Why haven't they been buried?" He was told that if funeral services were held for one or two persons there would be complaints from employers because a number of people would have to leave work to attend to duties connected with those funerals. Thus, he was told, when a number of corpses accumulated, a joint funeral was held. In Canete in those early years, it was not unusual for Japanese immigrants to die almost daily.

Mr. Yagi recounted that as he passed through the farming area of Canete he saw many grave markers on the hillsides. Some had names written in India ink on strips of wood taken from boxes; others had slips of paper pasted on with names written in pencil. Even though it does not rain too often in Peru, those flimsy grave markers seemed to be beyond civility. Mr. Yagi proposed that a common grave site be established.

When he spoke of that experience, I recalled that when I was a teacher at the Japanese elementary school in Canete, arrangements for improving the Canete Japanese Cemetery had been completed and a monument for the "unknown deceased" was erected. From every area in Peru many persons gathered and a solemn memorial service had been held. I recalled that I had taken the school children to attend the service.

Mr. Yagi recounted for me many other episodes and anecdotes from his experiences. I felt fortunate to have met him. I learned many things from this older, experienced and knowledgeable immigrant to Peru. Through my relationship with him, my understanding of the human experience in Peru and the world expanded immeasurably.

First Communications with My Family

One day, about three weeks after our detainment in Panama, we were informed that we could send letters to our families twice a week. Nothing was said about receiving letters, but we were grateful that we could report our situation to our families.

I immediately focused all my wit and energy to compose a letter to my wife. I knew that any information that openly touched on security matters would not reach her. Because of this I used every means I could contrive to communicate with her without being censored. I used innocuous terms and patterns of expression that only my wife and I would fully understand to send to her as much information as possible.

Two months later, the letters I had written every week reached my wife in a large bundle. Because I had used caution and had exerted myself to express matters in a way that could not be detected, my letters had reached her almost intact with only a few passages snipped out. The families of those "honest" detainees who had written without precaution were startled to receive letters that had been so heavily censored that even the original shape of the stationery could hardly be determined. Because my letters were almost completely intact, I later learned that families of those "honest letter writers" came to make many inquiries of my wife.

About two or three weeks after such letters were allowed we were told, "Those who wish to have their families join them should immediately send telegrams to them. A deportation ship is soon to enter Callao, so if they are not notified by telegram they will not have time to board the ship." Everyone could have leaped with joy; almost all rushed to send telegrams.

When I heard this, however, I had mixed feelings and did not know what to do. When I had left Peru, I felt that no matter what happened my wife and children should remain there and I had given my wife strict instructions that she was not to attempt to follow me. But, after more than a month in Panama, my feelings had changed.

For one thing, if the war continued over a long period I could not expect that there would be some simple resolution that would allow me to return to Peru. Furthermore, my life alone as a detainee was uncomfortable and difficult to bear. It had become clear that if we were detained for an extended period it would be under U.S. jurisdiction. America had initiated some very unreasonable actions, but I reconsidered the situation and came to feel that we might be safer there than in Peru. If other families were notified to board ship, and my wife alone did not receive such a notification, she would be greatly concerned. I decided that rather than have members of our family separated for many years it would be better to be together and pass through good and bad times together. I sent off a telegram.

I had told my wife very strongly, however, "Do not leave Peru at all." So the wording of that telegram had to be decisive. I focussed myself so that my true intent would be communicated in the limited space of the telegram. Finally, I sent a telegram that stated, "When ship comes in board all family. Leave even all assets. This is last chance."

That telegram was actually the first communication my wife received after I had left. The letters I had sent earlier still had not been delivered. When the telegram reached the Ica post office, the postmaster, Mr. Ramo, was overjoyed and personally delivered the telegram to my wife. At that time, my wife had just given birth to our third daughter, Marta Yoko, and was resting in bed.

My mother-in-law greeted Mr. Ramo. When my mother-in-law heard that it was a telegram from me, she asked to see it. She feared that if it contained bad news it would be a shock to my wife. "I wish very much to hand it over personally to the Senora," he insisted, and was finally allowed to my wife's bedside. The postmaster had been sorely concerned about my wife who had been alone and appeared overwhelmed by her responsibilities as she had bravely continued to operate our shop. When my wife read the telegram, I am told, the postmaster grasped her hand and repeatedly said, "No matter what, he is safe. He is safe." From that time, the postmaster stopped by every day to visit my wife. His kind words of encouragement, "It is all right. I"m sure you will be together," were words that even today my wife cannot forget.

Like the postmaster, our other Peruvian friends remained staunch supporters despite the anti-Japanese atmosphere in Peru. Even after I was detained, they all sympathized with my wife and made it a point to appear at our shops and give her words of consolation and support. They were truly magnificent friends . . . from the heart.

My Wife's Full Efforts—Closing the Business

What occurred in Ica after my telegram arrived has been told to me from a variety of angles. By reconciling such accounts, the following seems to have happened.

First, the telegram brought great confusion to the family. My expectations had been correct. From my wife's standpoint, only a few months earlier I had told her that she must never leave Peru. Now the telegram directed her to abandon everything, including our assets, and to board the next ship. She was naturally confused and uncertain about what to do. I had mentioned a ship, but where was it going? Was the telegram authentic? My wife began making long distance telephone calls to reach other families that had been left behind.

Although the circumstances and reasons for the telegrams remained unclear, she confirmed that similar telegrams had reached each family. Realizing that, she decided to move immediately as directed even if it was so soon after childbirth. My wife's parents also advised, "If he sent such a telegram, it is certain that he has some definite expectations. You must immediately close the shop." The entire family was drawn into tumultuous activity. Because of our earlier precautionary measures, our shop had not been ordered to close and, foreseeing inflation, we had bought large quantities of merchandise at every opportunity. Our storerooms were filled to the rafters. Now, everything had to be disposed of at once.

It would be an extraordinary task. First, my wife sent high profit items such as women's stockings and nylon articles to a friend's home in Lima. Since those items could easily be converted to cash, she decided to have an employee dispose of them at a later time and send the proceeds to us. Next, she went about selling items at cost to other merchants. She had tremendous quantities to dispose of but, fortunately, it was a time of rampant inflation. Since she was willing to sell off at our purchase prices, merchandise flew out of the warehouse.

With what she collected, she paid off our accounts at the banks and with our suppliers and managed to clear off all our obligations. The remaining items were taken to our two shops and sold to the public at give away prices. But, with such limited time, she could not sell everything. Finally, leaving merchandise in the shops, she sold the rights to our shops at a nominal price and left Ica.

When we look back on it now, we feel that it would have been better to have kept the readily saleable merchandise that had earlier been sent to Lima and divided it among our employees as parting gifts. We had not been able to do much for them and that would have been an appropriate expression of our feelings.

In the confusion of closing the business, my wife made the mistake of entrusting the disposal of the merchandise to an employee named Juan Yamashita. She asked him to send the proceeds to us when she notified him of our whereabouts. We later learned that Yamashita, a new employee, disposed of the merchandise and kept all the money for himself. Even today, I feel that by entrusting him with that task we rendered a great unfairness to our other employees.

Yamashita was the son of an acquaintance of my father-in-law. When we had learned that he and his younger brother were unemployed, we felt sorry for them and hired them. Shortly after that, I was detained, so the two had been in our employ only a very short time. Juan Yamashita happened to be the oldest among the employees, however, so my wife entrusted everything to him. That turned out to be a big mistake.

At the time, the entire society in Peru was in confusion. Among the Japanese, too, many got caught up with drinking and gambling. Some Japanese had even become involved in criminal activities. It was a time when honest people appeared to be fools; so, perhaps, we should not blame Yamashita too severely.

Twenty-five years later, when my wife and I were on a vacation trip to Peru, we accidentally ran into Yamashita on a street in Lima. As ever, he had a somewhat seedy appearance and walked along with his shoulders hunched. My wife noticed him immediately and started to go toward him to confront him with his dishonesty. But I pulled her sleeve and stopped her. Nothing would have come of it. Yamashita became aware of her and quickly disappeared into an alleyway, as if to escape. The war had distorted everything. Upon further reflection, we came to see that Yamashita was also a victim of the war.

A Tearful Adios

Having closed the business and concluded other necessary arrangements, my wife was ready to leave Ica. When the time for

Enroute to being imprisoned in Lima, Seiichi stopped at a photo studio to take this portrait to send home to his family. He thought it might be his last memento—if he never returned.

HIGASHIDE—153

departure came, those in the Japanese community did not appear; but our employees and many non-Japanese Peruvian friends came to see her off. Tears flowed freely from their eyes. "It is so sad that you have to go with a new-born child," they said. Everyone said, "When the war ends, you must come back." She came to understand directly and truly that people's kindnesses have nothing to do with race or nationality. They were simply good people. We eventually lost contact with many of them, but their warm friendship remains firmly in our hearts to this day.

My wife, her parents, my wife's youngest sister, and our five children filled the car. Leaving behind those who had come to say a tearful *adios,* the car moved forward. It was a final farewell to Ica.

When the group reached Lima only a few days after they had received our telegrams, they were told the last ship had already left on March 1, 1944. It was not, however, the last ship. So many families had come forth to join the deportees that the U.S. agencies had to arrange for another ship to follow. My wife had already heard through the Spanish Consulate that such arrangements were being made, so she was not particularly upset by the news.

If they had indeed missed the last ship, I would have been separated from my family for many years. But because she had received the report of another ship, my wife knew there was time to close the business and settle accounts. Even so, while remaining uncertain about the departure date of the next ship, disposing of a year's worth of inventory in such a short time was a tremendous accomplishment.

While her parents did help, it was my 27-year-old wife who, soon after childbirth, took charge quickly and astutely to close out our business. I came to see her abilities and her courage in an entirely new light. My family had quickly undertaken measures completely opposite to our earlier plans. They were to suddenly join me at an unknown destination. A few months earlier, we would not have even dreamed of such a move.

Chapter Eight. The Ordeal of "Utopia"

To New Orleans by Naval Convoy

From the time I sent my family that telegram I began to feel that Panama would be just a temporary stopping place. For one thing, the camp wasn't large enough and did not have facilities for us to live there with our families. For another, there were no signs of others from Peru who had been interned earlier; it was rumored that they all had been taken to the U.S. mainland. So we all felt that sooner or later we would also be moved there and that we would be allowed to reunite with our families at such a time.

Our expectations proved correct. In early March we were told that a ship carrying our families would soon enter port and that we were all to prepare to board that ship. It was almost certain that our destination would be the United States. I prayed that my family would be on that ship.

Finally, on March 6 the ship entered the port of Balboa. We were again placed on military trucks and taken to the port. We arrived just as a ship called the *U.S.S. Cuba* was about to dock.

It was the ship that our families were on. From the ship many Japanese enthusiastically called out their family names and waved to us. My eyes grew as large as saucers as I looked for my family. I stood up on the truck, searching for my wife, but I did not see anyone who resembled her. My family was not on that ship.

Other than families that were to join the Japanese detainees in Panama, the ship carried other recently detained Japanese and many detainees of German ancestry. The newly detained persons were accompanied by their families on the ship. There also appeared to be two or three Italian families among them. As had been the case with us earlier, they had been locked in the hold of the ship during the trip from Callao to Panama.

For those whose families were on board, it was a time for reunions. Although those family meetings were short periods of only 30 minutes, watched over by M.P.s carrying rifles, they were the first reunions for those families in the more than two months since our group had left Peru. Since my family was not on that ship, I would have to wait another four months before I would see them again.

We, 29 "single" Japanese detainees, who had arrived earlier, were ordered to board the *U.S.S. Cuba*. We were again placed in the hold of the ship, but were kept completely separated from the families that were on board. In the 17 days it took the ship to reach its destination, we were allowed to go out to the upper deck three times.

The *U.S.S. Cuba* left Balboa on March 6, 1944, passed through the Panama Canal, to the port of Colon where we anchored for three days. At Colon, a large convoy of ships assembled and we then moved out into the Caribbean where German submarines moved freely and undetected.

There were 17 or 18 ships in our convoy, led by two torpedo boats, followed by two destroyers. Following the destroyers were three fully loaded freighters; after them, in about the center of the convoy, was the *U.S.S. Cuba*. On both sides of us were other freighters and beyond them were additional destroyers. Behind us were three more freighters that were followed by more destroyers. The convoy was also assigned a small aircraft carrier and a cruiser. In the air, patrol planes kept pace with us, and below us, we were told, a submarine followed along. Full and detailed precautions had been taken. The large convoy zig-zagged through the sea as we moved northward through the Caribbean. It was a truly magnificent sight. During the voyage we were ordered to wear life jackets day and night in case of attacks or emergencies.

This was my first experience with actual war conditions and I felt an almost childish excitement. Surrounded by so many ships, I did not feel uneasy at all; the northward advance of the convoy proceeded with extreme caution. Because the zig-zagging continued the entire way, the voyage from Colon to New Orleans, with an intermediate stopover in Cuba, took over two weeks.

Westward, Not in a Freight Car but on a Pullman

After we reached New Orleans we went through entry procedures at an immigration facility near the docks. The officers of the Immigration and Naturalization Service (INS) asked us many question to confirm our identities. We were then taken to a temporary detainment facility and ordered into a shower room.

The shower room was a large, echoing place that looked like a warehouse; hot water continuously sprayed out of shower heads. If we had known then what had happened at the camp in Auschwitz, the simple mention of "shower room" would have made our blood freeze. But, fortunately, we knew nothing of that. On the contrary, we were happy to take a hot shower after a long period at sea.

After our showers, it was time for a "baptismal" in D.D.T. The powdered insecticide was poured on us until our heads were white. I felt like a modern day Urashima Taro, the Japanese equivalent of Rip Van Winkle. Our clothes were also dusted with D.D.T. Brushing out our white powdered hair and putting on clothes, we looked as though we had climbed out of a flour bin. We came out of the shower room, then assembled and were instructed about the next stage of our detainment. Finally, we were given small tags that we were to hang around our necks. On the tags were our names and the numbers of our seats on the train that we were about to board.

Soon, we were taken from the temporary detention facility near the docks to the railroad station. I was astounded when we reached the station—the train that awaited us was a splendid train with pullman cars. I had surely expected we would be herded into freight cars or something similar, so it seemed to be an unexpected stroke of good fortune.

I looked for the seat that matched the number on my tag and, with a sigh of relief, sat down. After a while, another group boarded the train. They were the family members who had been called over to join the detainees. They were finally being allowed to join their husbands and fathers. Family members had been assigned to the same compartments as their husbands or fathers. It had been arranged so that families were automatically reunited when seat numbers were sought out. I again marvelled at the superb planning demonstrated by the Americans.

After a time, the train moved out of New Orleans and headed westward. The pullman trip was wonderfully pleasant. With the exception of the armed M.P.s stationed between the cars, our trip would have been much like a luxurious trip to North America by a tour group of Japanese from Peru. The food in the dining car was excellent. After leaving Callao, on board ship and in Panama, we had had almost no fresh vegetables; the salads in the dining car appeared as marvelous delicacies.

That luxurious train trip came to a sudden end two days later. I can't recall the name of the station, but it was a small country depot where all of us "single men" were ordered to deboard the train with our luggage. The others with families continued on westward. They were destined for the "family camp" at Crystal City, Texas, not far from the Mexican border.

The Barbed-wire Enclosed Camp Kenedy

Those of us who were removed from the train at that small depot were taken to Camp Kenedy, a camp for single men in southern Texas.

Of the 27 detention camps that had been built in the United States, it was one of the smallest. Yet, basically, it was no different from the other detention camps.

It was fenced in on four sides with barbed-wire and within it were jerry-built barracks where detainees lived. The camp was, literally, for men who were alone. Married men such as I, who had not been able to be reunited with their families, were assigned to it. From what I heard, those who had been reunited with their families were almost all sent to Crystal City. Earlier, unmarried men and those who had left their families behind in Peru had been sent in random manner to camps built for U.S. residents of Japanese ancestry. After some time had passed, however, such "single men" were placed in specific camps, most notably that at Santa Fe, New Mexico, and Camp Kenedy.

Here, there were a number of others like myself who were waiting to be reunited with their families, but the great majority were young, high-spirited, unmarried males. It was in such an environment that I began my "second term" as a detainee. Here, everyone called the facility "the camp." The U.S. government agencies formally called it a "relocation camp," but we simply perceived it as no more than a "concentration camp."

Our arrival at the camp was much welcomed by those who had been placed there earlier. They were eager for news about Peru, which had been unavailable to them for over a year. In their words, they welcomed us because we had been "in the normal world of human beings" a year longer than they. Since they had no access to radios, newspapers or magazines in the camp, they were all starved for information. We tried to give them as much detailed information about Peru as we could.

Unlike the camp in Panama, everyday life in camp was completely unregimented. Here, we were not under the jurisdiction of the U.S. military, and there were no strict rules or procedures to follow, and we were not made to carry out exhausting work assignments.

We were given food and clothing, and all of our basic, survival needs were met. We had more than enough free time and, indeed, passed much of our time aimlessly. All we could do was gather in small groups to engage in foolish conversation, gamble, or participate in sports to keep us from boredom.

Vain Resistance from "Small Frogs"

High spirited, single young men who had been confined in that small detention camp had no constructive way of relieving their dissatisfactions, so they began to find outlets in unexpected ways.

I do not know who conceived it, but at one point it became popular among a group of internees to break chinaware. Calling it a "war of attrition," they would deliberately drop dishes and cups on the floor to shatter them after meals. Their absurd reasoning was that by such actions they would decrease the enemy's material resources and would eventually affect America's ability to carry on the war.

When it began, I did not pay much attention to it. Soon, however, petty boasts such as, "I broke such-and-such today," answered by, "Well, I broke more," and so forth. I grew irritated by such foolishness and warned them to stop. I "sermonized" to them that, as Japanese, they were representatives of a great civilization and were obligated to behave in a higher, more civilized manner.

Given our circumstances, I knew that they needed to release their frustrations, even through such absurd actions. But, given my nature, I could not remain silent. Eventually, such destructive behavior lessened and eventually ceased. But, after I spoke out, everyone came to believe, "He is pro-American," and most shied away from me.

I admired the response of the camp's administrators. After every meal, dozens of pieces of chinaware were broken, so they must have been fully aware it was being caused by deliberate actions. But no matter how many pieces were destroyed, they simply replaced them with new ones. They did not try to prevent such actions; they did not even complain about it. It seemed to be a case of tiny frogs attempting to make crazed resistances against a large water buffalo.

It was not that there was no work at the camp. Those who wanted to work were assigned different jobs and were paid wages at the rate of 20 cents per hour—regardless of age, sex, or type of work—in the form of tokens. Because all types of work was paid at the same rate, the detainees sought out the easiest jobs. Those jobs, however, had been monopolized by earlier detainees and were never available to those who came later.

In camp, however, one did not have to work to meet one's basic needs, so I did not feel a need to work. But there were others who seriously wanted the opportunity to work. We were notified of a recruitment program for farm workers who wished to go outside of camp to work. The wages would be the same as that for other workers outside the camp and during the period of employment living expenses would be guaranteed by employers.

For those locked up in the camp, the prospect of being "outside" was extremely attractive. Furthermore, it was promised that when their families arrived they would be sent to "family camps." I was somewhat tempted, but I recalled my work experience in Panama and put it aside.

Those who wished to take up the offer faced the general attitude in the camp that, "This was not a small matter. How could any Japanese hold up his head while collaborating and aiding the industry of an enemy country?"

Among those who hesitated because of such considerations were two detainees named Watanabe and Fukazawa. Although I was not particularly close to them, they came to me one day to ask my advice—perhaps because they thought I was "pro-American." They asked, "If we respond to the recruitment program, will that mean we are cooperating with the enemy?"

Watanabe had requested his wife children to come over from Peru and was waiting for them to arrive. Fukazawa said he had a common-law relationship with a Peruvian woman, but had given up on the possibility of calling her over. And since it did not seem possible to return to Peru, he had decided to go to Japan. When I inquired about their financial circumstances, both stated they had no funds at all and were concerned about their future. Both men wanted to work to build up reserve funds.

Even if they did not have to worry about their basic needs while in camp, they would eventually have to leave the camps behind. To be without a penny was, indeed, a matter of serious concern. Since I also had many children, I empathized with Mr. Watanabe's feelings. After considering the matter, I told the two that there seemed to be nothing wrong with their responding to the recruitment program.

Even if some had called it "the industry of an enemy country," it was not as though they would be working in a war-related industrial job. Nearby farms were simply pressed with labor shortages and had asked for voluntary workers from the camp to work during the harvests. It would have been different if they had proposed a discriminatory difference in wages, but the wages would be exactly the same as that paid to American workers. I believed one could engage in such work proudly, much more so than the work offered in camp. Moreover, since the camp authorities guaranteed their safety and reunion with families, there could not be better conditions. I told the two, "If you want to put in your names, do not hesitate at all."

Later, the two quietly left the camp to avoid notice by others. Watanabe worked on the farms for about three months and, when his family arrived, he was assigned as promised to the "family camp" at

Crystal City. I am sure that Watanabe was able to reunite with his family with a measure of financial security. Since he had not summoned his family, Fukazawa was not sent to Crystal City, but I believe that he returned to Japan with a good nest egg of U.S. dollars.

Reunion with My Family

I had grown accustomed to Camp Kenedy when, at the end of June 1944, I was informed that my family was about to reach Crystal City. I was overjoyed at the long-awaited news. The reports of a subsequent ship had not been just rumors after all. By that time, I had come to trust the actions of the U.S. government and I was sure I would see them again. Still, it was a time of war, so I had not been able to eliminate a lingering anxiety.

Finally, however, on July 2, 1944, I was transferred to the internment camp at Crystal City, where I was finally reunited with my family. It had been six months since I had left Peru. Happily, my wife, whom I had been much concerned about, was in good health and my children and in-laws were in good spirits. We embraced each other and rejoiced to be together again.

According to my wife, after the so-called "last ship" had left port on March 1, it had been more than three months before the next ship arrived. The ship they had boarded had left Callao on June 16, carrying many families on board. Most had been placed in its hold, but because my wife had a four-month-old child, our family was assigned a small cabin on the deck. But, because huge steam pipes ran through the small room and because the door and porthole had to be closed for security reasons nearly all the time, even they had to endure a stifling sea crossing, as in the ship's hold.

All of their possessions had been taken away when they boarded the ship. Because the amount of cash they could take out was restricted, my wife had converted almost everything into jewelry and precious metals and had placed them in a pouch. The officers had taken it away. What was more distressing, however, was the confiscation of their supply of canned milk, taken along for the new infant. The pouch of valuable items was returned after the ship left port. My wife was astounded that nothing was missing.

The ship had proceeded northward, through the Panama Canal, then up the Caribbean, as we had, to the port of New Orleans. They had then boarded a train westward and reached Crystal City at about the same time I had. The ship they had boarded had truly been the last ship. I had heard accounts that about six months later another ship left Peru, but I have not been able to confirm it.

Those who, for whatever reasons, had not been able to board that ship were placed in tragic circumstances. I heard that some were separated, never to be together again. Others lived separate lives in Peru and the United States for more than 10 years until the Japanese exclusion laws in Peru were revised to allow them to return. Other families, separated in Peru and the United States, made arrangements soon after the end of the war to leave those countries so that they could be reunited in Japan.

When we consider the fates of other families, we can only conclude that we were truly fortunate. We had always understood that whatever happened would have to be accepted. But we did not abandon hope, even at final, desperate moments. Our full efforts to pursue every possibility resulted in our family's reunion.

The Tragedy of Separated Families

There were a number of people who were pushed into unbearably sad circumstances, however, in spite of all their efforts. One of them was Kenzo Watanabe, who many years earlier had taken me from Lima to Canete when I first arrived in Peru. Circumstances had not allowed the Watanabe family to settle their affairs in time to board that final ship.

Mr. Watanabe explored various possibilities to reunite with his family, but nothing worked out. Eventually, he had to endure many years of being alone in the United States. After the war, the only possibility which would have reunited him with his family was for him in the U.S. and his family in Peru to arrange to return to Japan. But, if they returned to a defeated Japan that was in extreme confusion and economic desperation, even greater hardships would confront them. Because of such fears, he and his family decided to continue their separate lives, he in the U.S. and they in Peru.

There were a number of reasons deported Japanese could not return to Peru after the end of the war. The major reason was that before the war the Peruvian government had decided it did not want any further increase to the almost 10,000 Japanese already in Peru. Because the Japanese had made rapid economic advances in that society, the government had enacted laws prohibiting almost all entry of Japanese immigrants. Using that exclusionary law, the Peruvian government refused to allow the return of those deported during the Pacific War.

That Peruvian policy was recognized by a conference of Central and South American states held in Mexico City in 1945. At that conference, the 12 Central and South American states that had deported Japanese nationals to the United States confirmed that they would not allow the re-entry of such deportees. Despite several requests by the United States, they did not change their position.

On the other hand, because the United States continued even in the post-war period to handle us as illegal immigrants, it did not even recognize our families that had been brought over from Peru. The U.S. government had forcibly transferred us to the United States; thus, it seemed completely unreasonable to then classify us as illegal immigrants. But, we were told by officers in its bureaucracy, because we had not received visas from the U.S. government we were legally in such a position.

For a long time, because of such unreasonable excuses about our legal status, Mr. Watanabe endured a tragically unjust uncertainty. After we left the detention camp at the end of the war, we shared a common fate and experience. Still alone, he persisted in believing that, "Someday, our family will be reunited." I fully realized that if I had made one wrong choice I, too, would have been in Mr. Watanabe's position. It was not simply someone else's problem and I sympathized deeply with him. We invited him over for meals at every possible opportunity and tried to keep his spirits up.

From time to time, Mr. Watanabe received photographs from Peru. His wife, aware of his interest in photography, took special care to send rolls of films. He carefully placed them on enlargers to make prints. How he must have cried as he saw images of his wife and children gradually appear on prints floating in the developing fluid. Four or five years after the war, I also became interested in photography. Every time I developed prints, however, I was reminded of Watanabe and, although years had passed, my heart ached for him.

Mr. Watanabe's youngest child had been born, coincidentally, on the very day that he was detained by Peruvian authorities; he had never seen his last child. As he looked at photographs of his child growing up, how much did he yearn to reach out to embrace that child?

Everything had been brought about by the war. About 10 years after the war ended, Mr. Watanabe was given permission to reenter Peru and left the United States. But a life that had been disrupted could not be healed and reconstructed as before. After more than 10 years of separation he finally returned to his family in Peru. But, just as they looked forward to their remaining life together, his wife died. A few years later, Mr. Watanabe himself went on to join his wife. It was a tragic succession of fate that deeply pierced our hearts.

A City Behind Barbed Wire

Having escaped tragic circumstances such as those met by Mr. Watanabe, our family settled into camp life at Crystal City. Compared to Camp Kenedy, Crystal City was a major detention camp. The high, barbed-wire fences on all sides were the same, but in terms of its area, number of barracks, population and facilities, it was much larger than Camp Kenedy. Here, Axis nationals sent from Central and South America (mainly Japanese and German nationals) had to live together with many others. There were Japanese Americans whom we called "mainland people" and Japanese Americans who had been sent from Hawaii, whom we called "the Hawaiian contingent." Later, there were also a large number of single men who were sent from other detention camps.

I do not have accurate figures, but at its peak I would estimate there were much more than 3,000 people living there, mostly Japanese Americans. Because it was so large, it was not surprising that this detention camp seemed to have the characteristics of a town. Actually, it was the second most populous site within Zabara County, where the camp was located. Of Zabara County's total population of about 11,000, the size of the camp's population followed only the town of Crystal City's "civilian population" of 6,500 people.

A camp of that size engendered more than a few problems. Fortunately, its administrator, J.L. Oreck, was a very astute person who acknowledged the self-governing functions of the detainees. We were never afflicted with the confusion and anarchy that plagued other camps.

Self-governing groups were organized, for example, by the "Japanese section" and by the "German section" and above them there was an unofficial "central coordinating council."

The Japanese "self-governing association" was splendidly organized and superbly managed. If life in that restricted detention camp could in any sense be called agreeable, it was in large part because of the functions maintained by that organization. Everyone cooperated with the organization and exerted their full efforts to advance the health and well being of everyone there.

The Japanese self-governing association was based on the "Agreements of the Japanese Self-governing Association" that had been implemented in March 1943. At the center of the Self-governing Association was a general director elected by a general assembly of constituents and a number of administrative officers. Below them were a total of 14 divisions:

Maintenance Division. Completely responsible for the repair of roads and maintenance of sewers, etc.

Educational Division. Responsible for the operation of the Japanese school system and its library, guidance of children and support of facilities for Japanese martial arts.

Food Division. Responsible for the fair and equitable distribution of government issued provisions other than foods.

Housing Division. Responsible for all matters pertaining to housing, including renovation, repair, etc.

Community Welfare Division. Responsible for all efforts, including sports, performing arts, motion pictures, lectures, etc., for the community's social well being.

Medical Division. Responsible for all medical activity, including support of hospital facilities, concerns of hospitalized patients, public health, etc.

Security Division. Responsible for safety and maintenance of order in residential areas.

Other than these, there were an accounting division, postal division, agricultural division, women's division, etc.

Those who oversaw the administration of these divisions were in constant communication with the camp administrator, and they carried out the self-governing functions splendidly. From the scope and content of the Self-governing Association, the detention camp could well be called a town.

In 1945, the living areas had been divided into 24 precincts, each headed by a precinct chief. I recall that I had served as a precinct chief.

The facilities in such precincts were much better than what was available in any equivalent Japanese or Peruvian small town. In the southwest corner of the detention camp was a fully equipped hospital with an operating room and facilities for newborn infants. The schools handled children from kindergarten through high school. There was a library, a post office, and markets for food stuffs and stores for everyday necessities. As for recreation, there were basketball courts, volleyball courts, tennis courts, a baseball field, a sports arena, a swimming pool, and more. Of course, there were dining halls, a beauty shop, churches and temples and, necessarily, a cemetery. Indeed, a town enclosed in barbed wire had suddenly appeared in the Texas wasteland where only sagebrush and cactus had previously thrived.

Even a "Bird in a Cage"

Our family was assigned a corner of a barracks, and there we came to spend our days. There were many families who had come from Peru. Here and there, I recognized familiar faces from Peru. There were also many we had expected to see there but did not. Such persons had returned to Japan on exchange ships before U.S.-Japanese negotiations on exchange of detainees had broken off in the middle of 1944.

Our life in the camp continued peacefully. We were, without question, "birds in a cage," with our basic needs supplied by the camp administration. No physical labor or stringent regulations were forced upon us. Of course, as time passed, we became quite bored. But we were free to pursue anything we chose to without interference. We could read books, pursue special interests, engage in sports, indulge in simple conversation—anything was possible within the confines of the camp. If we had complained, indeed, we should have been "worthy of punishment from the gods." Some said that such a life would have indeed been impossible in "the real world."

Food was also available in good variety. Once a week we were issued tokens by a quartermaster and we used them to purchase food stuffs at the camp grocery store. The tokens were issued in dollar amounts according to the size of families and we were free to spend them in whatever way we chose. Of course, if they were all spent, there was no recourse but to wait for the next allotment the following week.

Our family never once suffered from any lack of food. There was adequate meat and fish. We could even afford the luxury of having sashimi with our beer ration. In the beginning, we were issued long-grain rice, which we were not accustomed to. But later, someone knowledgeable about rice negotiated to have California rice and Arkansas rice brought in and soon we had a more familiar, Japanese-style rice. We prepared it on government provided ranges and, as we were accustomed, had it with every meal.

Also available to us were *miso* (fermented bean paste) and soy sauce manufactured in Hawaii. Tofu and *aburage* (deep fried tofu slices) were made within the camp. Since we were blessed by the availability of such traditional Japanese food products, we could prepare almost any Japanese dish, including sushi and *tempura* and even special items such as *o-konomiyaki* and *osechi ryori* (special New Year's dishes).

We also had no problems with clothing. We were issued special tokens to purchase clothing. For other items, or to pay for service-related expenses, separate types of tokens were used. With the different tokens, one could go to a beauty shop to have a permanent, or go to a shop to buy a watermelon. Various types of traditional Japanese products manufactured in Hawaii or in the Denver area were brought in. Thus, we had almost every item we needed, from paper fans to disposable chopsticks.

Proportionate to available products, however, "currency" seemed to be insufficient, so within the camp trading of products flourished. Some, I heard, even initiated "international trade" practices by taking government issued butter, which the Japanese did not use much, to the area reserved for German detainees to exchange for fish, which they in turn did not particularly like.

Our living quarters came furnished with pots and pans, serving utensils, an ice box, a kerosene stove for cooking, furniture, blankets and sheets, etc. Each family had a "kitchen," but camp toilets and baths had to be shared.

The one significant inconvenience we all faced was the flimsy barracks, built with uninsulated roofs and walls. In mid-summer the barracks became a hellish oven. Constructed of thin plywood, the barracks stood in the middle of a desert where in summer temperatures reached 120 degrees Fahrenheit outdoors. In such ferocious heat, it became so hot that we were blistered if we touched metal parts of beds in those barracks.

When the sun went down, the temperature outside quickly cooled; but the interiors of the barracks remained unbearably hot. Every evening, we hosed down the roof of our barracks and cooled its floor by washing it with water. We then spread out thin straw mats on which to sleep, because the beds were too hot to sleep in.

Other than the extraordinary heat of summer, however, we could not complain about our lives in the camp. Compared with those in other detention camps who had to endure much more difficult conditions, we were well cared for.

Within Crystal City, however, we learned there were different conditions, depending on which section one lived in. Our experience cannot be generalized to represent the entire community. In particular, members of the "anti-citizenship" group that advocated renouncing one's U.S. citizenship were placed in extremely crowded conditions and were treated quite differently.

Provisions for "Cradle to Grave"

Superficially, at least, the forced detention camp at Crystal City was close to being a "utopia." Of course it was not, as its inhabitants had to make incalculable material and spiritual sacrifices before being forced into it against their will. Yet, materially, there actually existed adequate provisions to survive from "cradle to grave."

It was a large camp, so quite a number of infants were born there each year. Pregnant women all went to the camp hospital and gave birth under the supervision of qualified physicians; they also received advice from such doctors on how to care for those infants. Of course, the prenatal treatments, hospital fees and everything else from examinations to medications were all provided without charge.

There were outstanding doctors in the camp hospitals. While the head of the hospital at Crystal City was a Caucasian doctor who came in from outside the camp, all the other doctors were detainees of Japanese descent who lived in the camp. They had been solicited by the camp's Self-governing Association to serve in the hospital. Almost all medical specialities were represented. I also recall that there were two dentists. There were many persons who underwent life-saving, major surgery at no cost. Under normal conditions, such operations would have entailed enormous fees.

Besides their work at the hospital, these physicians also participated in public health activities. Whenever necessary, they went through the camp to check the health conditions of the detainees.

Shortly after we arrived at the camp there were a number of children from Peru who contracted measles. Since my family had come on the same ship, the doctors immediately established a quarantine area. Together with other members of the medical division, they warned us not to leave our barracks. The quarantine continued for two or three weeks. Since it happened to be the middle of summer, the heat was beyond description. But the doctors, with a number of assistants, went from family to family in the heat to examine the condition of each person. If anyone was infected, they immediately took appropriate measures. During that period, meals and other necessary items were delivered to us by the food division and the distribution division. Everything was handled with superb efficiency.

Despite the harsh natural environment, the children flourished with good health. When they reached an appropriate age, they entered school—all without fees or tuition.

The camp actually operated three school systems. For the sake of convenience, we referred to them by the language used: "Japanese school," "English school" and "German school." I don't know much about the German school, but the Japanese school and the English school included kindergartens, elementary schools (at the English school called grammar school), and middle schools (called high school in the case of the English school).

These school systems, under the direction of the "educational division" of the Self-governing Association, were operated at the same standards as schools in the outside world. The Japanese and English schools did not lack for teachers. Many outstanding teachers had been detained in the camp. They all responded to the requests of the association and gladly took positions as teachers.

Among the teachers of the Japanese school were many from Hawaii. Soon after the war ended the Hawaii group left the camp and the operations of the Japanese school became precarious; no matter how many teachers were recruited, a sufficient number could not be assembled.

Having been asked several times by the school superintendent, Mr. Seitsu Takahashi, I also temporarily took a position as a physics teacher at the Japanese system's middle school. But the number of students in the detention camp soon decreased and, finally, at about the middle of 1946 the school was closed. With that, my short stint as a teacher in the detention camp ended.

Our three oldest children attended the Japanese school until the end of the war; we then transferred them to the English school. After the Japanese American internees left the camp and the number of students at the English school became very small, the school was able to continue only because the camp administration took over responsibility for its operation. They brought in teachers from outside the camp. It was a blessing that our children were able to study English there until we left the camp.

The Burden of Free Time

In camp, other than those who had taken on special duties, the great majority could be said to have been completely at leisure. Everyone, from children to the elderly, actively participated in leisure time activities. Such participation, however, was not as simple as it sounds. We had to fill so much free time that it was actually more tedious and frustrating than having to endure some form of exhausting but productive work. We found that we had to always keep busy somehow.

The children's lives were very different from that of the adults. At least they were in school from eight in the morning until about four in the afternoon. On that point, their schedules were similar to those of children outside the camp. After they returned from school, small groups of friends would gather to occupy themselves with games and other things as do children anywhere. They also participated several times a week in organized boys' and girls' group activities so that they could receive training "in behavior worthy of Japanese in a time of war." Many devoted themselves to training in the martial arts, and sports activities, especially baseball, were extremely popular. They were able to release their youthful energies with such activities. They ate well, slept well, and led generally healthy lives.

It was not so for the adults, however. Many of them responded to requests from the Self-governing Association to take jobs in various occupational areas. In the camp, however, there was a limit to the number and types of jobs available, since almost everything was brought in from the outside. Moreover, one did not have to worry about basic necessities. Because all the better jobs were held by earlier detainees, latecomers could only select jobs such as field work. But it was beyond reason to expect that someone who had never held a hoe would volunteer for jobs such as tilling the ground in the blazing, desert sun. Thus, more and more became "unemployed persons."

For many who were caught in that situation, free time was no longer leisure time to be enjoyed. One might want to engage in aimless conversation day after day, but eventually one ran out of topics of interest. There were some who after a short period simply fell into silence. Others played baseball or tennis constantly as if they were obsessed. There were some who took great satisfaction in renovating and decorating their temporary living quarters until they looked like outlandish palaces. More than a few became afflicted with insomnia. Those were days spent in material plenty, but something was clearly distorted in our lives.

Fortunately, the camp was large enough and our time there relatively short, so that our family was not seriously affected. But, if it had been different, we all very likely would have been seriously affected emotionally and psychologically. There were such negative aspects to our barbed wire "utopia."

The overwhelming majority of the detainees, however, tried to find ways to maintain their physical and mental well-being and survived the trials of "utopia." In the camp, every sort of interest group was formed, covering such activities as tea ceremony, flower arrangement, judo, fencing and much more. Outstanding teachers could be found in the camp.

When it was proposed that a swimming pool be built, people who had never held a pick or shovel volunteered to work. The camp administrators cooperated, providing necessary materials. Detainees with professional experience in construction led the group, so that in a very short time a splendid pool was completed. I participated in the excavation, growing blisters on my hands. But, in the summers, happy shouts and laughter echoed from the pool.

Family gardens were an important part of the lives of most detainees. Almost everyone dug up an area in back of their barracks and planted vegetable and flower seeds purchased at the camp's general store. Although we were in the middle of the desert, the soil was extremely fertile, and as long as it was sufficiently watered almost everything grew marvelously. Watermelons and winter melons grew so large they could not be lifted up by one person. Long squashes grew two or three inches overnight and soon reached over one yard in length.

I found this phenomenon startling. In my childhood, I had experienced attempts to establish farming plots in the poor soil of cold Hokkaido. I was forced to reflect on the audacity of Japan to have gone to war against a country so bountiful that it could afford to let such fertile lands go undeveloped.

Although we were well provided for materially, there were many people who died in camp. The funerals within the camp were large, elaborate affairs. There were more than 40 Buddhist priests detained in the camp, and when someone died, all the priests participated in the chanting and general rites of the ceremonies. I have seen many funeral ceremonies in my life, but never before or after have I seen such solemn and elaborate ceremonies as within the detention camp. I wanted to take photographs of those ceremonies, but cameras were forbidden. Was it not the case, I thought, for those who must take their tears of frustration to their resting place in the barbed-wire enclosed camp cemetery, that those ceremonies brought some measure of consolation?

Mutual Suicide

The wealth and resources of the United States were awesome. Moreover, even if they were of an "enemy nation," I had to admire the magnanimity of the Americans who provided "prisoners of war" such decent material conditions. But even those actions of the American to so meticulously guarantee our material well being could, depending on one's standpoint, be seen in a completely opposite light.

When we entered the camp I had heard a person say, "The Americans treat us well because they are afraid of retaliation by the

Japanese government after the war ends." I was amazed at such creative reasoning. Later, as I became more familiar with the camp situation, I found that such opinions were not unique at all.

Because there were those who seriously held to such beliefs, one could not even hint of a Japanese defeat to those fanatical believers in Japanese victory. In addition to their absurd "war of attrition," consisting of breakage of American chinaware in the camp, they distorted daily news reports with their creative interpretations.

Anyone with clear eyes could see Japan's impending defeat, but those in that faction took any unfavorable news as being American propaganda. "The Americans are creating such false and unfounded rumors simply to cover their own desperate situation," they insisted.

There were, however, several reasons for their taking everything as "false rumors" created by the Americans. First, from childhood they had received a thoroughly militaristic education and the belief in the "invincible divine nation of Japan" had been instilled in them to the marrow of their bones. Second, shortwave broadcasts from Japan that they had heard while in Peru had repeatedly warned them not to be misled by "pernicious, unfounded rumors" perpetuated by the British and Americans. Third, in the early stages of the war, because the American mass media had been in considerable confusion, they had occasionally released reports that were inaccurate or could at the least be called journalistic sensationalism based on unfounded rumors.

For example, if one followed American reports, it would seem that the Japanese battleship, *Haruna,* was sunk two or three times. Also, bombing raids by Japanese naval attack squadrons in the early stages of the war had been so accurate that the American media had published reports, completely absurd to the Japanese, that "German aircraft carrier pilots must have been deployed." Because they had heard such reports earlier in the unreal and isolated world of the detention camps, it was understandable that such fervent believers in Japanese victory would doubt all American reports as propaganda.

That "end not long in coming" was not to be a U.S. defeat—it was to be disaster for Japan. In the detention camp, on August 15, 1945, we heard the report of Japan's defeat.

I was surprised by the reaction of the detainees in the camp to the news. They remained extremely calm; there were no overt disturbances. The great majority of detainees simply did not believe that Japan had surrendered unconditionally. Those who had continued to follow the war with any measure of objectivity had sad expressions on their faces that said, "Finally, what was to come has come." But for the fervent believers in Japanese victory, this was no more than another "pernicious rumor" created by the Americans.

It was clear, however, that the report of Japan's surrender was different from the reports of the "loss of Saipan" or the "loyal wartime suicides in Okinawa." Everywhere in the camp, small groups formed to discuss and analyze the situation. I joined a group of 15 or so people and quietly listened to what was being said. Included in the group was a former businessman from Peru who had assumed a leadership position among the detainees. Also participating was an influential Japanese American leader.

Speaking very loudly, the Peruvian businessman addressed the Japanese American, "If this report is true, we should take up short swords and mutually stab each other in suicide here and now. Is that not so? All of you here, would you not say so? What do you think?"

Unobtrusively, I left the group. Our leaders and advisors, for whom we had held great respect, had fallen to such a state. One could only infer what was occurring with other groups in the camp.

I believed the report. Later, as I had anticipated, the reaction to the news could not be suppressed by those in the camp. I again resolved to endure misfortune. Reports continued to arrive rapidly, and it became clear that there could be no doubt that Japan had lost the war. With every passing day, the atmosphere in the camp changed. Increasingly, despairing faces were seen and a heavy mood of sadness filled the camp.

But the rabidly pro-Japan faction would not retreat an inch. There were many who shouted, "We won! We won!" Apparently, it was to vent their disbelief. Most in that faction gladly went back to Japan on exchange ships in November and December of 1945. They had received a thorough indoctrination in militaristic ideology in Japan and had been confined to a closed-off Japanese community in Peru. I could not bring myself to accuse them of foolishness. They rejected advice from parents and words of persuasion from their children and simply returned to Japan. There were a number of cases where parents and children were separated by differing beliefs. They, more than others, became true victims of the war.

Partings Between Parents and Children

My wife was one of those who had to part with relatives because of the delusions about "Japanese victory." Soon after the end of the war, despite our repeated explanations and words of persuasion, my wife's father, mother and sister, who had become part of my family, decided to return to Japan.

They firmly believed that Japan had won the war. But, even more so, they simply wanted to go back to Japan—no matter what the situation. Since emigrating to Peru, they had not returned to their homeland for decades. They saw this as their chance to return. They felt if they missed this opportunity, they might never see Japan, or see relatives and friends in Japan, ever again. They felt very strongly that they wanted to be in their homeland once more and to be able to die there. With such thoughts, everything else seemed meaningless, so they decided to immediately return to Japan.

Even if one distrusted American reports, it could not be denied that much of Japan was in ashes. The country's government and economy was paralyzed, and its material resources had been completely depleted. Many defeated troops would return to a country in that condition. Civilians in Sakhalin, Taiwan, Korea, Manchuria, the South Pacific islands, and other places would also return. I had five young children, and I did not feel that I could survive in such a Japan. I was deeply concerned about my wife's position, but, as long as we were not forcibly deported, I decided we would remain in America. I worked to persuade my wife to see my position.

The wife of Yahei Ikenaga, who had been brought to the detention camp from Huancayo, Peru, was our neighbor who came many times to our home in the camp. "With so many children, what will you do if you remain in this enemy country? I am not saying anything against you, but please return to Japan with your parents," she would implore.

The evening before my in-law's return to Japan, Mrs. Ikenaga came to our home to make a final appeal. "There are reports that there will be another ship," she said, "so please return to Japan on that ship." She was sincerely concerned about us and spoke out of kindness. I finally said to her, "Yes, we shall do that," but there had been not the slightest change in my determination to remain in America.

For those who returned to Japan during that period from the end of 1945 through early 1946, those of us who insisted on remaining in the United States must have seemed totally unreasonable. To them, we were not even worthy of being considered non-citizens, or even traitors. We were great fools who were simply beyond reach. We were pitied or detested, and were laughed at even to our faces.

When I look back on it now, it all seems so absurd. Yet, when I assume their viewpoint at that time, it is not beyond understanding.

It was, after all, a time when people in the camp would say, "An exchange ship sent by Japan is waiting in San Francisco harbor." There were other rumors that an Imperial Japanese naval fleet was anchored outside San Francisco bay. Many took such rumors as absolute truth.

My wife's parents quite clearly believed that Japan had won the war. After they returned to Japan, they were fortunate to be taken in by relatively well-off family members and did not suffer severe hardships in comparison with others. It was good that they did not suffer any more trying hardships than what faced us who remained in America.

Crystal City internment camp school photo, 1945.

Chapter Nine. From a Barbed-wire "Town" to a Chain-link Town

Provisional Release into American Society

The forced detention of Japanese Americans who lived on the West Coast was based on Executive Order No. 9066, issued by President Franklin Delano Roosevelt on Feb. 19, 1942. The exclusion program was carried out by the military's Western Defense Command. The administration of the internment program in the 10 inland camps and its satellites was transferred on March 18 to the War Relocation Authority (WRA), supervised by civilian officers. The camps, however, were eventually declared "military areas" and were guarded by MPs.

In addition to the WRA operated camps, there existed many camps under the U.S. Justice Department, such as Camp Kenedy, where I had first been placed, and Crystal City camp.

As the 10 WRA camps began to close down by the end of 1945, those who were still interned were transferred to Justice Department camps. Crystal City internment camp was the last to remain open. Eventually, those at the other Justice Department camps were all transferred to Crystal City, which became the major site for transferees. In the spring of 1946, a large number of Japanese from Peru—almost all single men—were transferred to Crystal City from Santa Fe, New Mexico, and other Justice Department camps.

By the end of 1945, about 20 to 30 percent of the total 112,000 Japanese American internees remained in camps. Most of them were older persons or children who had no families to take them in; another large group was comprised of those who had renounced their U.S. citizenship while detained.

By March 20, 1946, when the relocation camp at Tule Lake was closed, the few thousand who remained to the very end were transferred to Crystal City. These were special cases among those who had renounced their U.S. citizenship—they were then in the process of attempting to regain their citizenship. Until their cases were decided, the U.S. government would not release them from the camps.

The detainees from Hawaii comprised the first large group to leave Crystal City at war's end. Approximately 1,900 leaders of the Japanese community in Hawaii had been sent to detention camps on the U.S. mainland. Later, those who were reunited with their families sent to Crystal City. After the Hawaii group left, those from the U.S. mainland began leaving in small groups. By the middle of 1946, the camp was emptying out, and a lonely, forlorn feeling fell over us.

The Fate of Japanese from Central and South America

Some 2,118 Japanese had been deported to the United States from 12 countries in Central and South America. Of these, 1,024 were arrested by authorities of the countries they had resided in and had been removed to the U.S. mainland. The remaining 1,094 were family members who responded to the U.S. State Department's summons to voluntarily join their interned fathers, following a scathing protest by the Japanese government that the U.S. was inhumanely allowing women and children left behind to suffer.

Peru provided 84 percent of the total number. Others came from countries such as Panama, Bolivia, Nicaragua and El Salvador. Perhaps because it was not on the Pacific coast, Brazil, which had the largest number of Japanese in South America, did not deport any Japanese. Mexico moved its Japanese to inland areas, but did not take the hard policy of deportation. Argentina and Chile, which remained neutral until very late in the war, did not send their Japanese residents to the United States.

Those who remained in camp were mainly Japanese from Peru. Using its exclusionary laws against Japanese immigration promulgated in 1940, however, Peru rejected the U.S. government's request to allow re-entry of all Japanese deportees. Peru even took the issue to the United Nations. Only in 1946 did the Peruvian government finally agree to allow the reentry of 79 persons (those who held Peruvian citizenship and their families), but would not accept anyone else. Three-hundred and sixty-four of the original 2,118 detainees remained in the United States with no place to go.

The Question of "Illegal Entry" and the Efforts of Wayne M. Collins

Soon after the end of the war, the Japanese from Central and South American countries in Crystal City were summoned to hearings held by officers of the U.S. Immigration and Naturalization Service (INS). At that time, the great majority expressed their desire to return to Japan. Since I could not return to Peru, I strongly asserted my desire to remain in the United States. At subsequent hearings, I never once changed my position. Even when I was asked, "What would be your second choice?" I insisted, "I can't think of any place other than America." I believe I was the only person who, from his first hearing, continued to insist that he remain in the United States.

Gradually, however, those who had first stated that they wanted to return to Japan became aware of the situation and a number of them later said they also wanted to remain in the United States. I believe the INS officers were aware of the unreasonable actions of the U.S. government that had brought us to forced detainment. One of the officers, Ms. Anderson, showed concern and sympathy for our situation. Speaking in fluent Japanese, she said, "If you want to return to Japan, that can be arranged at any time. There is no need to make a hasty decision." She made sure we fully understood our position and tried to disuade us from hastily deciding to return to Japan.

But, even if she and other INS officers privately sympathized with us, they were still officers of the U.S. Justice Department and were bound by the restrictions of the federal government's immigration laws and the anti-Japanese naturalization laws then in force.

According to the law, we were illegal aliens. The irony of the matter was that the U.S. government had illegally and unreasonably forced the matter upon us. The INS was thus placed in a very difficult position. The hearings always began in the accustomed way, with questions about place of birth, date of birth, citizenship, date of entry, port of entry, etc., and inevitably ended in silence. "You are illegal entrants to these United States. Therefore, the INS shall deport you to the country of your birth," the investigators always concluded.

"How can we be illegal entrants? No one could have entered this country more openly. When we landed in New Orleans, we were amazed to be met by so many INS officers. There was no reason for officers of the Justice Department to have overlooked our 'illegal entry.' It is absurd to label us 'illegal aliens.' "

"Well, then, show us a passport with a valid visa," they would respond. "We don't have such a thing. We were forced to enter this country against our will by armed American M.P.s."

At that point, most of the INS officers fell silent, with forced smiles on their faces. With the issuance of Executive Order No. 2662 on September 12, 1945, the U.S. government had already formally decided that we were to be removed to areas outside the western hemisphere. The government wanted to force the return of the last 364 detainees to Japan as quickly as possible to bring its legal nightmare to an end. Thus, INS officers were under pressure to persuade us by any means possible to agree to be sent to Japan.

In the process of such hearings, Wayne M. Collins, an attorney from San Francisco, became aware of our situation. Mr. Collins had been involved in efforts to restore U.S. citizenship to Japanese Americans who had been misled into renouncing their citizenship while detained in the camps. When he visited Crystal City to consult with some of his clients, a representative of the Japanese from Peru was able to speak with him.

Mr. Collins immediately began to prepare legal action. On June 25, 1946 he filed a writ of *habeas corpus* on behalf of the 364 Japanese from Peru in the federal Circuit Court in San Francisco. When I heard that the court had accepted it, I breathed a sigh of relief. I knew that as long as the case was in court we at least could not be sent to Japan until a decision was rendered.

They were willing to place us under "relaxed internment" with the status of "restricted parolees." We were then allowed to leave camp and remain in the U.S. if we could find employment guarantors. This was a major development that was brought about entirely by the efforts of Mr. Collins.

For the U.S. government, the matter came to be provisionally resolved by such measures. For the Japanese from Peru, however, who had spent years in detention camps in a foreign country and were without any resources, the decision that allowed us to leave the camp was simply the beginning of enormous hardships.

How did the U.S. government intend to compensate us for our incalculable spiritual and material losses? How did it intend to make clear its responsibility for taking such unjust and unreasonable actions? Although we were to be allowed to leave the camp, such questions remained in our hearts.

To Seabrook—From Confinement to Partial Freedom

We were informed of the decision granting us restricted parole in August 1946. Our immediate problem was to find a guarantor in order to meet the primary condition for our provisional release. Luckily, a guarantor soon came forth. Seabrook Farms, a large food processing company located in southern New Jersey, agreed to become our guarantor if we worked for the company. Although there were strings attached, we were finally going to leave Crystal City and re-enter the outside world.

It was September 1946. Almost all of the more than 300 Japanese from Peru who had been confined to the camp decided to leave for New

Jersey. Our family joined the group after two-and-a-half years of incarceration. The camp was closed a year after we left; we had literally been one of the last detainees.

We left the camp in cars that had been arranged to take us to the railroad station at San Antonio. Although the old and dirty train that awaited us there did not have first-class pullman cars, it did have other amenities similar to what we had experienced on our earlier trip from New Orleans. The difference now was there were no M.P.s with rifles standing between the cars. We were no longer "prisoners of war." The strings still attached to us had been transformed into invisible restraints.

Our trip was extremely pleasant. We left San Antonio and rode for hours through oil fields covered with forests of derricks. Eventually, we entered the vast green areas of the Midwest. Although we continued on and on, the green farmlands seemed to extend endlessly. I was again struck by the vastness and bountifulness of America. It is good, I thought, that we chose to remain in America. As I looked out over that great vista, I became more confident that we could survive in a country such as this. My attitude was transformed into one of optimism and I resolved that we could rebuild our lives even if we had to start with almost nothing.

On the second day, the train reached St. Louis, Missouri. There, we were to transfer to another train that would take us further eastward. We had a three-hour stopover before departure. It had been such a long time since we had been in the outside world, so the prospect of spending three hours in an aimless manner seemed wasteful. On the spur of the moment, I decided to take the children to the zoological gardens.

We went outside the station and I signalled for a cab. Since my English was almost completely useless, I tried speaking in Spanish. But I had no luck. Summoning up my limited knowledge of English, I said, "Zoh, please." But this also brought no response at all. The driver just shook his head and shrugged his shoulders. Yet, I was sure that in English the zoological gardens were called "zoh." I thought the driver might be dull witted, but the same thing happened with every other driver I tried.

Brought to a halt by the "wall of language," we were about to give up. Just then, another taxi came by, driven by a brown-skinned man. I automatically began speaking Spanish. This time, I was correct. The driver, who was Hispanic, immediately turned on the meter and off we went out onto the streets of St. Louis.

I had no specific knowledge about the St. Louis zoo, but I simply had a hunch that a city of that size would have one. It did in fact have a very large zoo. It could not be viewed in just two or three hours, so, keeping track of time, we looked at the elephants and other exhibits and returned to the station. When we found a cab to take us back, I simply said, "Station, please," and was immediately understood. In my youthful days in Tokyo we had often used terms such as "Ueno Station," but this was my first actual confirmation that "station" was the correct English term.

We reached the station five minutes later than our scheduled departure. In Japan, the train would have left and, in all likelihood, a search for us as "escapees" would have already been initiated. But, here, the train was waiting for us. The conductor had trusted the others when they said, "They'll be back soon," and we escaped becoming "fugitives" by a hair's breadth.

The train continued eastward. Three days and three nights after we left San Antonio, we reached New Jersey and arrived at our destination, Seabrook.

Located in Cumberland County, Seabrook was a small town of less than 2,000 residents, about five miles north of the city of Bridgeton. The people living there all had some relationship with the frozen food company, Seabrook Farms; there were no outsiders. With everything centered around a single company, Seabrook was a typical company town, as they existed in various areas of the U.S. in the early decades of this century.

As its name indicates, Seabrook Farms operated huge farms in that area, where it raised different types of fruits and vegetables. It employed approximately 3,000 people, who worked on the farms and in the factory.

Previously, the company had employed many German prisoners of war at its frozen food plant. At the end of the war those employees returned home. Because immigration from Europe had stopped during the war, the company faced a severe worker shortage. Soon after the end of the war, mainland Japanese Americans from various internment camps went to work there.

Even at that, however, the labor shortage persisted, and company officers came to consider recruiting Japanese from Peru who were still in camp. They even came out to Crystal City to make a "connection." The majority of employees at Seabrook were Japanese. The next largest group, a distant second, were black workers.

Upon reaching Seabrook, we were given three days to settle in. During that period we were assigned living quarters, applied for Social Security numbers, signed work contracts, and generally adjusted to our new environment. The living quarters to which we were assigned had been used as a base camp for the Civilian Conservation Corps (CCC), established in the 1930s by the administration of President Franklin Delano Roosevelt. The CCC had been organized during the Great Depression to activate large numbers of unemployed young men. In conjunction with "New Deal" policies, they planted forests and opened farmlands as part of government work programs.

After the CCC was disbanded, the camp was sold to Seabrook Farms, which converted the existing barracks into living quarters for its employees. It was partially enclosed by a high, chain-link fence. It had no watchtowers or guards, but it was similar in other ways to the detention camp in Texas.

We were assigned to one of the barracks and began to settle in. As in the detention camp, we had to share bath and toilet facilities with a number of other families. The roof and walls of the barracks were not insulated, so we were again subject to changes in climate. Because New Jersey is much farther north than Texas, here, winter was more of problem than summer. Areas near a pot-bellied stove or heater were warm enough, but at night it sometimes got so cold that ice even formed indoors along cracks in the walls.

This time, however, we had "voluntarily" come to live in this town of chain-linked fences. The transfer to this place from our former life behind barbed-wire fences was no more than a shift from complete confinement to partial confinement. One big difference was that, here, we were completely responsible for our own survival.

Days of Trial

On the fourth day after we arrived in Seabrook, we came face-to-face with the realities that confronted us. My wife and I were assigned to work at the frozen food factory on different shifts. Men could earn higher wages by working on the farms, but, after my experiences in Panama, I decided to work at the factory. Except for the winter months, the factory operated continuously, 24 hours a day. The change over between the day shift and the night shift was at 6 a.m. and 6 p.m. Those on one shift were moved to the other shift every two weeks.

We were required to work 12 hours a day. Initially, men were paid 50 cents an hour and women 35 cents an hour, with no overtime pay or differential for night work. If one arrived at work late, or if one went home sick, that portion would be subtracted from his hours in five-minute units. We had only one free day every two weeks, when we moved from one shift to the other. There were no paid holidays, no sick leave. Even for that time, these working conditions were considered to be severe. It was not surprising that the company faced a shortage of workers and had to extend its recruitment across the country to "prisoners of war" in Crystal City.

Although we worked at the same factory, my wife and I were in different sections and were on different shifts; we seldom saw each other except for the one free day every two weeks. If we needed to communicate with each other, we left hastily scribbled notes on the kitchen table before we went to work.

We divided the care of our children equally between us. When I was on day shift, I would take our two youngest children, 3-year-old Arturo and 2-year-old Marta, to the company's children's center before rushing over to the factory. They would stay there all day until I picked them up at the end of my shift. The three older children, Elsa, Carlos and Irma, went to the Seabrook Elementary School.

Life at Seabrook was hard on our children. The three older children did everything within their capacities, from cleaning the house to preparing meals for themselves. Without complaining, they endured days when they barely saw their parents. Even if we did not explain it to them, they fully understood our circumstances and did not once make tearful or resentful complaints.

The two younger children, however, could not be expected to be so understanding. Those two, who until then had not been away from a parent for even an hour, suddenly were left in a children's center enclosed by a chain-linked fence. They were left there with children they had never seen before. It could be expected that their tears were ever present.

It was painful for me to leave Arturo and Marta at the children's center in the morning. Arturo was a child who listened well, but Marta was still too young to fully understand what was explained to her. Marta would hold on to Arturo—who would press his face up to the chain-linked fence at the children's center to watch me leave—and she would begin to cry. Every day I had to force myself to become a monster and not turn back to look at them while I hurried off to work.

With tears welling up in his eyes, too, Arturo would set his lower lip to ward off tears as he watched me go.

Even while enduring such trying circumstances, however, my wife continued to smile to cheer up all of us. She showed superhuman strength, working 12 long hours every day at the factory, taking care of the housework, and looking after the children. Although prices were low, it was not easy to maintain our family of seven with our two small incomes. My wife did everything she could to get us through our difficult situation. Watching her struggle to save on our food expenses, tears came to my eyes. Yet, everyday, nutritious and tasty Peruvian dishes appeared on our table. We never lacked sufficient food. She would smile and say, "After all, am I not the daughter of a fonda?" Fonda were places where Peruvian workers could get cheap, one-dish meals.

My wife had helped her parents prepare food at a *fonda* that they had operated. There, she had learned the special ways of making inexpensive but tasty Peruvian meals. My wife was an extremely careful and thrifty shopper. Since Seabrook was a typical "company town" there were a grocery store and several other company-run stores near our living quarters. Prices at these stores were much higher than at other places.

If we could shop at Bridgeton, five miles away, everything would be cheaper. We had no automobile, however, so we had no alternative but to shop at the more expensive company stores. The system was such that the wages the company paid out would return to its own pockets.

No matter how hard my wife tried to reduce expenses, there was a limit. Fortunately, everyone in our family remained in good health and endured our poverty with a sturdy resistance. Some of the other families received assistance from the company's social services office. Workers in the social services office also made frequent inquiries about our family.

At one point, Miss Chapman of that office asked our oldest daughter, "Elsa, what did you have for breakfast? Did you have milk? Do you have enough to eat every day?" She raised such questions often. On each occasion, Elsa would ask me, "Papa, why does Miss Chapman ask me those questions? Why does she?"

To pass over it, I would answer, "She must have thought you were ill, because you didn't look healthy and fit." But it was, without a doubt, an expression of concern on the part of the social services office. I was grateful for that concern. Given our income and the size of our family, it was obvious that by American standards we would not be able to maintain even minimum living standards. For whatever reason, at that time I could not accept a handout from the higher authorities.

When I consider it now, it seems that I may have merely been indulging in a foolish pride. In this country the higher authorities are not higher at all; here, the authorities are basically "we, the people" and nothing more. Because "the people" are the authorities in a democracy, it would not have been wrong for us to have sought out entitlements from our own representatives. We had insisted on maintaining an anachronistic pride while living in an America. By the time we became aware of this point, however, we had already been transformed from "persons eligible for welfare assistance" to "persons who can contribute toward welfare assistance."

When we began our life in Seabrook, I was still a proud and strict, first generation issei. It was unthinkable that we would receive the kindness and concern of the company. As long as we had our health and could work, that would be a great shame—we absolutely would not allow it.

A Flood of Beans

At the food processing plant, I was first assigned to the freezing section for lima beans. The rather large, whitish, flat-shaped beans first had to be separated according to quality before they were boiled and frozen. On the third floor of the plant, the lima beans were cooked in great vats. They were then emptied out and came flowing down to the second floor. My job was to take up buckets to scoop up the beans as they came down and pour them into trolley containers.

On the second floor, the lima beans were received through five openings. I was stationed at one of those openings. Others were assigned to the remaining openings to do the same type of work. The other workers all seemed to be much older than I.

If the beans had come flowing down in a consistent manner, the work would have been manageable. But, because they would only be sent down when they were adequately cooked, they did not come down to us in a steady manner. A great flood of beans would be sent down, accumulating at one opening. Even a young person could hardly keep up when they came down in an enormous rush. When it happened at the stations of the older workers, I did not know what to do. Even if a person exerted his entire effort, the flood of beans could not be managed. The beans would spill over from our overflowing buckets and form large mounds on the floor.

When the beans flooded out of one opening, the other employees felt they were lucky it had not been at their stations. After a while, janitors would come over and, with easy strokes of their mops, push the heaps of lima beans on the floor into sewer openings. I saw that as extremely wasteful. During my childhood in Hokkaido I had experienced periods of scarcity of food and I could not endure such waste. I also could not stand seeing those older workers become red-faced with effort while they furiously tried to cope with the intermittent flood of beans. When beans began flooding in, I sped over to help them. I could not understand why the others who were standing nearby did nothing.

Four or five days after I began work, beans were flooding out to a station, as usual. Whenever that happened, I flew over to help. When the flood of beans had been taken care of, I would return to my station. This happened several times before the older worker whom I had helped stopped me. "You are a good worker," he said. "That is admirable, and I'm grateful that you helped me. However, I don't think you understand the American system. Whatever happens, do not interfere with the job of another person. In this country, this is what is understood as 'consideration.'

"The company will not raise wages," he continued, "but will do almost anything to raise our work output. If they find out that you are running around to help other workers such as us, they will simply increase the rate of beans sent to us. If that happens, what is the result? You just strangle yourself by your own efforts. Since the employers are the way they are, those who are used—we employees— must respond in like measure."

The old man had said this for my own benefit. I thought about it and came to see that in our situation what he had said was true. But, as someone from Japan, the matter did not sit comfortably with me. What that older worker had called the "American system," definitely functioned as he had explained. I could see that. If there was anyone who seemed to have free time in the plant, the foremen began raising the tempo of work by degrees. It was also evident that even if they had actual work or not the employees always took care to seem to be working. If they could fool the foremen or supervisors, they willingly did so.

In that situation, if one made an effort to help other workers one ultimately, as that old man said, "strangles oneself" and also takes away from co-workers their short rest periods. From that time, even if I saw mounds of beans growing on the floor, I made no move to help anyone and felt little regret about the waste.

Something, Somewhere, is Wrong

I still could not understand, however, what exactly was happening at the plant. Something, somewhere, was wrong. In order to raise profits, management pressed its own workers and capital to an extreme degree. In so doing, they did not seem to care that the "humanity" of the workers was being completely neglected or that material was being wasted. From their point of view, it seemed, the only concern was to increase profits, even if it be only a penny.

When production slowed down, management laid off workers without warning. On the other hand, workers did not care at all about the company's welfare—they simply sought out new employment and moved on. This was accepted as completely normal in an American society that is premised on a thorough-going individualism. All that existed was a piece of paper called an employment contract. When that paper linkage was severed, the individual was completely cut off from his work. In the workplace, complicating bonds such as duty and human affection did not even exist. In exchange for the absence of such complex bonds, the individual was completely isolated. He was not allowed to be dependent on anyone, nor did he seem to want it.

On that point Japan was completely different. Although it had become Westernized during and after the Meiji period, it had undergone no more than a "Japanese-style" of Westernization. Basically, it ran no deeper than adopting Western types of buildings and Western styles of clothing.

Although they donned Western clothing, the people were not much different from the earlier villagers clothed in Japanese costumes of *hakama* and *haori*. They remained tightly bound to each other with innumerable social linkages. They could only exist as elements of basic units which, in turn, existed as part of the communal entity that was the village. Apart from that social organization there was no individual.

Japanese business enterprises, of course, had corresponding structures. Even the most modern and Westernized companies would not have been able to function if they had ignored the village communal unit that was Japan. Modern businesses in Japan were called "modern" only because they carefully and subtly substituted traditional practices with applicable Western procedures. Thus, even the enterprises with the most Westernized operations continued with many non-Western elements, such as lifetime employment, promotion according to age, familial management principles, and others.

While not all traditional aspects of Japanese businesses were worthwhile, at least it held human and social elements lacking in American business organizations. Human beings must engage in productive activity in order to exist, but precisely because human beings participate in that activity, productivity must not be allowed to become non-human or inhumane. I recalled my job at the lumberyard at Fukagawa in Tokyo. The work there had been many times more severe and physically taxing than slinging beans in the factory at Seabrook. But that work had been made bearable because of the human warmth and concern shared by co-workers and by the owners of that business. In comparison, what could be said about Seabrook? I could only conclude that at a fundamental level, over which we as workers had no control, something was definitely wrong and was distorting all relationships.

Those Who Steal—Those Who are Stolen From

The first two or three months at Seabrook were truly difficult. We had left the detention camp with only meager funds and almost immediately had to see to the survival of our family.

If I had been alone it might not have been so difficult, but with a family of seven, even small miscellaneous expenses added up everywhere. Since we were making a completely new start in the outside world, buying such necessities as pots and pans, beds, tables, dishes and cups, clothing, etc., added up to a staggering amount. Of course, daily needs such as food, heat and lighting had to be taken care of on a continuing basis. We considered every purchase carefully and put off getting items we could manage without; that was the only way we could survive that initial trying period.

Although still difficult, by winter our lives had stabilized. As winter progressed, our work hours were shortened until, finally, the factory closed down for its annual winter break. Our lives seemed to be less desperate. By that time, my wife and I had become accustomed to our jobs and our circumstances. The children had adjusted to their school and the children's center. A certain rhythm had become established in our daily lives. Although still unsure about many things in our community, we had come to know the town of Seabrook. Our family could now breathe with a small measure of normality.

One day, we went to Bridgeton to purchase some clothing. It was the first American town we could freely explore and come to know. We had been in America for three years, but had never fully experienced a "normal" American environment.

At that time Bridgeton was a small country town of about 10,000 people. In spite of its size, it served as the judicial and administrative center of Cumberland County. Near the county office buildings, the streets were lined with a variety of shops. The people there were unhurried and relaxed; the town seemed to be peaceful and had an air of being long-established and settled in its ways.

What first amazed us as we walked along its streets was the seemingly unending variety of merchandise available. At the clothing stores and in the markets, items were stacked in enormous quantities and our eyes opened wide at the many types of items offered. My wife and I were also amazed to find that, despite the large size of the shops, only a few employees were needed.

A good example was Montgomery Ward which, based on catalog sales, had established a chain of stores throughout the country. In its large store, an astonishing variety of merchandise was displayed. Many customers entered and left, but it had only three or four employees stationed at cashier's counters near its entrance. Customers freely inspected items, took them to the counter, made their payments, and left. I looked intently at the system and thought to myself, "So, this is what is called 'self-service.'"

Even some rather expensive items were placed on display counters and shelves where the customers could handle them freely. If it had been Peru, I am sure the merchandise would have been pocketed by thieves and the store would have been emptied in less than a week. I was astounded and felt much admiration; I felt that this was only possible in America where private property was respected. I had heard that in America property was considered to be sacred, but I had not even dreamed that the capitalistic ethic would be so thoroughly instilled as this.

In Peru, the accepted attitude was that those who were stolen from were more wrong than those who stole. The concept was accepted openly by the police in Peru. When I lived in Canete, I caught thieves in our shops many times. At first, I handed the thieves over to the police. But the police would scold me, not the thieves. They would say, "It is you who are wrong for creating the opportunity for the thief. You have created a criminal." I could only apologize and say, "I am very sorry. I shall be more careful in the future." When I thought about it, there seemed to be a measure of truth in what the police said. The same thing happened to me two or three more times and I saw that there was no other recourse. I accepted the warnings from the police and became more attentive so that I would not "create criminals" any more.

The Price of Abundance

Another thing I noticed during our shopping trip to Bridgeton was that American business methods were functional, yet cold and impersonal. When one entered a shop no one said a word. When one brought an item to an employee, they took your payment and without a word put it into a paper bag, folded over the top of the bag, and handed it over. That was all. Even in big, well-known department stores that was the accepted practice.

Basically, business is the selling of merchandise, and in that sense American business practices were superb. By having fewer employees and by not indulging in wasteful wrappings it is true that prices might be lowered considerably. The paper bags that they used were very plain, but they were sturdy and served their purpose. There was really no reason to complain. Yet, I also saw that there was nothing "human" about transactions in American stores, only an exchange of merchandise for cash. The price printed on a small paper tag was absolute. Employees could not make any adjustments based on their own judgment. A large "system" had made decisions that they could not alter or influence. They simply had to perform as the system required.

This was in striking contrast with how business was conducted in Peru, where each transaction began with conversation and ended with conversation. Of course, Peruvian shops also had established prices, but they were not absolute or "sacred." They were not beyond the influence of the customer or shop clerk. The items bought and sold were wrapped carefully and the shop clerks passed them with care from their hands to the hands of the customer. At that point, for both the seller and for the buyer, that item clearly came to have a different significance from similar items displayed in the store. That was the way business was conducted in Peru.

Of course, I do not think that simply because of those procedures Peruvian business practices are better than American practices. For the general consumer, needless to say, American practices work to his advantage. But, it seemed to me, with such American practices one felt no human warmth or contact. I am sure that the coldness I felt during our initial shopping trip to Bridgeton derived from this.

America was in all aspects extremely product-and function-oriented. Probably, in large measure, it is because of such an orientation that America was able to become the wealthiest country in the world in only a relatively short period of 200 years. Certainly, as never before seen in history, it is a country blessed with material plenitude. But what the American people pay in return for material comforts is not at all insignificant. It is that deep isolation and loneliness I saw among the workers at the Seabrook factory and the structured coldness I encountered on our shopping trip to Bridgeton.

I found it sad that within such a system trying to be human almost always meant making material sacrifices. If one tried to attain material security, one had to face the necessity of neglecting his own humanity. Through history, human beings have still not resolved that contradiction. Yet, it seems to me that we have to work to coordinate, even if only partially, these seemingly incompatible goals.

Flower-viewing in Washington

In April 1947, we took our first small pleasure trip after moving to Seabrook. We were told that the cherry blossoms in Washington were about to reach full bloom and, taking up a friend's offer to drive us there in his car, we went to Washington to view the cherry blossoms.

It was a short trip, but since we rarely had a chance to leave Seabrook it was a matter of great anticipation and excitement. Adults and children alike were quite worked up about our first automobile trip. We left Seabrook early in the morning. The car raced along on a splendid highway and passed along a river to enter Delaware. We then passed through Maryland to reach the nation's capital, Washington, D.C.

The cherry blossoms were indeed in full bloom. Those trees, which had been sent from Japan, were covered with blossoms even to their stems. Their beauty was reflected in the calmly flowing waters of the Tidal Basin. The people were all finely dressed and strolled in small groups under the flowering trees. I had expected to find the banks of the Potomac transformed into picnic grounds, with flower-viewing parties taking place under the cherry trees. But I was wrong. There was no one there having loud parties. If it had been Japan, the trash bins would have been overflowing from several days of flower-viewing parties; trash and litter would be everywhere. But, here, not even a cigarette butt could be seen. When I saw those immaculately kept surroundings, I came to feel that I had seen another face of America.

Our group, carrying large baskets filled with o-bento (box lunches), bottles of beer, and *goza* (thin straw mats) to sit on, must have appeared barbaric and foreign to those who strolled by. Eventually, we walked over to a less conspicuous area to eat our lunch and then returned to the banks of the Potomac. Our expectations of having a happy, "drunken" party under the cherry blossoms were completely unfulfilled. But I felt a small response of pleasure and was satisfied.

That sense of pleasure and the fact that the cherry trees in Washington still were there were enough to make it a happy time. When I was in Peru, I had heard a shortwave report from Japan that every cherry tree in Washington had been cut down. I remember feeling an indescribable anger when I heard that report. Even if they had come from an enemy country, I felt there was no need to destroy the trees. I was saddened that war could bring such hatred to people that they would even cut down such trees.

When I heard that the cherry trees in Washington were in full bloom, I thought only a few trees had escaped destruction. But, marvelously, those expectations were wrong. I learned later that a few trees had been cut down by fanatics, and that fair-minded people in Washington, D.C. had rigorously opposed all proposals to cut down the rest of the trees.

During our little excursion, I suddenly remembered that dogwood trees had been sent from America to Japan in appreciation for the cherry trees. In the ashes of Tokyo, I wondered, would the dogwood trees show their white blossoms? There in Washington, I prayed from my heart that this year they would again do so.

Snapshots from 52 Hoover Annex, Seabrook Farms, 1946.

Chapter Ten. A Concrete Frontier

A Plan to Escape Seabrook

As we entered our third year at Seabrook, our lives had become fully settled and we could, to a certain degree, gain some perspective of our future there. If we stayed, our family would not be faced with basic problems of survival. In the future, we might leave the company's living quarters, rent an apartment in Bridgeton, buy a car, and enjoy a simple American lifestyle. As long as we continued our relationship with Seabrook Farms, however, we could not look forward to much more than that. We would not be able, as we had when we started our business in Ica, to dream of broader possibilities.

We were mainly concerned about the future of our children. They would be able to finish high school at Seabrook, but if they were to continue their education further we almost certainly would have to move on quickly to establish a basis for other opportunities. If they did not go to college and simply took jobs at Seabrook then, of course, we could not expect that their futures would be much better than ours. As we entered our third year at Seabrook, I began to consider ways to escape the dead end that was our situation in Seabrook.

In order to open up our future possibilities, it was first necessary to sever our ties with Seabrook. With so many children to care for, it was not an easy decision to abandon the security we had established there. Although I worried endlessly about it, I knew from the start what we had to do. If we did not engage in a new challenge, there was no way of removing ourselves from that cul-de-sac that restricted our future.

Once I decided we must leave Seabrook, many possibilities seemed to open. One easy possibility was to find a job in Bridgeton. But if we were to leave Seabrook, I thought, why not go to a larger city? Finally, I decided to move the family to a large metropolis.

The first place that came to mind was Los Angeles. In Los Angeles there were many mainland Japanese whom we had come to know at Crystal City. A number of them had returned to restart businesses that had been successful before the war and were now making small but sure advances. They had all kindly urged us to join them in Los Angeles when we left the detention camp. I felt sure that if I went to Los Angeles, I would be able to quickly find a guarantor and a job.

But the West Coast was so far away. We were on opposite coasts of an America that was so vast as to have four time zones. If we were to go from New Jersey to California, even the train fare for our family would add up to more than what we had managed to save in more than two years at Seabrook. If we continued to save for our train fares and for some reserve funds to tide us over after we reached California, it would be several more years before we could leave. When I thought of this, I had to put off all considerations about going to Los Angeles.

On the East Coast, within a 150-mile radius of Seabrook, were New York City, Philadelphia, Baltimore and Washington, D.C. Unfortunately, I knew no one in those cities. Because we could speak almost no English, it would be impossible to find a guarantor, a job and a place to live if we did not have someone we knew to help us get established when we moved.

The next possibility was Chicago. There we had Kunio Takeshita, who had shared times of hardship and happiness with us in Crystal City and then at Seabrook. Takeshita had already found a job in Chicago. Takeshita, still unmarried and not burdened with a family, had quickly seen the hopelessness of Seabrook and had gone out alone to Chicago. I felt that it would be well for me to ask Takeshita for help and for me to go out to Chicago to check out the possibilities there with my own eyes.

If our family went to Chicago, I thought, it might be possible to eventually reach my dream of going to Los Angeles. If we set our preliminary goals on Chicago, we would not have to wait too long to save for our train fares and our initial living expenses.

I decided to wait for winter, when the Seabrook plant closed down, to make a trip alone to Chicago. The food processing plant at Seabrook laid off almost all of its employees for the three or four months of winter, when there were no products to process. When we were laid off we received no pay from the company but we all applied for unemployment insurance benefits and were almost automatically approved; so we did not have to worry especially about basic living expenses for our families. I felt secure in leaving my family at Seabrook to go out to Chicago to inspect actual conditions there.

The Kindness of Old Mr. Iida

When I reached Chicago, I immediately went over to see Takeshita. He lived in what is commonly called the near Northside of Chicago and worked at a nearby factory. His small rented studio apartment was in a low income area, where many different ethnic groups lived in a bewildering variety of cultural behaviors.

Through his efforts, I found a night shift job. While I worked on that job I began to explore Chicago during the daylight hours. I worked all night and returned to Takeshita's apartment in the early morning. We exchanged greetings as he went off to work. I slept in his bed until about noon and then went out to explore Chicago until I had to go to work in the evening.

Chicago was, as could be expected of a metropolis second in America only to New York City, full of bustling activities unimaginable in Seabrook or Bridgeton. People walked about briskly and impatiently; its streets, without let up, were filled with automobiles moving in every direction. The downtown area, which was oriented in a north-south axis along Lake Michigan, had an astounding activity that made me appreciate that this was the commercial and industrial center of the American Midwest.

When I saw such hectic activity, I felt instinctively that there would be no lack of job opportunities. Takeshita and two or three others told me that as long as I was not picky about the type of job, it was not a problem to find employment. If necessary, there were also many night shift jobs. Wages were much higher than at Seabrook. I began to feel that we could move out to Chicago and survive.

While inquiring about job possibilities and wages, I also checked living costs. Whenever possible, I went into markets and department stores to study prices for clothing and daily necessities such as milk and vegetables. Prices were generally higher than at Seabrook, but in such a great metropolis I also saw stores that handled second-hand items and many discount stores. It seemed that if we were frugal we might be able to survive in that city. Although reassured by those possibilities, more immediate and complicated problems remained to be resolved. First, if we were to go out to Chicago we needed to find someone who would be willing to be our guarantor.

Luckily, this problem was solved more easily than I expected; we found a guarantor quite quickly. The remaining problem was to find a place to live. When I arrived in Chicago, I saw many "for rent" signs on apartment buildings so I had been somewhat optimistic about finding living accommodations. Unexpectedly, this became a big problem that remained unsolved until the final stages before our family moved to Chicago.

Although "for rent" signs could be seen everywhere, wherever I inquired, when it was learned that we were a family of eight (at Seabrook our third son, Richard, had been born) the landlord just shook his head. I felt no objections to living in a black section of the city if a landlord would only accept us into an apartment; many times

I went into such sections of the city which seemed gradually to be deteriorating into slums. But even there the landlords refused. In the case of apartments in the black areas, rather than the size of families or anything else, the main obstacle was the iron rule, "for colored only."

Everyday, I walked through different areas in search of an apartment until my legs ached but was unable to find any that would accept us. It was a time when it had become common for landlords to divide family-sized apartments into single rooms. I finally concluded that it was futile to continue searching for an apartment and decided to end my exploratory visit to Chicago. Disappointed, I decided to return to Seabrook. On the night before I left, however, a completely unexpected offer came to me. An elder person named Iida had heard of my difficulties from Takeshita and, sympathizing with us, offered to rent a place to us.

Mr. Iida owned the apartment building where Takeshita lived. It had many large flats for families, but some of them had already been divided into individual rooms; it had begun to be transformed into the then popular rooming house type of business. Thus, its tenants ranged from large families to single people.

A couple who lived in the building was about to move out and Mr. Iida very kindly said, "If you find it acceptable until you find a place more suitable for your needs, why not live here?" Even as a desperate person clings to straws, I instantly accepted Mr. Iida's warm concern. He said, "It is a very small place, you understand." But I was in no position to complain. I immediately gave him a deposit of a month's rent and left the next morning, as planned, to return to Seabrook. I was overjoyed that my month-long stay in Chicago had not been in vain. With a buoyant heart, I returned eastward.

Start From Zero Again

It was January 1949 when, buffeted by biting north winds, we ended over two and a half years at Seabrook to seek a new life in Chicago. When I told our friends at Seabrook that we were moving to Chicago, they were truly concerned and repeatedly advised us to set aside our reckless plans.

By that time, many of the Japanese living at Seabrook were leaving to pursue their own dreams, but they were all single people or couples whose children were already grown and independent. There were none among them who had six young children as we did, who had left for a city as large as Chicago.

"You should give it up, Higashide. Chicago is very different from Seabrook. First of all, it would place your children in a pitiful situation. Here, we have farms and open spaces and almost all the workers are Japanese. If you go to Chicago, it won't be the same. You don't know what to expect. Chicago is a city of mobsters. If you go to such a place, how would your family with six children survive?"

Everyone came to us with such opinions. But we, as a family, had come to our decision after considering and reconsidering our plans. We felt badly about doing so, but we firmly rejected the pleas of our friends who were so sincerely concerned about our fate.

Moving to Chicago was literally like starting from zero again. When we reached Mr. Iida's apartment, we purchased only items that we absolutely needed. Even at that, we depleted almost all our savings. Even my wife, who always managed to present an optimistic outlook, seemed worried.

As Mr. Iida had warned, the apartment we moved into was truly very small. It had one room about 12 x 15 feet and another room about 12 x 12 feet, which also included a kitchen. Our family of eight had to live in those two rooms; it was almost unbearably crowded.

When I had gone out to look for an apartment, I quickly found that the size of our family was a problem and had soon fallen into the habit of saying that we were a family of five. Mr. Iida thought that we had only three children and probably assumed that we would be able to manage even with only those two rooms. When he learned there were actually eight of us, Mr. Iida became upset and expressed his dissatisfaction. We had already moved in, however, and he eventually accepted the fact that we were a much larger family.

Fortunately, adjacent to that apartment, next to our kitchen area, there was a rather large, unused pantry of about 9 x 6 feet. Knowing that I might be refused, I went to Mr. Iida to ask if I could remodel it into an addition to our apartment. Mr. Iida replied that he had no objections if I did the work by myself. Whenever I had free time I removed shelves from the pantry and used those planks to make a "built-in" bed. Soon, our two-room apartment became a three-room apartment.

Arturo and Marta slept on a sofa in the 12 x 15 foot room, and the other three children slept on the floor wrapped in blankets. My wife and I and our newborn son, Ricardo, slept in the remodeled pantry. The remaining room served as a kitchen, dining room, study room, and a place for all the other activities necessary for our life as a family. The bathroom was in a separate location; we shared it with the others who lived on our floor.

With that small apartment as our base, we took our first steps in our new community, Chicago. The children enrolled in a new school and my wife and I found new jobs. Our situation was indeed miserable, but if we had complained or felt sorry for ourselves that would have led to endless self-pity. If we did not survive those first difficult months in Chicago, we knew we would be left with the fate of being buried for the rest of our lives in Seabrook.

I told myself that in Chicago something good would surely come to us and resolved to endure our initial period of adjustment. The possibility of that hope would be our only reward for leaving Seabrook to embark on this reckless adventure toward a better future for our family.

A Life of Ultimate Poverty

Our first two or three years in Chicago was a time of complete and ultimate poverty. We did not have stable jobs; we did not have a real home for our family; we did not have fluency in English. In everything, it seemed, we were lacking.

There were jobs available, but the jobs we were able to find were only temporary. We considered it good when a job continued for five or six months. In the worse cases, we were laid off after only a week of work. It was not that our work attitudes or our ability to do the work were inadequate; it was the American system which immediately released new workers when the need for them lessened. We were part of the group described by American workers as "last hired, first fired."

During our first two or three years in Chicago I held a great variety of jobs. Most involved simple physical labor and needed no language or technical skills. With that type of work the increase or decrease in business directly affected the workers. When work increased, owners hired new employees to cope with the increase in business and when business slowed down they unhesitatingly laid off employees.

At that employment level, where no skills or experience was necessary, a complete newcomer and a 10-year veteran did the same work; managers readily hired persons and just as readily fired them. If they said, "You need not come from tomorrow," they were being tactful. Many times I was simply told, "Your job ends tonight," or "It ends at three o'clock." Although I moved from job to job, I was never unemployed for a long period, so our situation did not become completely desperate.

As we did at Seabrook, my wife and I took jobs on different shifts in order to care for the children. After we moved to Chicago, I worked only at night. Although my jobs were unstable, it was fortunate that such night work was constantly available. It was well that we had come to a large city, I thought; if it had been a small town such night work could not have been found.

Wages in Chicago were higher than at Seabrook, but the correspondingly higher prices for everything and the instability of our jobs ate into our higher wages and our living standards fell to the lowest and harshest levels we had ever experienced since we were married.

While we were at Seabrook we had been able to send small packages to Japan every week to friends and relatives struggling through the devastated economic conditions of postwar Japan. At that time small "care packages" could be sent free to war-recovering countries, as postage was absorbed by the U.S. government. As much as possible, we had sent clothing and food items. After we moved out to Chicago, however, those packages became drastically fewer, until, finally, we were forced to discontinue sending such packages.

Our material conditions were that desperate. What we found more difficult to endure, however, was the feeling of isolation brought on by being alone in a large city in a foreign country. There were few Japanese in Chicago, and they were scattered in different areas of the city. In truth, it seemed there was no Japanese community there.

The people around us all looked different and spoke different languages. Further, people who lived in large cities kept to themselves and did not readily form relationships with others. Even if they lived in the same apartment building, many people would pass by without a word of greeting. Although we had moved of our own free will, we regretted that we had come to such a world. We felt a certain nostalgia for Seabrook, where we had been surrounded by fellow countrymen with whom we could share our joys and sorrows.

An Unexpected Visit

Not even two months after we moved to Chicago, while we were still in an unsettled state, a cousin from Tokyo unexpectedly visited us. Norio Higashide came to America as the manager of the Japan Student Wrestling Team. One stop on their goodwill tour of the United States was Chicago.

According to Mr. Ichiro Hatta, the businessman who sponsored the goodwill tour, my cousin was quite a businessman himself. During the war, Norio had established contact with the military. After the war, he maintained relationships with the Occupation Forces. He became extensively involved in business operations. Before the war, Mr. Hatta's family operated businesses in Sakhalin, Manchuria and North China, but at war's end, they had been forced to return to Japan. With Norio's help, they had made a new start. They were making small but steady business advances in Japan.

Norio, who had been successful in business dealings, had visited our family which was then in the depths of poverty. We were very embarrassed. He sympathized with us and repeatedly urged us to go to Japan. "Japan has become relatively stable after the initial confusion of losing the war. Although it may not be much, I can be of help," he said to me kindly. I knew we were in a pitiful situation, but I did not waver from my resolve to make a new start in Chicago.

Norio stayed in Chicago for three days. Since I was working at night, I was able to take him out to see Chicago during the days. Most of all, he wanted to see a manufacturing plant for ready-made clothing. At that time his businesses were focussed on such manufacturing and he wanted to inspect American approaches and procedures in that line of business.

At that point, of course, I did not even know whether such manufacturing plants existed in Chicago. I did not know what to do to fulfill Norio's request. I took the matter to a number of acquaintances, but no one could offer any help. Not knowing what else to do, I looked at the Yellow Pages of the telephone directory and picked a few large firms. I decided that we would visit them unannounced and see what would happen.

One such firm was a large manufacturer which had its plant not far from the downtown area of the city. We entered its offices and, in my poor English, I explained, "We have come from Japan to study the manufacturing of ready-made clothes. If it would not be an inconvenience, could we inspect your manufacturing plant?" The person who received us was very nice and took care to understand my simple English. She immediately arranged for us to meet the manager of the plant.

The manager seemed to be very pleased that we had come all the way from Japan to inspect his plant. He immediately assigned one of his secretaries to show us the plant and said, "Please feel free to inspect the plant at your own pace and in terms of what interests you."

Taken around by the secretary, we inspected the flow of manufacturing from the cutting of materials to the final sewing of the items. Being knowledgeable in the area, Norio grasped important points that would not be obvious to an outsider and, when he was not clear about something, he asked me to inquire with our guide. I became an instant interpreter and struggled to communicate his questions with my poor English. To my surprise, my English was understood. After that experience I began to have a little confidence in my English.

What excited Norio was the procedure of using paper patterns as a guide to cut through many layers of material to make multiple pieces for large scale manufacturing. Those patterns were based on numerous decisions made by fashion designers, but had been extrapolated to accommodate the cutting of materials. For each design there were many adjustments in the patterns for different sizes. At that manufacturing plant there were dozens of patterns available so, when necessary, large quantities of popular sizes could be manufactured immediately.

Norio was astonished by the many different designs and sizes for each design made possible by the patterns. He wanted to have the patterns and asked me to negotiate so that he could purchase them. When we returned to the plant's office, I began negotiating with my limited English. Fortunately, the manufacturer very kindly entertained our request and agreed to pass over the patterns. Delighted, Norio immediately selected a number of patterns for designs and sizes that seemed suitable for the Japanese market. We then paid for those patterns and took our leave of the plant.

Excited and happy about acquiring the patterns, Norio said that our inspection of the manufacturing plant had brought "great significance to his trip to America." In our state of utter poverty, this had been the only thing that I could offer him during his visit to us. Norio, who was extraordinarily involved with his work, returned to Japan and immediately used those patterns to formulate a better procedure for manufacturing ready-made clothing.

According to a letter he later sent us, he modified the patterns to manufacture items suitable for the Japanese market. At a business convention held in Tokyo he subsequently had been awarded a prize for excellence in innovation. When I received the letter, I felt gratified that I had been able to fulfill our obligations to our visitor from Japan even in our desperate financial situation.

In the following years Norio repeatedly expanded his business activities and opened the Sennariya Clothing Shop in the Ginza area of Tokyo. He soon built the seven-story Sennariya Building nearby. Sometime later, Norio was involved in an aqualung diving accident, but his family still continues his business.

An Unendurable Homesickness

I had left Japan in 1930 and Norio was the first blood relative that I had seen in 20 years. It was painfully embarrassing to meet him while we were in such a state of poverty, but seeing a relative again was a great joy. I inundated him with questions about my father and younger sister in Hokkaido, my older sister in Tokyo, and about my mother and older brother, both of whom had died much earlier. I asked him one question after the other, as I recalled members of the family. To each of the questions, Norio provided detailed answers. Those answers touched me with nostalgia and longing and a long surpressed "homesickness" began to fill and overwhelm me.

In addition to my personal inquiries, it was a rare chance to learn more about conditions in Japan, so I also felt moved to invite five or six friends to our home to meet Norio. Norio gave us a detailed description of the period immediately after the war and the period of reconstruction under the Occupation Forces.

A new constitution had been promulgated; democracy had become the guideline for the country. The giant *zaibatsu* (business cartels) had been dismantled, leading to increased democratization of the financial and business sectors. The Japanese population of approximately 100 million persons had focussed all of its energies to rebuild the country. Everything he described seemed hopeful and we felt a certain pride and strength. "If that is the case," I thought, "Japan will surely recover." I was happy and grateful that we had received such a sure and positive basis for hope.

After three days in Chicago, Norio left with the wrestling team to continue the tour of goodwill matches. Unfortunately, while on the tour, he received a telegram from Japan informing him that his mother had died. He left the tour and immediately returned to Japan.

When Norio left I entrusted $100 with him to give to my father in Hokkaido. I expected that when my father came out to attend my aunt's funeral in Tokyo, Norio would be able to pass it on to him directly. At that time, $100 was a very large sum for our family. But I had left home at a very young age and had never been able to do anything substantial for my family. Even if it was only a token of filial regard, I felt at that time that whatever funds we could spare should be offered to my father.

Several weeks later, I received a long letter from my father; he also enclosed with his letter a number of photographs. In the photographs were many familiar faces that I had not seen in many years. In the letter my father wrote about how touched he was by my gift and repeatedly asked that I "forgive him for not having been able to do for me what a parent should have done."

"You wanted to go to school so much, but we could not afford to send you to a proper school. When you left for Peru we could not help you nor give you a parting gift. We took the salary that was given to you at the dairy plant, yet did not even give you a gift when you departed to a foreign land. I can understand what feelings of resentment you must have held against your father.

"When you left, our financial situation had improved somewhat so we could have given you some help; but I felt then that if you had to rely on your family you would never be able to endure the trials of life in a foreign country. I steeled my heart in a monstrous way and watched silently what you did. When I look back on it now, however, I have endless regrets for my cruel actions. What I did was unforgivable; yet, I hope that you will find a way in your heart to forgive me.

"We have not used a penny of the large sum that you sent; it has been placed in an account for you. We have also reserved for you your share of the family property. I am quite old; while I am still in good health and active, please come back to Japan. Let me see your face once more. As for travel expenses, we will be able to manage it so do not be concerned about that. Just quietly return to us."

As I read my father's letter, tears streamed from my eyes. I had not known that my father, who had seemed so strong-minded and aloof, had cared so much and had been so concerned about my hopes. While my eyes moved over the shakily written script that continued line after line on simple stationery, an overwhelming desire to return to Japan came over me. I wanted to reach out to embrace him. But in our situation at that time that was an unfulfillable dream.

The homesickness that was touched off by Norio's visit was intensified by my father's letter. I gazed many times at the photographs that had been sent and read and reread my father's letter. Each time, tears filled my eyes. Eventually, however, in our daily struggle to survive, those feelings had to be put aside. I could not afford the leisure of remaining consumed with homesickness. Several years later, without seeing me again, my father died. I was an unfilial son who had not been with his parents when they passed on.

My Sister-in-law's Illness

About a year after we moved to Chicago, we received a letter from my wife's parents, who had returned to Japan at the end of the war, informing us that my wife's younger sister, Fumiko, had contracted tuberculosis and was confined to bed. New medications had been developed to treat tuberculosis and it was no longer an incurable illness. At the time, however, Japan was still plagued by material shortages, and it was difficult to obtain those new drugs. There, tuberculosis remained a dreaded disease, contagious and fatal. My wife's parents were greatly concerned.

Fortunately, Fumiko's husband was a physician who was knowledgeable about new methods of treatment. But even he could not obtain the necessary medications in Japan. It was then that they turned to us in America for help. They wrote, "There is a particularly effective medication for tuberculosis called 'streptomycin.' Knowing it is a burden we place on you, we ask that you forward some to us."

Almost everyone has heard of streptomycin these days, but at the time very few people had heard of it. I immediately went to a nearby drugstore to inquire about it. The pharmacist knew about such a drug but would not sell it to me. I went around to several large pharmacies, but the replies were the same. I did not know what to do.

About that time, I happened to have suffered a mild case of insomnia and was being treated by a Dr. Nakaya, whose office was near where we lived. Dr. Nakaya was an outstanding physician, who was extremely warm and personable as well. Even in those days, unless one had an appointment, it was difficult to see a doctor. But Dr. Nakaya was an exception. Whenever we went to see him, even without an appointment, he made time to see us. Even when we had unpaid bills, he never demanded payment. He often said, "Don't worry about it; you can pay me when you have the money." While searching for streptomycin, I suddenly thought of consulting Dr. Nakaya.

I soon learned why I could not find the medication on drug store shelves. According to Dr. Nakaya, it was available only with a doctor's prescription. He kindly said, "I'll arrange to get some for you." The doctor quickly obtained a rather large supply, explaining that tuberculosis needed to be treated over an extended period and that a constant supply of medication was necessary.

I divided the precious supply of medication into several carefully wrapped packages and sent them off successively to Japan. The streptomycin had quick results. A few months later we received a letter from my wife's parents informing us that my sister-in-law was recovering and had regained much of her strength. I quickly went over to report the good news to Dr. Nakaya and to thank him again. The doctor said, "That's good; that's good." He seemed as delighted as if it was one of his own patients who had recovered.

Sometime later my sister-in-law recovered completely. I felt that this was all due to the kindness and help of Dr. Nakaya. Dr. Nakaya was an especially outstanding physician, I felt, because he managed to combine the latest medical techniques and treatments with a warmth of human concern. He addressed patients by their given names and established a direct, personal relationship. At his office there were no complicated application procedures nor many documents to read and sign as was inevitable at other hospitals and clinics. I felt that he was a person who truly could be called a "physician."

"If There is no Home to Rent. . ." A New Challenge

In Chicago, our biggest problem was finding a suitable apartment for our family. For two years, whenever I was able to find time, I continued to search for a suitable apartment, but was unable to find one we could afford. Mr. Iida's apartment was simply too small for our family. The children were rapidly growing up, and we could not forever confine them to one room.

Yet, that did not mean that we could simply give up. If we could not find a place to rent, why not raise our sights and consider buying a home? I suddenly came to see that buying a home was possible and began to investigate ways to reach that goal.

We had almost no savings. When I looked into different possibilities, however, I found that there were ways of buying a home even without much capital. We could borrow money to make the downpayment to buy a rooming house. Then, with the rent we collected, we could pay back the loan and the mortgage over a number of years. By utilizing that method, it seemed, owning a building in 10 or 15 years might not be a mere dream. I immediately began to look at properties and began making detailed calculations. The result of my study did not make us overly optimistic, but we had no alternative. I decided that we would buy an apartment building.

My attention soon focused on a three-story building located not far from Mr. Iida's property. It was an apartment building that had been divided into six rooming units on each floor, for a total of 18 units. Although the building was over 50 years old, I could see that it was solidly constructed.

I borrowed funds from the Japanese Trust Association and from a finance company. For the former, a sympathetic friend agreed to co-sign the loan as a guarantor. For the latter, we eventually reached an agreement by my signing a second mortgage to the building. When I think of it now, I can see we made some extremely risky moves, but, at that time, there were no other alternatives. This is how we came to own and operate a rooming house.

There was a housing shortage in Chicago at that time so we never lacked tenants. For the most part, we were blessed with good tenants, and there were only a few cases of tenants being overly late with rents or absconding without making payments. We were able to pay our debts, make our mortgage payments, and meet maintenance expenses with the rental income. Except for rare emergencies, we did not have to put in additional capital.

We were, however, swamped with additional work. Since rooming houses at that time were operated like apartment-hotels, we had to take out the trash for the tenants and provide changes of linen such as sheets, pillow cases, and towels. Common areas such as the staircases, hallways and bathrooms had to be cleaned by the owner. Just washing the linen for 16 units was a major job.

Almost all the units had a sink and refrigerator, so when problems occurred with the plumbing or electrical system I quickly had to make repairs. Luckily, I had worked at various types of jobs, so I was able to handle almost all the repairs without outside help. In America, where labor costs are high, we would never have been able to meet expenses if we had to hire professional workers to do repairs. Entering this new business activity, I again became a jack of all trades.

There was a lot of simple carpentry to be done, but I was able to handle almost all of it by myself because of my experiences in Canete. I also did all of the painting, whether it was interior or exterior work. Except for exceptionally difficult problems, I also did all the repairs to the gas lines, water lines, and electrical wiring. If there was a leak in the roof, I went up to coat it with tar. I learned the technique of "tag point," so I could maintain the brick and brownstone exteriors of the buildings. When the sewer lines clogged or the heaters broke down, I did whatever was necessary to restore them to working condition. Because of this we managed to get by, even with our lack of capital.

At first, I was so overwhelmed with work that even if I had been blessed with two bodies I would not have had the time to attend to everything. Although I was now a rooming house operator, the rental income all went to pay off loans, so my wife and I could not quit our other jobs. Our family would have starved if we did. Continuing our separate day and night work schedules, we took on the additional work necessary to operate the rooming house.

Fortunately, by that time our children were old enough to help us with the work. If not, we would not have been able to manage, and our "reckless adventure" of operating a rooming house would have probably ended in failure.

A Concrete Frontier

On the surface, operating a rooming house seemed to make our lives more hectic, with no apparent benefits to be seen. But, actually, there was a decisive difference in our circumstances. First of all, we acquired a true home; we no longer needed to be careful about what a landlord required. When I first went to inspect the building, I immediately noticed it had a large, empty basement area. I believed we could convert it into an adequate living quarters for our family. By living in the basement, we could rent out all of the 18 units. We would be acquiring a three-story apartment building and a home for ourselves. Eliminating the need to pay rent for our small, crowded apartment in Mr. Iida's building would be a very big financial advantage for us.

As soon as we signed the contracts to obtain the property, I bought some inexpensive lumber and, whenever I had any free time, began building living quarters for us in the basement. There was a large boiler in the basement, as well as pipes and utility lines for electricity, gas and steam heating, but they were concentrated in one corner. Blocking off that area still left ample space for a three-bedroom apartment. I first built a kitchen, then a living room, then one bedroom. We then moved from Mr. Iida's apartment to what we could truly call our own home.

When we first moved into the basement our living space was not much different from what we had in Mr. Iida's apartment. But we were not completely hemmed in by neighbors as before, and our new home had space for expansion. More importantly, it was a place that nurtured hopes and dreams, and the faces of my wife and children glowed with happiness. I accepted the responsibility of nurturing their hopes and expectations, and whenever I found time I worked to add on rooms one by one.

Eventually, our home was completed. Even if it was my own work, I must say that it was splendid. I had to exert myself to do all the work, but I had the satisfaction of knowing that I was actually building our home. I looked at my self-built home and was content. I imagined that this was what the pioneers moving westward in America must have felt when they opened new lands and built log cabins with their own hands. This home, I thought, was our log cabin that we had built in a concrete frontier. We were new settlers who, in a concrete frontier, continued to build on a legacy established by many forbears who had built this country. Operating the rooming house definitely required an extraordinary effort that seemed to parallel the superhuman effort necessary to open out the western areas of the country.

At the same time, our efforts opened up endless possibilities before us. I felt that in our urban environment we were standing on frontier lands and experiencing something similar to the feelings of those pioneers who had looked out to the opportunities of the great land that spread out endlessly to the west.

It was, of course, only a building that was encumbered completely with borrowed money. Yet, its title was in our names. In 15 years, if we did not fail in our efforts, it would be all ours. While we labored, we did not have to worry about a place to live. For the first time since coming to Chicago, I began to see a glimmer of light and hope in the darkness of our struggle to survive.

We bought that first apartment building in the summer of 1951. Those early days were extremely trying times, both financially and physically. Soon, however, we adjusted, and things fell into an established pattern. We began to feel more stable.

We were able to invite to our home the members of the wrestling team from Japan that Mr. Hatta brought to America every year; we could welcome and entertain them with a small party. I regained a certain measure of security and equanimity and began to feel that I had a leeway to begin deliberately to consider our future.

The rooming house operations, which we had entered in desperation in our quest to find an adequate place to live, had brought good results beyond our fondest imagination. If things continued well, I thought, we could acquire one or two more buildings and make such operations our main source of livelihood.

Because I had no viable capital or skills to market in this country, operating rooming houses might be the most suitable recourse in our circumstances. Using the same methods that we had used to acquire the first building, I could add other buildings and I could maximize my abilities as a jack-of-all-trades. Owning our own business might also open up other possibilities and free us from the uncertainties of the labor market. I was grateful and excited by thoughts of such prospects.

When our rooming house operation reached a point of stability, I quickly sought to buy another building. Fortunately, I found an affordable property nearby, almost the same size as the first. Because the second building was almost completely financed with borrowed monies, I still could not abandon my night shift job. Handling its management by myself kept us very busy, but our financial condition improved markedly. Finally, our family was beginning to move out of our "frontier" conditions.

Moving "Uptown"

Operations at our two buildings proved to be very stable. I grew more confident in my ability to handle the business. By the latter half of the 1950s, I began to expand our operations as much as possible.

We sold our first two buildings. With the proceeds, I bought two buildings of the same size in the Uptown area of Northside Chicago. The two buildings had been built at the same time, side by side, so it was convenient to service them. By that time, our family finances had improved, so we no longer needed to live in a basement. We decided to occupy the entire first floor of one building as our living quarters. Our new home was a six-room flat, about standard for a family of our size. We had finally achieved a "normal" American standard of living.

We settled into our new home on Racine Avenue in the Uptown section of Chicago, about a three-minute walk from the Wilson Station of the Chicago "El." The area had formerly been known for its high-priced homes, but from the period just before the war, because of a pressing housing shortage, family-style apartment buildings had gradually been converted into rooming houses. Most of the previous well-established residents moved to the suburbs or to luxury apartments along Lake Michigan.

When we moved Uptown, some long-time residents still remained there, but quite a large number of Asians and Spanish-speaking people had moved in. A number of years later, many hillbillies (mainly from the mountains of Kentucky and Tennessee), who were looked down upon by other whites, moved into the area.

Because of such trends, the area was a far cry from the high-priced residential area that the term "Uptown" had earlier connoted. But since the apartment buildings had been erected during the height of prosperity, almost all were of good quality with magnificent exteriors. The two buildings we bought were elegant, three-story brick buildings with wide verandas. Although they were about 50 years old, the buildings had been so well constructed that, with proper maintenance, they easily could have been used for another 30 or 40 years.

At that time, agreements, both formal and informal, existed within the business and financial communities to exclude property ownership by persons of particular races in certain areas of the city. That "red-lining" was primarily a strategy to prevent blacks from entering white residential areas; in certain areas, Americans of Asian or Latin ancestry were also excluded. I do not know whether such agreements or covenants would have had the binding force of law, but when we bought the two Uptown buildings the sales contract contained a clause that stated that we "could not rent out or transfer the property to colored persons."

Such discrimination was a large barrier for black persons and, at times, also for those of Asian ancestry. From the point of view of white Americans, once Asians entered an area, other racial and ethnic groups would gradually follow and real estate values would fall. Thus, they felt that Asians had to be excluded as a preventive measure. This, of course, was rarely stated openly, but it was an undeniable fact that such racial discrimination limited our choice of living areas.

Starting in the 1950s and continuing through 1960s, however, areas which excluded Japanese were steadily eliminated in Chicago so that such discrimination was not a major handicap for our business. It must be noted, however, that even in areas other than exclusive, high-priced areas, some sections of Chicago continued to bar Japanese from residing or owning property. We probably were able to move to the Uptown area because Hispanics and other ethnic groups had already broken through the color barrier. In any case, we settled into the Uptown area and established our base for expanding our rental operations.

In the late '60s, we decided to establish financial security for our family by operating rooming houses. Whenever we accumulated even small amounts of capital we invested everything back into the business. Fortunately, our rental operations continued without disruptions; we were able to expand it gradually.

When the operations of our first two Uptown buildings became financially stable, I arranged to acquire another large apartment building less than a 10-minute walk away. The three-story building, located on Lakeside Avenue, had as many apartments as the two buildings on Racine Avenue combined.

Sometime later, we purchased a fourth building, about a five-minute walk from our home. It was about the size of the building on Lakeside. Then, we bought another large building on Racine Avenue. In this manner, we came to own five apartment buildings. While they were all acquired with borrowed money, their value at that time nevertheless totaled $250,000.

Almost all the units in the five buildings were one-room apartment-hotel types, so we would not have been able to handle maintenance and supervision by ourselves even with extraordinary efforts. We placed managers in the buildings to be responsible for daily maintenance. I continued to work eight hours a day at my evening job, and handled only repairs, the regular collection of trash, and other such miscellaneous tasks. Winters were especially busy for me, as I also had to clear snow from walkways.

The business continued to operate smoothly, however, so such work did not seem to be a hardship. If things continued in that way, I thought, I would soon be able to leave my job to devote all my time to our rental properties. Perhaps, I hoped, we would not have to worry about our retirement years. I set a goal to retire at age 60. To fulfill that goal, I resolved to concentrate all my energies on our rental operations and on my night shift job.

Life, however, inevitably does not work out as one might expect. Along our chosen path, we were to meet an unexpected ambush. By the early '60s, municipal ordinances governing the operation of rooming houses in Chicago were drastically revised. The reason for the revisions was mainly to reduce overcrowding and correct undesirable health and fire hazards. By early '60s, the population had shifted significantly to the suburbs, and housing problems in the city had been alleviated. It was at that point that the municipal agencies began proposing stricter regulation of rooming houses.

The new regulations restricted the use of communal bathrooms, required that fire escapes be placed in certain locations, specified new requirements for units with kitchens, and more. When I received the new ordinances, I felt, "Well, that's the end of rooming house operations."

City inspectors were right in that there a number of problems with the way rooming houses were being operated. A few points seemed to be overly strict, but the general approach of the new ordinances seemed to be appropriate and proper. I accepted what the city inspectors pointed out and began, one by one, to make changes to conform with the new regulations. Given the configurations of our buildings, conforming to the new regulations would require decreasing the number of tenants. Whenever a tenant moved out, we left the room empty. Gradually, a floor that once had six rooming units would be remodelled into two apartment units.

Such large scale remodelling required a great deal of carpentry, plumbing, and other construction work. By that time, I had left my outside job, so I managed to do most of the work by myself, with only a small amount of professional help, mainly to deal with large technical problems. Over a period of years, the rooming houses were converted into apartments.

Of course, the new ordinances greatly impacted our income. While the larger, remodeled units commanded higher rents, and the decrease in the number of tenants reduced maintenance and supervision demands, these factors could not match the loss in income due to the decrease in rental units. It was a severe setback for us.

By that time, fortunately, our family's finances were secure enough so we could absorb the loss in income. If we had started in the business a few years later than we did, we would have certainly been confronted with financial disaster. In that sense, we had to still count ourselves fortunate.

It is undeniable, however, that the new ordinances completely halted any further expansion of our rental operations. Taking my age into consideration, I decided to shift my philosophy from one of expansion to one of safety and stability so that my wife and I could begin to enjoy our modest security.

We could not expect to increase our income from apartment operations, but if we were not extravagant we would have no problems in providing for our family. It was no longer necessary for both of us to hold outside jobs. We could now enjoy some leisure activities and, for the first time, we now had opportunities for the whole family to be together. The setback, I realized, had turned out to be an unexpected blessing for our family.

Soon after the new ordinances were enacted in the 1960s, rapid inflation afflicted the economy, bringing about huge increases in income taxes, property taxes, and conveyance taxes for real estate transactions. But we had already shifted from a policy of expansion to that of maintenance, so we did not feel the full brunt of those tax increases. I came to feel that even setbacks could be blessings in disguise.

Chapter Eleven. Becoming Americanized

The American Work Ethic

Since its founding by Puritan immigrants, America has held an honored tradition of viewing all work as sacred. This is in marked contrast to the general attitude found in Japan and Latin America, where some types of work are to be respected and other types are despised.

Of course a clear authority relationship existed between workers and their employers in the United States as elsewhere, but the value of work in itself was not deemed "honorable" or "base" on the basis of employer-employee status. As I began to work in America, I often witnessed workers and employers speaking to each other casually— and as equals. I admired and appreciated the fact that neither party seemed particularly self-conscious of the egalitarian nature of their attitudes.

In America, moreover, there was a tradition of encouraging young children to strive toward economic independence. Parents explained the importance of work to their children. Thus, when they were old enough to do so, children helped with household chores or took part-time jobs to earn their own pocket money. For most children at that time, pocket money was something they earned and not something simply given to them.

Not long after we moved to Chicago, I saw a boy obviously just starting to deliver newspapers. He was being followed by his father, who was driving a Cadillac. The boy, who could only have been about 10 years old, went about checking a piece of paper and carefully throwing newspapers onto particular doorsteps. His father, following behind him, also looked at what seemed to be a delivery list to be sure that the boy made the correct deliveries. After a few days, the father was no longer seen and the young boy freely delivered the newspapers without even looking at a list.

In Japan, a poor family might have been forced to have its son deliver newspapers, but it would have been unthinkable that a father who could afford such an expensive car would have his son do so. That would bring "shame" to the parents, and would have been impossible simply in terms of maintaining the family's reputation within the community.

But in America, it was different. Here, the tradition of Adam Smith, who emphasized the iron rule that "those who do not work will not eat" and even demanded that even aristocrats work, had continued for over three centuries. It was held that all types of work had value and that sloth and laziness were sins.

When we first left the detention camp at Crystal City, my wife was not familiar with the American work ethic. She did not complain nor even mention it, but I could see that she felt that being forced to do the lowest type of physical labor was insulting and degrading. She grew up surrounded by nurses and maids and, having had the experience of managing a shop with many employees, she had not personally done any housework or laundry, or even handled the day-to-day care of our children while we were in Peru. That was the normal situation for those of the middle and upper classes in Peru.

Given that background, it was understandable that she felt it degrading to have to mix with general laborers and engage in physical labor. Even with that background, however, having once been forced to do such work because of economic necessity, my wife somehow assimilated the American work ethic and came to feel that work was not degrading, but was even a basis for pride.

It was the same with our children. Our poverty taught them to accept the proud American tradition of valuing work. From their earliest years they were raised to understand that they must work hard, study hard, handle material things with respect and care, and to live simply and frugally. Our family was able to pass through the depths of poverty because each of us, at our respective tasks, gave our utmost efforts.

Without a complaint, the children cooperated by doing household chores while my wife and I went out to work. They even handled miscellaneous tasks made necessary by our rooming house operations. They did menial cleaning chores that would have disgusted people in Japan, but none of them complained.

Our Children Grow Independent

Because my wife and I had always held outside jobs, our first daughter, Elsa Yukiko, had from an early age become a second mother to our other children. From the time she was old enough to understand our circumstances, she saw our difficult situation and had always stood with us to explain our position to the other children.

Elsa was also an independent child and, even at an early age, wanted to shape her own future. Even when it was not legally permitted, she somehow found a part-time job and managed to pay for part of her school expenses. In high school, she found a part-time job at a small publishing firm that put out public relations information for the Chicago Police Department. Every day after school, she worked two or three hours at that office handling monies, answering telephone inquiries, and taking orders.

Once, with the income from her part-time job, she invited my wife and me to an ice skating show. I think she felt sorry for us, as we only continued at our jobs and did not even go out to see a movie. Wanting to give us some enjoyment, she bought tickets to a very good section at the ice skating show. I knew she must have spent a very large part of what, at that time, she could have saved. She had done this for parents who could not even give her a decent allowance. I was moved with gratitude at the thoughtfulness of our first daughter who must have saved a long time to make this happy time possible for us. Unexpectedly, tears came to my eyes.

Elsa graduated from high school and advanced to college. I had felt, from an earlier time, that in order to live in America it was necessary to have higher education. I welcomed her desire to move on to higher education. It was, however, something that my wife had not expected. She had looked toward a time when our oldest daughter would find a job and help with family expenses. But our daughter had said, "After I graduate from college, I shall work with all my effort and send my younger brothers through college." My wife had been persuaded by that argument and, reluctantly, gave her approval.

In this manner, Elsa entered the School of Education at Northern Illinois University, located about 130 miles west of Chicago. We paid her dormitory fees, but she paid her own tuition and other school fees with funds she had earned from part-time work. Every summer, during school vacations, she returned to Chicago to work to earn her school expenses and returned to school in the fall.

A few years later, a year before she graduated, she told us that she had a boyfriend and the two later became engaged. Her fiance was Eigo Kudo, who was majoring in accounting at the University of Illinois.

Eigo was the fifth son of Rokuichi Kudo, who had shared common experiences with us from the time we had been in Peru. After graduating from high school, Eigo had spent two years in the U.S. military and had used the opportunity of the G.I. Bill to enroll at the university. He was a few years older than our daughter, but because he had entered high school late, and because of his military service, he was two years behind our daughter at college. Eventually, when she graduated, the two were married. Leaving our family, our daughter found a position as a teacher at an elementary school near the university and helped to support her husband who was still a student. Because of this, she could not fulfill her promise to send her younger brothers through college.

But her younger brother, Carlos Shuichi, was not waiting for her help—he had already enrolled in the School of Engineering at the University of Illinois on his own. He had begun studying toward a degree in electrical engineering. Like his older sister, he earned his school expenses by taking part-time jobs and finished the four-year college curriculum on his own.

While still in school, Carlos had landed a position with a large electronics firm headquartered in Chicago. Soon after he graduated, however, it was discovered that he had tuberculosis and his employment had to be postponed while he entered a sanitarium for treatment.

We faced the situation with deep regret and blamed ourselves. As parents, if we had supported Carlos adequately, he would not have had to suffer such an illness. To have worked his way through college, and to have landed a position with an outstanding corporation, then to have all of this come to nothing because of his illness must have been a great disappointment. Fortunately, he recovered completely in about a year and found a position in Chicago with the Honeywell Corporation, a large electronics manufacturer. Carlos moved forth to build his own independent life.

One after another, our second daughter, Irma Setsuko, our second son, Arthur Hideki, and our third daughter, Martha Yoko, then entered colleges in the city. Our second and third daughters finished their lower division courses and then married. Our second son later transferred to Roosevelt University and graduated from its business school. In this manner, in the late 1950s and early 1960s our children each established their own independent lives.

A Generation Gap

Inevitably, as our children gradually became self-supporting and came to lead their own lives, a communications gap widened between us as parents and children. Even American families, where parents and children shared the same culture, felt a generation gap. Our family did not even have a common language anymore, so it was not surprising that a gap would develop.

From the time we had been in Peru, I had observed a wide gap

The family's first building on Burling Street, Chicago, 1951.

between the first generation immigrants and their children who had been born and raised in Peru.

Before the war, matters in Peru were handled so casually that everything could be set aside with, "Hasta manana (Till tomorrow)." The second generation nisei were naturally influenced by Peru's unpressured lifestyle and tended to be easy-going about things. That attitude and lifestyle seemed irresponsible and lazy to the quick-tempered issei immigrants who had been born in Japan.

To the nisei, the precise and ordered lifestyle of their first generation parents was hard to accept. They came to hold unexpressed resentments toward those of the first generation who demanded such Japanese sensibilities and behavior.

The gap between the first and second generations was made worse by the language differences and by the circumstances of their lives, which left them little time to adequately communicate with each other.

Before the war, the Japanese community in Peru was still run by issei immigrants. Those of the second generation were almost inevitably excluded from decision-making in the Japanese community, further deepening the generation gap. More and more, the first generation came to look down upon the second generation as un-Japanese. This attitude, of course, only increased the resentments held by the second generation niseis.

These attitudes were clearly reflected in the help wanted advertisements of the Japanese language newspapers in Peru. Advertisements of the time often contained the phrase, "nisei may also apply." While it was thought to be completely acceptable by the issei, the phrase of course implied that the employer did not really want a nisei employee, but would consider a nisei better than a non-Japanese Peruvian.

The nisei did not overlook such attitudes. Victor K. Tateishi, a nisei attorney who had graduated from Colegio Modelo and studied law at San Marcos University, became so provoked by the demeaning of niseis that he finally responded with a stinging attack on such attitudes in a newspaper article. Tateishi stated that niseis should not be looked down upon and that niseis had abilities equivalent to those of the isseis. When I read the article I felt a sense of exhilaration and admiration at his well-reasoned, detailed arguments. Tateishi's points struck me as being true. At the same time, however, I saw the newspaper article itself as evidence that the generation gap had widened to such a degree that I could not put aside a sense of apprehension.

The split between the first and second generations had occurred in the Japanese Peruvian community, which emphasized human relationships to a degree greater than in Japan. It could be expected that it would be a larger problem in America, which embraced a thoroughgoing individualism.

Unlike in Peru, nisei in the United States could not receive their compulsory education through courses conducted in the Japanese language. Thus, nisei in the United States were further separated from the issei than their Peruvian counterparts. They knew almost nothing about their parents' homeland and could not even adequately use their parents' language.

In our family, too, the language spoken in our home gradually shifted from Japanese to English as our children grew up. At some imperceptible point, English became the common language in our home. Of course, when my wife and I led the conversation we mainly used a brand of broken Japanese that embraced an odd mixture of English and Spanish. But even that gradually lost its ability to communicate our thoughts and feelings accurately. After a certain point, if we wanted to communicate with our children at all, we were forced to rely on the English language.

The Price of Americanization

The shift from one language to another in our home was completely natural in an America which sets its perspective in the future. America is a dynamic society that constantly looks toward an ideal future age; it is a society which repeatedly experiments and reaches out toward unlimited progress; it is a society where the past is ruthlessly abandoned if it would impede progress. In Japan, society sets its foundations on the traditions of the past; in America, history and traditions soon fade away. Rather than becoming teachers or models for the young, in America, the older generation merely establishes what the young should surpass.

For new immigrants, these developments meshed with their own hopes, because they sought, as did other Americans, to be a part of a more perfect society in the future. Such progress was almost inevitably seen as being part of the process of Americanization.

In the United States the attitude which underpinned the phrase, "Niseis may also apply," would never exist. In America, the second generation who spoke English and were more American than their parents held the upper hand. In fact, Japanese language newspapers in the United States contained advertisements that included the phrase, "Japanese speakers may also apply." I never saw the phrase, "Nisei may also apply."

In that sense, there was a big difference between the issei in Peru, who always looked back to their homeland and rejected assimilation with Peruvian society, and the issei in America who were forced to look to the future and, whether they wanted to or not, were under great pressure to assimilate into American society.

In our home, our children went beyond their parents and, one by one, became more American. Of course my wife and I were happy about this, but since we could not express the finer nuances of our feelings in English, it also distanced us further from our children. This, indeed, could be called the price of Americanization.

America is a society where constant change occurs. This definition of progress, seems to me like a multi-staged rocket which expels its earlier stages of power to fly off into the openness of space, into the universe that extends into infinity.

As I watched the launching of such space missions, I noticed that the focus was always on the space capsule's spectacular flight into space, and the secondary rocket that gave it strength and then was ejected soon disappeared from the TV screen and no one knew its fate. That indeed was a characteristic facet, I felt, of American futurism.

In our home there was no true common language. This was a severe handicap, but our family was unifiied by or having shared the tough conditions of poverty together. Such experiences probably helped our family to survive the generation gap better than most American families which shared a common language.

This is not to say that there was no gap between us and our children. In particular, our third son, Richard Daisuke, our fourth daughter, Deanna Mitsuko, and our fourth son, Mark Yoshio, were born in the U.S. and were completely American. In many ways their outlook differed from our older children, who had been born in Peru. In that sense, they were more distant from my wife and me emotionally and in ways of thinking.

We felt, however, that this was normal. It was more amazing to us that they had come so far and still had not abandoned us. If they had not shared our experiences during our early years in Chicago, I felt, our relationships would probably have been quite different.

Our Children's Marriages

In the late '50s and early '60s, our children got married and became independent. I tried, as much as possible, not to interfere with their personal affairs. I would express my feelings, but I believed that each of them would have to make their own decisions. At times, I worried about them. Yet, while aware of my feelings, they began to make their own decisions.

Because they were fully Americanized, I was fully prepared that our children might marry partners who were not Japanese. In America, where so many different ethnic groups co-existed, it was to be expected that persons of different races married. It would be impractical to insist that our children marry only those of the same ethnic group. I only trusted in the good sense of our children and hoped, in my heart, that they would be blessed with good marriage partners.

Happily, our children were level-headed in their relationships with those of the opposite sex. Whenever they had a boyfriend or girlfriend they brought them to our home to be introduced. Some of them quickly married, but others had two or three "friends." Whatever the case, we as parents, never objected about their "friends."

Our daughters wanted to go out alone with their boyfriends, but we did not allow it until they became 18. There were those who warned us, "If you insist on holding on to those old, Japanese attitudes, your girls will soon run off." As a parent, however, I still felt responsible and I did not give in on the issue of "unaccompanied dates." Fortunately, our daughters did not run away. All of them made happy marriages and I was much satisfied.

As mentioned earlier, our oldest daughter, Elsa, married Eigo Kudo when she graduated from college. Kudo graduated two years after her, passed the difficult certified public accountant examinations and was hired as an auditor by the Arthur Andersen Company, one of the major U.S. accounting firms. Kudo was fluent in Japanese and Spanish, so he was assigned to audit multi-national companies. He worked in Japan, Central America, Europe and other foreign countries. He later left that company to move to Hawaii and works for Deloitte, Touche and Tohmatsu. He is now a partner of the Hawaii office of that company in charge of the Japanese Division which he developed.

Our daughter Elsa worked toward a real estate license when her two children no longer needed her daily attention and received a Hawaii state license. She is a realtor with a local firm, Marcus and Associates, Inc. She believes that "women's liberation" is possible only with economic independence, and she says she feels gratified that she can test her own abilities in the "real world" of business. Although she has a somewhat "Japanese" outlook toward things, she is splendidly American and independent.

Our oldest son, Carlos Shuichi, got married after graduating from the University of Illinois. After a number of years, however, he was divorced and subsequently married Chie, the first daughter of Roy Ishiwari. Chie is a third generation sansei who graduated from the University of Illinois. Chie taught for many years, until she retired a number of years ago to open a travel agency in Chicago.

Our second daughter, Irma, was married soon after she finished lower division courses at the University of Illinois. Her husband, Shiro Kudo, is the older brother of Eigo Kudo. To our surprise, we experienced the rare case of having our two daughters marry brothers. Shiro Kudo majored in commercial art at the American Academy of Art and has been involved with businesses in that field. Our second daughter is an active career woman who currently holds a major position as executive director of the American Association of Endodontists.

From the time I met Mr. Kudo at the Kurotobi Company in Lima shortly before I was deported to the United States, the Kudo family shared a common fate with us at the detention camp in Crystal City, at Seabrook in New Jersey, and in Chicago. Still, I never dreamed that in our children's generation a tie with the Kudo family would come into being.

Our second son, Arthur Hideki, graduated from Roosevelt University in Chicago and is the owner of Principal Properties, Inc., a realty company in Honolulu.

In the early 1960s, our third daughter, Martha Yoko, married Don Shigio, the oldest son of Mr. Shigetoshi Shigio. Martha completed lower division courses at Illinois State College and then married to become a housewife. Her husband, Don, is a sansei who is in computers.

By the early 1960s, four of our eight children were married and began building their own homes and families. They had put down firm roots in American soil and were beginning, confidently, to establish their own lives.

From "Illegal Immigrant" to Naturalized Citizenship

As our children were putting down roots in America, so were my wife and I gradually becoming Americanized. The basic tenets of American democracy and individualism imperceptibly became a part of our basic outlook. As with other new immigrants to this country, we had to overcome repeated difficulties. Such experiences were part of the process of our assimilation into American society.

The U.S. government, which had determined while we were still at Crystal City that the detainees from Central and South America were "illegal entrants" to this country, could no longer disregard the fact that we were all becoming "Americanized." Even before they were allowed citizenship, the Japanese from Peru were already fulfilling the duties of citizens. Who could refuse citizenship to our second daughter's husband, Shiro Kudo, who had joined the U.S. Army and fought in the Korean conflict?

Since immigration laws were first enacted in 1790, soon after the U.S. Constitution was ratified, such laws strictly enforced exclusionary principles for more than a century and a half. Essentially, those laws did not allow the right of naturalization to those other than "free, white persons."

In 1870, after the American Civil War, the laws were revised to extend naturalization rights to African Americans. In actuality, though, there was very little change in the application of the law. For Asian immigrants, these exclusionary policies remained a major barrier.

Finally, in 1952, for the first time in American history, the revised naturalization laws allowed first generation Asian immigrants to be naturalized. For us, if the United States recognized the legality of our entry into the country, we also would be allowed, as with other new immigrants, to become naturalized American citizens.

It took another two years of advances and setbacks before the U.S. Congress formally passed a bill that recognized the legality of our entry into the country. It was only then that the Justice Department acknowledged the legality of our status. In 1954, "illegal entrants" from Central and South America were formally given entry visas and the large stamp, "Illegal Entrant," no longer appeared on our documents.

We had finally been freed from a lingering fear of possible forced deportation; we had been allowed the right of acquiring permanent residency in the U.S. and were now equal in status with all other new immigrants. Acquiring U.S. citizenship was no longer merely a dream; it now depended only on the wishes and efforts of each of us as individuals.

At that time, we were struggling in poverty to adapt to our new life in Chicago and could not afford to be caught up in the rush toward citizenship. Since we intended to live permanently in this country, however, we decided we should make the effort. We began studying whenever we could find time, so that we could become citizens. In order to pass the citizenship test, we had to learn English and have a basic knowledge of the American political and economic systems. In 1958, my wife and I took the test and passed.

The test was not difficult at all. It even seemed anti-climactic after our more than 10 years of hardship and struggle. In this manner, however, we ended our detention period. On August 25, 1958, at the Immigration and Naturalization Office in Chicago, we recited oaths making us American citizens.

To my surprise, the event was accompanied with emotion. The citizenship test had been only a minor obstacle, but as I looked back at the long and difficult road we had traveled to be able to take that test, I was struck with deep emotions and I could not prevent tears from misting my eyes.

"Divorce Can Be a Strategy for Survival" —An Aspect of America

When we received our citizenship, America was the most powerful country in the world. When I look back on that period, however, I can see that early indications of the problems that America would face 20 years later were already evident. The decline of the work ethic, the wanton use of resources and energy, the transformation of individualism into a kind of self-centeredness, social problems brought about by divorce, increasing crime and violence, the deterioration of the cities, racial discrimination, etc.—even I, who did not know America well, was aware of such problems because of my everyday experiences in Chicago.

Of course, I had no reason to expect that those seemingly minor incidents that I experienced were part of trends that would, in the 1960s and 1970s, become large problems that would threaten the foundations of the country. But, as someone born and raised in Japan, those social phenomena seemed so different from what could be expected in the older Japan that I knew that I could not dismiss a feeling that something was wrong. They remained in a corner of my mind as irksome incidents that could not be overlooked.

All I knew about America was what I dealt with directly in my everyday life. My perceptions of America may therefore be quite different from those with more balanced views. Yet, because my daily experiences were the only way I could know America, I valued and reflected upon those incidents and encounters that I experienced.

After we began our rental operations we came to learn many significant things about America. In the course of managing such a business we were provided numerous opportunities to see aspects of America that the average family would not have had. For example, after we acquired our second apartment building I became aware of a unique type of couple. In our apartment building on North Clark Street there were three divorced women who each had two or three children. Since each of these single-parent families had no one who worked to bring in an income, government agencies paid their rent directly to us. At first I felt this was a good arrangement and was quite happy that we would not have problems collecting the rent. What I discovered, however, brought me to complete exasperation.

At first I felt sorry for those three single-parent families, but, to my surprise, I soon came to see that the three families lived more luxuriously than my own family. Their apartments were the larger units in the building and they owned large television sets and FM radios, which were very expensive items at that time. The government agencies paid their rent, but I still wondered how they could afford such a standard of living.

I came to see that the women all had "husbands." I later learned they had been legally divorced, but the couples continued to live as before, sharing an apartment and maintaining the same family budget. The "wife" was legally divorced and claimed that she was without financial support for her children. She thus received rental payments, child support, medical coverage and other assistance from the government. Yet, she still had the income of her "husband."

Through this method, they all managed to own fine automobiles and, at different times of the year, each of the "families" went off on vacations. For them, divorce was a way of maintaining a comfortable, American lifestyle.

Of course, even if they were divorced, as long as they maintained a common household for their children they could not legally receive public assistance. Government investigators always came during normal working hours, precisely the time when their "husbands" were away at work, so the women were always alone. If investigators came when the "husbands" were home, the "husband" instantly became an "older brother" or "cousin visiting from the country."

The social service workers also came to inquire with the landlords a number of times each year. But we, of course, were in business and did not want anything to disrupt it. The three "families" were fully aware of our situation. They were indeed shrewd and worldly-wise.

I felt that the struggling poor, who worked honestly, were being taken as fools. They continued to pay taxes that maintained the comfortable style of life of such manipulators of the system. Although we benefited by receiving the rental payments, I was disturbed by the implications of that system.

Later, the abuses practiced by this type of supported families increased greatly, leading to criticism of social service agencies and the social welfare system. Unfortunately, those who truly deserved assistance were affected by the backlash against such abuse. I believe no modern nation can survive without some form of social services, but I also came to understand the difficulties of effecting that function equitably.

America: A Country Where the Poor are Strong

We experienced repeated incidents involving such "well-provided poor" people. Our loss of rental payments for an apartment in our Uptown building on Malden Street was another such instance. The apartment was different from the units in the usual rooming house. It was a three-bedroom family flat. The rent was higher than for rooms, of course, but it was not that the tenant was destitute. The tenant was a nurse who worked at a nearby hospital. She had a number of children, but was divorced and seemed to be living without a "husband." After staying in the apartment for about six months, she failed to pay the rent for two successive months, so we asked her to leave. She agreed, but made no move to vacate the apartment.

After it became clear that she did not intend to leave, I went to an attorney, who petitioned the courts for an eviction order. But even after the 30 days that had been stipulated by the courts, the tenant continued to remain in the apartment. She gave various reasons and asked that we wait for a period of two weeks. I was quite exasperated by the situation, but I agreed to allow the two weeks.

Two weeks passed, but she did not appear to be ready to move at all. I asked the lawyer to have the courts enforce the eviction order. On the day of the eviction, however, the woman said that one of her children was ill with a high fever and would not allow the deputy sheriff to enter her apartment. The forced eviction was postponed. But the courts were not to be disobeyed. A week later, several deputy sheriffs appeared and carried out all her belongings to the street.

The woman then began saying that she had no money to move her belongings. Finally, she went to a government agency to weep and petition for assistance because of her "emergency." The city hired a moving company and all her possessions were moved somewhere completely without charge. We lost more than five months of rental payments and had to pay expensive attorney's fees and the charges for the time expended by the deputy sheriffs to evict her. It was a complete loss for us.

Yet, if she had been truly destitute I would have accepted it as a business loss. This incident, however, had a follow-up. A person from the moving company that had transported her belongings later told me that the woman had bought a large house in the suburbs and that all her things had been taken there. From other information that later came to me, it seems that from about the time she stopped paying her rent she had been looking for a house in the suburbs. She had refused to move out because she needed time to find a home to her liking.

In a situation such as hers, if one does not pretend to be completely penniless, there could be harsh consequences. One could be forced to pay the accumulated back rent, the expenses for the deputy sheriffs and the moving costs. But the woman seemed to be fully aware of this and put on a skillful act of being a destitute person. In that deliberate manner, she managed to join the ranks of the suburban middle class and even had her moving costs paid for by the government. The victims of her shameless performance were, ultimately, we as her landlord who suffered individual losses and everyone else who, as we did, honestly kept on paying our taxes. It is said that America is a country where poor people have rights; but when I see such "well-placed poor" outwit well-intentioned citizens, I cannot help but be exasperated and angered.

Tenants from Japan

We learned quite a few things by managing our rental units. On the positive side, such operations allowed us to also function as a liaison that kept us in touch with Japan. There were always one or two tenants who were company employees, academics or students from Japan. We were able to receive from them direct, detailed information about conditions in Japan.

In particular, during the late 1950s, perhaps reflecting the recovery of their country, they came in increasing numbers. One by one, they stayed in our apartments. Our family invariably became friendly with such visitors, and we often heard updated accounts of Japan from them.

From about that time, in the late 1950s, the attitudes of the people from Japan changed—they no longer seemed to be self-conscious about Japan's defeat in the Pacific War. This heartened me, for I took it as an indication that the chaotic and unsettled post-war period in Japan was now a thing of the past.

One of the visitors from Japan whom I still recall vividly is a Mr. Ogawa. A graduate of Tokyo Shogyo University, Ogawa was employed by the Daido Corporation and was sent to represent his company in Chicago because of his language abilities.

Although he had good command of English, Mr. Ogawa still felt that there were problems with his understanding and use of spoken English. He quickly acquired a small transistor radio to improve his understanding of spoken English and, at night, began attending English language courses that were offered to new immigrants. Together with young immigrants from Europe, he began practicing English conversation and written composition.

I went with Mr. Ogawa to the evening English classes but could not match his fervor. His abilities in the language rapidly improved and he also worked hard to become accustomed to American attitudes and ways of thinking so that he could better carry out his duties as a representative of his company. Undoubtedly, he is now active in the top management levels of the Daido Corporation.

From about the beginning of the 1960s, we saw not only employees of large Japanese corporations but also professors from Japanese universities who came to do research in Chicago. The professors, who seemed to replace each other at the beginning of every school year, had different areas of specialization, but they all had words of praise and admiration for the research facilities in the U.S. and educational and research conditions in the U.S. We learned much from our associations and conversations with those professors. I expect that many of them are now leaders in Japan and internationally famous in their specific areas of research.

Our relationship with those business people and professors was simply that of landlord and tenant; but they all visited our family freely and, while relaxing perhaps over glasses of beer, often stayed late into the night to converse with us. Even today, after 20 years, a number of them still send greeting cards during the holiday season to maintain ties.

Poor Foreign Students

Our apartments also housed students from Japan, Korea, Taiwan, Iran, South America and even Hawaii. Differing from the employees of large corporations and the professors from Japan, almost all of the students were poor, struggling to acquire an education. Most held part-time jobs while continuing their schooling. Since I had also experienced being a struggling, destitute student in my youth, I rented rooms to such students at a 20 to 30 percent discount.

One student whom I cannot forget is the Rev. Paul Yamasaki, who had come over from Japan in the late 1950s to study at a seminary in Kentucky. Every year, when his school went on summer vacation, Reverend Yamasaki would come to Chicago and stay for two months in one of our apartments while he worked to earn school expenses. He would arrange earlier to reserve the apartment and, on precisely the day school ended for him, would start out to Chicago with his wife in their battered, old car. Early the next morning they would reach Chicago and from that very morning he would go out to work at a job for which he earlier had made arrangements. He did not waste even a day before going to work.

I had to lower my head in admiration at his complete willingness to work to reach is goals. He usually found two jobs and from the day he reached Chicago would work at both from early morning and into the night. He was receiving no support from his family in Japan, it seemed, and during his two months in Chicago had to earn most of his school expenses. Reverend Yamasaki eventually completed his studies and graduated from the seminary. He returned to Japan, where he received an appointment with the Nihonbashi Church in Osaka. In a letter we received some time after he returned to Japan, he wrote, "We have been blessed with a child and the church we have longed for has been built." I was much impressed by a photograph he enclosed of his newly built church.

Soon after Reverend Yamasaki returned to Japan, another foreign student came to stay with us from the seminary in Kentucky. We had been asked by the Reverend Kuzuhara of the Lakeside Japanese Christian Church to take in a Reverend Kim who had come from Korea to continue his studies. At that time, Reverend Kim was already about 45 years old. When his period of study in the U.S. was completed he was expected to return to Korea to become the vice chancellor of a Christian university in Seoul. He and his family were struggling financially, however, and he had hoped to find a job, even if only for the summer, so that he would be able to send funds back to his wife and five children who had remained in Korea.

It happened that we were in an economic recession at the time. He could not find a suitable job and began to spend his days aimlessly. Sympathizing with him, I told him that if it was acceptable there was a job available to help paint in our apartment buildings. Reverend Kim was overjoyed. For two weeks he worked with me, painting in our buildings. Fortunately, during that time, a suitable job became available and he began to go out to work steadily. I, too, was happy and much relieved that he had found a proper job.

At that time it was not unusual for older persons, such as Reverend Kim, to come to America to study while supporting themselves with part-time or summer jobs.

There were many young students who rented our apartments and rooms during the summer. They came from Japan, Korea, China and other foreign countries. During the summers, our apartment buildings seemed to be transformed into international houses"and were filled with lively activity.

Other foreign students stayed in our apartments over a long period while they attended school in Chicago. Yukinori Koyama, who edited the Japanese version of *Adios to Tears,* is one of the students who stayed at our apartments while he attended school. He had married my niece, Junko, the third daughter of my oldest sister, Misao Sakaguchi, and came over to America in 1964 with her. The young couple supported themselves while Yukinori attended Roosevelt University in Chicago, where he majored in American history.

Another relative who stayed in our apartments while studying in Chicago was Jorge Nishii, a son of my wife's younger sister. Nishii had remained in Peru during the war years. He was the grandson of Tajiemon Nishii, an outstanding member of the third group of Japanese emigrants to Peru, who built the Canal de Nishii, a major irrigation facility at the Quebrada Hacienda in Canete. Nishii and his wife came to study in Chicago about the same time as the Koyamas.

By receiving people from different countries into our apartments, we built friendships with many people, so our circle of friends and acquaintances expanded greatly. If I had been working at a factory or in some similar job, those opportunities would not have been possible. This was an unexpected benefit that arose from our rental operations. We had started in desperation in order to solve our initial difficulties in Chicago, but I truly came to feel that in our lives we cannot know what things and what actions will bring us happiness.

Madre Francisca and Professor Shochi

As we entered the 1960s, 15 years had already passed after the end of the Pacific War, and visitors from Japan and South America increased considerably. They brought us detailed information about current circumstances of relatives and friends scattered in Japan and Peru.

In a number of cases, the news they brought us evoked regret and sadness. Those of an earlier generation and friends who had helped us in our youth in Japan and Peru were reaching a time when they passed on. I was greatly moved when I learned of the passing of the beloved Madre Francisca, who had been revered by the Japanese in Peru.

In 1899, Madre Francisca left France for Peru, where she had devoted her entire life to aiding and nurturing Japanese immigrants. 1899 was precisely the year when the first Japanese immigrants set foot in Peru. For over 50 years, Madre Francisca worked at the Dos de Mayo Charity Hospital, where she treated and comforted thousands of Japanese. Upon reaching Peru, many contract immigrants soon fell ill with contagious diseases such as malaria, typhus and dysentery. Most of them were taken to Madre Francisca's hospital.

In the early days, I have been told, because the equipment and everything else at the hospital was inadequate, the Madre used her own funds to purchase necessary items and medications. She even went out to buy meat and eggs for the patients. Among the many Japanese immigrants who spent their last hours at the hospital, there were many who, in high fever, grasped her hands and called out, "*Okaasan!* (Mother!)," as she kept vigil over them.

Not long after we opened our shop in Ica in 1936, I came down with typhus and also came to receive the care of Madre Francisca. Everyday, the Madre would come to see the patients one by one. She would put a hand on a forehead or say in encouragement, "You will soon be well." In 1957, at the age of 91, our Madre also passed on.

Visitors also brought us heartwarming news—there were many happy reports of marriages, births and success in business. An incident that vividly remains with me was the visit of Professor Shochi, who had devoted his life to developing a unique method of educating children with birth defects. Professor Shochi was then the head of the Handicap Shinomi Gakuen in Fukuoka, Japan.

While on a lecture tour of the United States, he stopped in Chicago and visited us at our home. Professor Shochi brought a 16-millimeter film and many slides from Japan. He wanted to show the Japanese in Chicago what was being carried out at his school. I immediately brought the matter to the attention of Reverend Kubose of the nearby

Chicago Buddhist Association. Reverend Kubose kindly allowed the use of the association's auditorium. The next day, the large hall overflowed with listeners. Much moved by Professor Shochi's lecture, everyone expressed support for his efforts; many immediately made monetary contributions. I was happy that I could be of some assistance to Professor Shochi.

Although my role had been only a minor one, I felt some satisfaction that I had been able to be of assistance to people. By that time, however, I was no longer a youth looking forward to a life of unlimited potential; white threads were now interspersed through my hair and I knew that my physical strength and stamina had passed their peak. This was natural. Although my outlook and emotions were the same as when I had immigrated to Peru as a young man, I was now well past the age of 50. It had come time to seriously consider what I would do in my retirement years.

Our first home in Chicago at Sedgwick and Division streets.

Chapter Twelve. Hawaii—A Paradise of Sea and Sun

Facing a "New Life Cycle"

By the late 1960s, our life in Chicago had become financially secure. My wife, no longer tied to the care of our children, still went out whenever she found an opportunity to work, but it was no longer an absolute necessity that she did so. I had stopped working at outside jobs, for it had become financially feasible that I concentrate only on our rental operations.

By that time, however, I had to seriously consider what I would do after retirement. During the latter half of the 1960s I began to take trips whenever possible. Along with enjoying the sightseeing, I kept an eye out for an appropriate place to settle in our later years. I traveled to many places throughout the United States, Japan and in South and Central America.

I still had not made a definite decision when, on Jan. 18, 1969, I reached my 60th birthday, a time in Asian cultures when one begins a new cycle of life. I had forgotten that it was my birthday and had, as usual, been involved with my daily activities and concerns. Much earlier I had assumed that my children would not understand the significance of the 60-year, Asian calendrical cycle; yet they remembered that it was an important event in Asian lives and had secretly arranged a surprise party. They took me to a large restaurant and celebrated the beginning of my new life cycle in a big way.

Made to wear an infant's red cap and red vest, I was moved to emotion by being surrounded by my children and so many friends. But I was made aware, again, that my later years were not far away and I felt some ambivalence. I welcomed the event, yet I did not feel completely happy about it.

At that time, the biggest problem for us was deciding on an appropriate place to retire. Of course we considered spending our retirement years in Chicago. We had many friends and relatives there and all our children were there. We knew that in our old age we would not be alone in Chicago. At Thanksgiving, Christmas, New Year's, or on other holidays we could expect to spend lively and happy gatherings with our children and their families.

We felt, however, there were a number of problems with spending our leisure years in Chicago. First of all, it was too far from Japan. I could not deny when I thought of our retirement years that I retained a longing to visit the places of my youth.

Also, while we could bear Chicago's wintery conditions while we were in good health, it would become a problem if our health declined.

Chicago is commonly called "The Windy City." Often, it is buffeted with fierce winds that come in over Lake Michigan. I had once undergone the unnerving experience of being buried in snow while in my own automobile and having to be rescued by the Chicago Fire Department.

At my 60th birthday party, one of my friends said, "With this new cycle one returns to childhood." In my first childhood, however, I knew I had already passed through many trying days of winter in Hokkaido; I did not look forward to facing such severe winters again during my "new childhood."

As I grew older, the hectic activity and noise of Chicago had gradually come to seem bothersome. Like many other retired persons, the dynamic "busy-ness" of a gigantic, constantly changing metropolis now seemed to be burdensome, and I began to long for a place where we could lead a settled and quiet life.

Postponing Retirement

The first alternative to retiring in Chicago that came to mind was Japan. For some time, I had held vague expectations that eventually we might spend our later years in Japan. I began to seriously investigate that possibility.

In 1971, I returned to Japan by myself to look for a place where we could retire. I traveled throughout Japan, from Hokkaido to Kyushu, to find a suitable site.

I decided that a likely site for our retirement might be the prefecture of Izu. I spent two nights in the city of Ito and went to five sites along the Izu Peninsula where vacation homes were being sold. Izu had a relatively mild climate and was not far from Tokyo, yet had vacation homes available at prices we could afford. Those homes were not far from shopping areas and medical facilities. And, most importantly, I felt certain that my wife would like the area.

As I narrowed my choices, however, I began to feel an inexplicable uneasiness. I had dreamt for so long of retiring in Japan, but now I felt reluctant to take decisive action. I was not uneasy because we would be separated from our children or because we had no friends or acquaintances in the area. Financial concerns or our health were not factors, either. Even so, I remained troubled.

A number of our friends had urged us to retire in Mexico or Spain, but I had felt a similar uneasiness when I considered those countries as retirement sites. Was it an attachment to America, where I had spent a quarter of a century? Or, was it that I had lost my attachment to my original "motherland" in my close to 50 years of being abroad?

I had felt that I was truly Japanese, but I knew now, without a doubt, there had been a decisive change within me. It may be, I reflected, that Japan had become for me, just another country.

While I hesitated to make a final move, I received an urgent telegram from my wife in Chicago: "Lakeside building burned down. Return quickly." Without making a decision about acquiring a home for our retirement, I dropped all negotiations and returned to Chicago.

The Lakeside apartment building had not completely burned down. The fire had apparently started near a back porch, destroying six apartments at the rear of the building. By the time I reached Chicago, attorneys were handling the matter of damage and insurance payments, so there was nothing compelling left for me to do. There had been no need for me to return; but because of that incident our plans for retirement in Izu were postponed.

Two years later, I made a third trip back to Japan with my wife and her sister from Peru. It was a wonderful, happy occasion. The Yoshinagas, my wife's family, which had been scattered in Peru, Japan and the U.S. since 1944, was reunited after 30 years. But, yet again, we returned to the U.S. without deciding to retire permanently in Japan.

In this way, my goal of retiring at the age of 60 was postponed. Days passed without reaching a decision. The question was settled, unexpectedly, during the fall and winter of 1973 when my wife began to suffer from severe neuralgia. We took the advice of her physician and decided to spend some time in the warmer climate of Hawaii. With only one suitcase, we boarded a plane to leave Chicago, which was being buffeted by fierce Arctic winds, to fly to an entirely different world.

We were able to go to Hawaii, as if on a casual vacation, because of the concern and kindness of our second son, Arthur. After graduating from college, Arthur worked as an accountant in Chicago and had also spent some time with the Internal Revenue Service. He had long suffered with an asthmatic condition, however, that had been made worse by the deteriorating environment in the city. Besides, he had grown weary of being part of a "minority group" in Chicago, and, in February 1972, he had left by himself to move to Hawaii.

Arthur found a position as an accountant in Honolulu and had settled there. When he learned that even with much treatment his mother's neuralgic condition was not improving, he immediately sent us two airline tickets and invited us to stay in the condominium apartment he had just bought in Waikiki. Tears came to my wife's eyes when she learned of her son's concern for her.

A "Guarantee" from Another Retiree

Just as Arthur had assured us, Hawaii was a wondrous place, so different from Chicago, where bitter, cold winter winds swept in over Lake Michigan. It was the middle of January, but people were surfing on the waves off of Waikiki, while others were relaxing and playing on the beach. Sunlight poured down and the pure, blue sky seemed to reach up forever into space. "In this environment may wife's illness might improve," I thought, and was again grateful for Arthur's concern.

Our days during that first trip to Hawaii were like a dream. My wife, who had been so afflicted that she had difficulty walking, began to improve with every passing day. In two or three weeks she was able to leave the apartment to take walks along the nearby beach. Such walks became a part of our daily schedule. We had come to Hawaii for the sake of her recuperation, but now it began to seem that we were on a vacation.

I immediately took a liking to Hawaii, but I did not even think we would retire here. We needed to know more about Hawaii before we could even consider it as a retirement site.

One day, we went out on our usual walk along the beach at Waikiki and sat down on a bench in the shade of coconut trees to watch people surfing and swimming nearby. An older couple sat near our bench and serenely looked out to sea. I forget who initiated it, but we began casually to converse with the other couple.

The man and the woman, who seemed to be in their late seventies, were visitors from New York. The husband, now retired, had been a business executive with many international contacts. They said they were enjoying their later years by taking trips to different locales all over the world. Because he had traveled so extensively when he was active in business, the husband was very knowledgeable about different places. When I mentioned that I was originally from Hokkaido, he said that he had traveled to Sapporo and also mentioned Nemuro and other towns in Hokkaido. When I said, "Before the war, I had a business in Ica in Peru," he responded, "My grandfather had an importing business in Arequipa, so I know Ica well."

We found ourselves completely compatible in spirit and outlook and spoke a while about Japan and South America. The conversation then turned toward our stages of life and I mentioned that we were looking for a place to retire. He immediately said, "Then, it must be Hawaii. I guarantee that. . . . You are Japanese," he reasoned, "but when you have lived abroad as long as you have, you are different from the Japanese who lived their whole lives in Japan. Especially because you've lived in America for more than 25 years, if you return to live in Japan, you are sure to run into unexpected problems. I know it's hard to cut off your attachments to Japan, but you can go back on trips to Japan. You don't have to move there permanently. . .

"Hawaii is the perfect place for you two to retire," he continued. "This is part of America so, basically, even if you move from Chicago to Honolulu there'll be no problems of adapting or changing your attitudes and the way you live. All these will be necessary if you move to Japan. And, Hawaii is different from the mainland, where everything is controlled by Caucasians. In politics, business, the social and cultural areas, second and third generation Japanese here have built leading roles. You won't have to be always conscious of being in a small, minority group if you move to Hawaii.

"And, look, as you can see right now, the climate is perfect; there's no pollution, no typhoons, no earthquakes. Can there be a better place than this? Hawaii is really a paradise that brings with it a real understanding of Japanese feelings and Japanese thinking; yet, it has a very stable American political system and an American economic system. The climate is as warm as Peru. And, Japan is not so far away."

There was so much truth in the words of this older couple, who had traveled throughout the world and came every winter to spend a month or so in Hawaii. Although we had come to Hawaii to help my wife recover from her illness, we began to seriously consider Hawaii as a place for our retirement.

Mass Relocation of Family Members

My wife and I grew more and more inclined to the idea of retiring in Hawaii. For a retired couple, living on old age benefits, the living costs in Hawaii, 25 to 40 percent higher than on the mainland, would be a matter of concern. But we had the income from the apartment buildings in Chicago, so finances were not a big problem.

We decided, finally, that we would retire to Hawaii and began looking for a home. At first, we thought of buying a single-family home; but we then considered the effort needed, even as we entered our later years, to maintain such a home. We decided that a condominium apartment might be more suitable. We bought a two-bedroom apartment on Kuhio Avenue in Waikiki in June 1974, five months after we arrived in Hawaii.

Soon after we bought the apartment, we returned to Chicago to settle our affairs there. It took about a month to arrange to make our move to live in Hawaii permanently. Moving was quite simple. For the two of us, standing at the edge of retirement, there were not many possessions that we could not abandon. Everything could be placed in two trunks. Our apartment in Honolulu was completely furnished. Although they were only items of modest quality, we did not need to take much clothing to the "nakedly" casual, warm environment of Hawaii. We distributed our furnishings and everything else in our home to our children in Chicago and with only two trunks, as if going on a vacation trip, my wife and I went to O'hare Airport in Chicago. It was a lighthearted move to retirement that needed no pomp or ceremony. We became, in this manner, residents of the "Paradise of the Pacific."

Our life in Hawaii fully met our expectations—my wife and I were content. We felt a little lonely because our children and grandchildren could not come to visit whenever they wanted to, but there was more than enough to make up for it. We wrote to those in Chicago about our truly wonderful life in Hawaii and related our satisfaction with our decision. We felt that our children would be reassured by such reports and that they could, without concern over our circumstances, focus attention on their lives and work.

Instead, our move to Hawaii brought about an unexpected response from members of our family. Even before we could get settled, members of our family began, one by one, to ask whether they could follow us and move to Hawaii. I knew that the cost of living in Hawaii was much higher than on the mainland, that employment opportunities were generally more limited here, and that wage levels were lower than in Chicago. Of course, I was happy that our children and grandchildren wanted to be near us, but I could not agree wholeheartedly that they should move to Hawaii if it would create hardships for them. In spite of our concerns, however, our children grew more and more enthusiastic about moving to Hawaii.

Actually, the first to move to Hawaii was not one of our children but Rokuichi Kudo and his wife. Mr. and Mrs. Kudo had retired many years earlier and had been living in Chicago. Like us, they were severely inconvenienced by winters in Chicago. They joined us soon after we settled in Hawaii. Then, their fifth son, Eigo, who had married our oldest daughter, Elsa, moved to Hawaii. In the following four years, our third son, Richard, came over alone, then our third daughter, Martha, and her family and our fourth daughter, Deanna, moved to Hawaii. Of our eight children, five followed us to Hawaii. Only our oldest son, Carlos, our second daughter, Irma, and our fourth son, Mark, remain in Chicago.

The "Closed" Nature of the Hawaiian Community

As I had warned, our children who came to Hawaii faced many barriers—many times, they thought they would have to abandon their dreams of living in Hawaii. We were retired, but they had to find means to support themselves and their families. The problems they faced were different and much deeper than ours. Because of their situation, they became aware of an aspect of Hawaii that my wife and I had not seen.

One of the first problems our children faced when they came to Hawaii was their inability to find suitable employment. I had expected that they would have such problems, but the reasons for the problem were not what I had thought. They were not hindered by the limitations of the job market in Hawaii, but because they were "outsiders" who had no "connections" in Hawaii. In other words, they found that in Hawaii there was a special type of "exclusivity." The people of Hawaii fostered strong relational bonds, similar to what I had seen in Japanese villages. One consequence of that was the extreme caution they used when dealing with "outsiders."

The same type of closed, tightly knit communities can also be found in ethnic communities and in small rural towns on the mainland. It is, in that sense, not particularly extraordinary. But in Chicago we had constantly been under pressure to conform to the dominant white culture and its behavioral patterns to the point that it had become "common sense" to think and behave and even to respond emotionally in such a manner. We were not ready for the situation in Hawaii.

In the white-dominated society of the mainland United States, irrational racial discrimination pervaded everywhere, so it could not be called a completely open society. Although white culture was not dominant in Hawaii, I nevertheless found barriers that were different from the racial discrimination on the mainland.

Many times I heard Caucasians from the U.S. mainland complain about their difficulty in finding jobs in Hawaii. They tended, short-sightedly, to take this as a form of "reverse discrimination." But one must consider the special characteristics of Hawaii. The problems that Caucasian newcomers from the mainland face in Hawaii are not unique to them. Our Japanese American children, without exception, had great difficulty in finding jobs in Hawaii because they did not have "roots" or "connections" when they first arrived.

Surprisingly, even in such a modern and Americanized place like Hawaii, there remained a "closedness" similar to that of an ancient Japanese village. In Hawaii, the special human ties based on family, geographical origins, etc., are not as clear and strong as in Japan—but similar human relationships are woven into a complex network, forming an "organic entity." Our family, having just arrived in Hawaii, did not have points of contact with this organic and living network which formed Hawaiian society.

This type of "closed" society, however, differed from the discrimination based on race in that it was not absolutely exclusive. If one, through some opportunity, gained a link with one point of the network, it became possible to make contact and gain acceptance with all other points of the network. One is no longer an "outsider."

This is evidenced, I feel, by the experiences of our oldest daughter's husband, who has become widely accepted as a member of the Hawaiian community and has even become active with the Honolulu Chamber of Commerce. This would have been impossible in the white society of the mainland, where race is often a major condition for becoming an "insider" in the community.

Moreover, on the mainland, even if one had extraordinary talent and qualifications, not all areas of society would necessarily be open to him. But, in Hawaii, all one needed to do was to build relationships with those who had firm roots in Hawaii.

Our son, Arthur, who was the first to move to Hawaii, spent several weeks looking for work. He could not find anything appropriate and nearly gave up hope of moving to Hawaii. But on the night before he returned to Chicago he met a Japanese American attorney in a bar at his hotel and, through that acquaintance, found a job as an accountant in Honolulu.

Once in that job, more avenues opened up to him and he now has many connections within the Honolulu community. As can be seen from his case, the "closed" Hawaiian society is different from that of white society in the mainland United States.

"Kotonks" and "Buddhaheads"

Another aspect of the "closedness" which members of our family encountered in Hawaii is the result of the antagonism that Japanese

Americans in Hawaii retain against Japanese Americans on the mainland. In Hawaii, Japanese Americans from the mainland are referred to as "kotonks." On the other hand, Japanese from the mainland use equally derogatory terms such as "Buddhahead" or "pineapple" to refer to Japanese Americans from Hawaii. I have heard that these terms originated among the youths of both areas who first were forced to have continuing contact during WWII. It then gradually entered general usage, I am told, in both communities.

During the war, Japanese Americans were assigned to special military units. Often, I have heard, because of differences in upbringing and ways of thinking, misunderstandings arose between the Japanese Americans from Hawaii and those from the mainland. When those differences developed into physical confrontations, those from the mainland usually could not contend with the more robust Japanese Americans from Hawaii. When they were knocked down against walls and floors in their barracks, there was a hollow sound, "kotonk," when their heads hit obstacles—implying, of course, that their heads were empty.

On the other hand, Japanese Americans from the mainland held the attitude that even if they were physically stronger, Japanese Americans from Hawaii were headstrong and stubborn and could not accept other views. They labelled the Hawaiians "Buddhaheads" and also called them "pineapples," viewing them as persons who had only "the ability to raise pineapples."

These derogatory epithets still have currency at a time when there is much movement between the mainland and the islands. The sense of alienation and opposition expressed by such terms still remain to some degree. According to Hawaii Japanese Americans, the Japanese Americans from the mainland are "flashy" dressers and talkers, and try whenever possible to express disdain for Hawaiian Japanese Americans. At the same time, Hawaii Japanese Americans perceive their mainland counterparts as being subservient to white cultural patterns and as having no confidence or fundamental self- respect.

We were unaware of such differences in attitudes and relationships at first. Our children felt confused when they were treated as "kotonks" and, in some cases, were regarded as even more foreign than whites from the mainland. They were accustomed to being regarded as "alien" by whites on the mainland, but to face similar prejudice in Hawaii by those who had the same ancestors and same physical features, they naturally did not know how to respond.

We eventually came to see, however, that these types of problems were essentially different from what we had encountered elsewhere in our lives. When we became accustomed to wearing "aloha shirts" and "muumuus," when we came to understand that "no more" meant in Hawaii that "something is lacking" and not that something "no longer exists," when we came to understand that the Hawaiian usage of "the kind" was equivalent to the Japanese term *"ano"* to make unspecified but understood references, and came to use such terms naturally in our speech, we no longer were "kotonks" and had already become full "citizens" within the Hawaiian community.

A "Tropical, Ocean Culture"

It has been almost 10 years since I have moved to Hawaii. If I have learned one thing, it is the obvious fact that Hawaii is one corner of an ocean-oriented Polynesian cultural area. This, of course, is a major factor in any understanding of Hawaii. Hawaii is basically a place where the ocean-oriented Polynesian culture had come to fuse with other cultures in complex ways.

Differing from Japan, Peru or the U.S. mainland where I have lived, everything in my life in Hawaii has been tied to our tropical sun and sea. The people here are, as it were, "naked" or almost so and their basic mode of life is one of uncovered and open living; it may be taken as life as open and natural as for a newborn infant.

Before Westerners arrived, Hawaiians had no strong custom, I am told, of distinguishing the inside of a home from the outside. For them, the inside of a home was simply an extension of natural, environmental space; they lived in conformity with nature.

In not differentiating between interior and exterior space, indigenous Hawaiians had, I feel, something in common with white culture. Westerners built homes with walls on four sides and were much involved with the idea of "privacy," yet they wore the same clothing and shoes whether they were within the home or outside the home. If we hold that Hawaiians lived in an overwhelmingly open and natural space with no "inside" space, whites can be said to approach the question from the opposite direction—that is, they tended to extend their interior space to embrace the entire "outside space."

In contrast, Japanese culture was different in every way. For the Japanese, who actually speak of their homes as the "inside," the distinction between "inside" and "outside" is extremely important. Japanese culture prescribes a difference between life "inside" the home and that "outside" the home. When one returns from "outside," one removes one's shoes and "steps up" into the home. It is also common for one to also change into a different set of clothing inside the home.

In Japan, however, at the boundary between what is completely "interior" space and what is completely "exterior," there are areas which belong to neither. There are, for example, areas of the traditional Japanese home with earthen floors and engawa, or walkways extending outward around the Japanese home. The areas with earthen floors are probably an extension of "outside" into the "inside." On the other hand, the outside walkways constitute a projection of "inside" space outward. Similar spaces exist in Polynesian and white cultures—porches, sun rooms, atria, etc., all fall into such an "in-between" category.

In Hawaii, such elements from different cultures blended to form a unique culture. In the early 19th century, Puritan missionaries from New England made a strenuous effort to have the half-naked indigenous Hawaiians wear more clothes. But the stifling and restrictive clothing they brought were not suitable for Hawaii. Such clothing became accepted only in the altered form of "aloha shirts" and muumuus.

The Western custom of wearing shoes, with noticeable Japanese influences, became more accepted when sandals and slippers became available. At almost every home in Hawaii today, it is the custom to remove one's shoes before entering, due in part to the ease with which sandals and slippers can be put on and removed, combined with the Japanese custom of making strict distinctions between "inside" and "outside" spaces.

This interesting blend of cultures can also be seen in Hawaiian architecture. The basic style in Hawaii is Western, in which all sides of a house are enclosed by walls. Many homes, however, have large sliding glass panels which create a feeling of extension of "outside" space. Often, fixed interior walls are kept to a minimum in order to further promote a sense of openness through the interior spaces of a home. There is also the "lanai," which seems to corresond to Western porches, the Japanese areas with earthen floors, and the Polynesian home itself.

Modern Hawaiian lifestyles, therefore, can be viewed as an adaptation of Western and Asian cultures to the tropical climate of Hawaii's tropical and ocean-oriented culture. What is interesting is the fact that in the process of blending elements from many cultures, everything is still fundamentally influenced by the sun and the sea.

I presently live on Ala Moana Boulevard in Honolulu in a condominium apartment. When I go out on its balcony, or "lanai," the unending, open Hawaiian sky and deep blue sea spread out before my eyes; the inland vista provides a backdrop of muted, green mountain patterns often found in the tropics.

As I sit out on the balcony by myself and look out over the ocean, images of my past arise as an enveloping mist to fill my mind. Someone said, "When one recalls experiences of the past, they light up in themselves to be like dreams." My dreams, quite definitely, span many changes and different backdrops. Filled with impossible hopes, encountering obstacles to attaining such hopes, then resurrecting such hopes again, the days of my past form a continuum. Now, looking back at earlier days, I feel no regrets. After all this, I feel, it is well that I have had this life.

Of course, Hawaii has its own limitations, but for me, Hawaii is literally "a paradise on earth." I have found, here, a word that is appropriate to end these recollections. The term is "aloha," and it best expresses the essence of Hawaii. I have heard that "aloha" basically means "love," but in this case it differs from the Christian understanding of "love." Here, the term seems to be more directly connected to the earth that sustains us and to acceptance of human emotions. In that sense, "aloha" includes everything that I have sought for over many years. If that is true, I need not now write more words. Simply to say "aloha" suffices—with it everything else that I feel is communicated. I feel much happiness that I can end my recollections with this word. So, again, I shall say, "aloha. . . ."

Seiichi Higashide
August, 1981
Honolulu, Hawaii

Afterword

I am now 84 years old. Our oldest daughter and son are both blessed with grandchildren. The children are now mature enough, spiritually and materially, to want to read an English account of their father's book and to make it available to friends and acquaintances who have requested it. They began working on the English translation of *Namida no Adios*.

Much earlier, friends in Central and South America suggested that if an English version were prepared, it could readily be translated into Spanish and Portuguese so that the hardships encountered by the early Japanese emigrants could be appreciated and understood by their children and grandchildren. Many persons have looked forward to it, so I am very grateful that this English translation now can be offered.

It is over ten years since the original Japanese volume was published. During that period, the question of forced internment of those of Japanese ancestry during the Pacific War was brought to consideration in the U.S. Congress, which debated the illegality of the internment and the issue of reparations to the internees. From the start, I sent letters to members of Congress and to others closely concerned with the matter to request that internees from Peru and other Central and South American countries be included in their considerations. Despite such efforts, those of us who were interned from "third countries" were denied inclusion under redress legislation.

For a time, I felt that all avenues for redress had been exhausted, but I recalled the Japanese tale of "Sakura Sogoro" and decided that there still was the possibility of making a direct appeal to the President of the United States. I sent a letter addressed directly to President Ronald Reagan, asking him to take measures to correct the inequitable decision made by the Congress. My letter was eventually forwarded to the U.S. Justice Department.

As much as I was elated to see that a few exceptions were made for some of the Peruvian deportees, including us, it is incomprehensible that not all of the Latin American internees were included. The irony of this plight is that within a family some have been included while others have not. As an example, a mother has been included but her children, who were minors in camp, were not. Her oldest son, after serving in the Army during the Korean Conflict, was told by the INS to re-enter via Canada. Consequently, the date of his entry does not reflect the retroactive date to the internment period. There are many other similar stories. It is imperative that the U.S. proceed to complete the repair by extending redress to all the Latin American deportees whose rights, wealth, homes and reputation were taken away. It is my fervent prayer and request of this my third and final motherland.

Acknowledgements

The work on redress and the English publication of my book were made possible by our daughter, Elsa, and her husband Eigo Kudo who both cooperated in every way with my wife and me, even while pressed with the many requirements of their individual lives. I am forever grateful for their efforts and wish here to express my appreciation.

I also wish to express thanks to my translator, Clifford Miyashiro, and Arnold Hiura, editor.

Human memories seem to be accurate, yet cannot be fully relied upon. Should there be any errors in this text, the responsibility is solely my own. To reawaken and to relive memories, I have often consulted the works listed in the following bibliography. If these works had not been available, I do not know how many inaccuracies I would have perpetrated. I have not annotated my statements, but I would like to assert that many of them are supported in those works. I wish to express my gratitude for the efforts of their authors.

Seiichi Higashide, 1993

Bibliography

1. Ito, Rikiya, et. al., *Zai-Peru Hojin Nanajugo-Nen no Ayumi* (Seventy-five Years of Experiences of Japanese in Peru), (Peru Shimpo-sha), Lima, 1974.
2. Weglyn, Michi, *American Detention Camps* (translated into Japanese by Seiji Yamaoka), Tokyo (Seiji Koho Center), 1974. (English title: *Years of Infamy: The Untold Story of America's Concentration Camps*)
3. Koyama, Yukinori; *The Detention in the U.S. of Japanese from Peru—The Case of Rokuichi Kudo,* Rekishi Hyoron (July, 1981).
4. Barnhart, Edward N., *Japanese Internees from Peru,* Pacific Historical Review, 31 (May, 1962).
5. Daniels, Roger, *Concentration Camps, U.S.A.: Japanese Americans and World War II,* New York, Holt, Rinehart & Winston (1971).
6. Emerson, John K., *The Japanese Thread: A Life in the U.S. Foreign Service.* Holt, Rinehart & Winston, New York. (1978).
7. Gardiner, C. Harvey, *The Japanese and Peru: 1873-1973,* Albuquerque, University of New Mexico Press (1975).
8. Girdner, Audrie and Loftis, Anne, *The Great Betrayal,* Toronto, MacMillan (1969).
9. Petersen, William, *Japanese Americans,* New York, Random House (1971).

Epilogue

Just as certain individuals championed the Japanese Americans' right to gain an apology and compensation from the U.S. government for violations they endured during World War II, Seiichi Higashide pioneered in calling for similar redress for the Japanese Latin Americans, many of whom lived side-by-side with Japanese Americans in Department of Justice camps.

In 1981, Congress formed the Commission on Wartime Relocation and Internment of Civilians to assess the impact of Executive Order 9066 and similar government directives that led to the wartime imprisonment of persons of Japanese ancestry in the United States. To carry out their job, the commissioners heard twenty-two days of testimony from more than 750 witnesses, of whom Higashide was one. During the time of the congressional hearings, Higashide also corresponded with other former internees to urge them to participate in the redress struggle and sent the Commission telegrams urging inclusion of the Japanese Latins. His efforts contributed to the first official acknowledgment of the prisoner exchange involving Latin Americans, contained in the Commission's report, *Personal Justice Denied* (p. 305). The report greatly aided subsequent efforts to achieve redress for Japanese Latin Americans, a struggle Higashide participated in until his death in 1997.

The Commission approved an official apology and individual reparation payments by the U.S. government to Americans of Japanese ancestry and permanent residents who were of Japanese ancestry, and approved the establishment of a community education fund. In 1988 Congress passed the Civil Liberties Act (Public Law 100-383) to implement the recommendations of the Commission. Two years later, the government began to distribute letters of apology and a token compensation payment of $20,000 to each survivor or heir. During the interim, however, the government declared that, as the Japanese Latin Americans were "illegal aliens" at the time of their imprisonment, they were not eligible for redress. The former internees were able to win only two exceptions to this order of exclusion: persons who had remained in the United States and been awarded permanent residency retroactive to their date of entry, and children born in the camps. Eventually 189 Japanese Latin Americans were included in the redress under these provisions and received the same redress as Japanese Americans.

It was not until after the government issued the first reparation payment in 1990 that the majority of the Japanese Latin Americans became aware of their exclusion from redress. As more internees received letters from the government denying their applications, the momentum of redress activism grew.

In 1991 a group of Japanese Peruvian families formed the Japanese Peruvian Oral History Project (JPOHP) to collect and preserve interviews with former internees. As the scope of the redress denials came to light, the group expanded its purpose to provide internees with legal and referral information. Because of the educational and community outreach efforts of the JPOHP, Japanese American groups in the forefront of the redress movement embraced the Japanese Latin American internment experience as a part of Japanese American history and a part of the larger redress struggle.

By 1994 the JPOHP had participated in two Japanese American redress delegations to Washington, D.C. Government representatives maintained that overturning the denials of redress under the Civil Liberties Act would not likely be achieved by administrative or legislative efforts. The JPOHP decided to put the Japanese Latin American issue before the court.

A legal team, composed of civil rights attorneys in Los Angeles and aided by the American Civil Liberties Union of Southern California, formed to research and craft a complaint for a class action lawsuit. Carmen Mochizuki, Alice Nishimoto, and Henry Koshio Shima, former internees living in Los Angeles, stepped forward to act as named plaintiffs. Sumiko Tsuboi and Masaji Sugimaru of Japan also joined the suit to represent persons deported to Japan during the war in a hostage exchange program.

Recognizing that a lawsuit might take years to resolve, the JPOHP recruited a group of community volunteers to launch a public awareness campaign to urge the government to grant redress to Japanese Latin Americans. The group named itself Campaign for Justice–Redress Now for Japanese Latin Americans! The JPOHP, the American Civil Liberties Union, the Japanese American Citizens League, and the National Coalition for Redress/Reparations became founding organizational members of the coalition and provided support for grassroots organizing, lobbying, and media relations.

On August 28, 1996, the attorneys for Japanese Latin Americans filed a class action lawsuit *(Mochizuki et al. v U.S., No.)* in the

United States District Court of Southern California. The case began its slow progress through the courts.

In the meantime, Campaign for Justice was building on grassroots lobbying and educational presentations to community and academic groups, in all conducting nearly two hundred presentations in the United States, Japan, and Peru. The Campaign garnered national and international media coverage through dozens of press conferences and actions. The coalition sent nine delegations to Washington, D.C., which gained the support of more than eighty members of Congress, as well as White House and Department of Justice officials.

In 1998, when parties settled the *Mochizuki v U.S.* case, the Department of Justice offered a letter of apology signed by the President and $5,000 to each eligible Japanese Latin American internee or surviving heir, to be paid from the remainder of the Civil Liberties Act Public Education Fund. If funds ran out before all Japanese Latin American claimants received the reparation, however, the government assumed no legal obligation to pay the remaining claims.

To Japanese Latin Americans, who sought the same redress as Japanese Americans, the settlement offer seemed bleak, but the end of the Civil Liberties Act was imminent and the future of the litigation uncertain. The highest priority was that internees, many of them elderly or ill, receive some measure of justice while they still lived. The settlement, if not equal, would provide something for everyone. The majority of Japanese Latin American internees decided to accept the offer. Four factors influenced their decision: (1) the U.S. government gave repeated assurances that the money left in the Civil Liberties Act fund would cover all the Japanese Latin American claims; (2) the White House Administration was willing to issue a statement promising to support legislation to augment the fund should the money run out (statement issued June 12, 1998); (3) the settlement included a provision that the internees were not barred from seeking further reparations through an act of Congress; and (4) internees also had the right to refuse the settlement and continue litigation.

The final settlement agreement gave former internees less than six weeks to apply. Despite the Campaign for Justice's vigorous efforts to publicize the settlement through press releases and community forums in the United States, Japan, and Peru, seventeen internees missed the deadline to apply. The U.S. government denied their claims. Hundreds more survivors are believed to exist, but because they did not know about the lawsuit, they were not able officially to refuse the settlement and have lost their legal right to sue the government. The Department of Justice also refused to allow attorneys for Japanese Latin Americans to ensure proper processing of claims.

Seven hundred and thirty-one Japanese Latin Americans filed to claim the benefits. More than thirty people were deemed ineligible; the government was unable to locate twelve people; and five applicants died awaiting redress. Nineteen of the Japanese Latin Americans rejected the settlement; several filed lawsuits to continue the struggle for redress.

On August 10, 1998, the Civil Liberties Act expired. Within two months, the Department of Justice announced that they could not pay the majority of the Japanese Latin Americans. The Office of Redress Administration, which ran the reparations program, closed its doors on February 5, 1999. Its final report stated that, of the 731 Japanese Latin Americans who filed for the settlement, only 145 were paid. In September 1999, the Department of Justice approved the use of agency funds to cover the remaining claims. Payments were scheduled to be sent to 528 Japanese Latin American claimants by March 2000.

The Mochizuki settlement provided internees with an acknowledgment that a wrongdoing had been perpetrated against them by the United States during World War II. The settlement did not, however, admit or recognize any legal obligation by the United States to provide redress for those violations and fails to address the gravity of the human rights violations committed. The forced deportation of civilians, thrusting civilians into a war zone, and putting civilians to hard labor, all violate the Geneva Convention and existing international customary law. The U.S. government characterized the settlement as a complete resolution. Others, including many of the internees felt the settlement did not resolve the issue and should not set the standard for redress of war crimes. Even those who agreed to the settlement did so with the intent to fight for a more just resolution.

Seiichi Higashide passed away in 1997, before his dream of redress for all interned Japanese Latin American could be realized.

He had faith, however, that the United States would rise to its responsibility and provide just compensation to all.

Campaign for Justice continues through litigation and legislative efforts to secure redress for all Japanese Latin American internees of World War II.

JULIE SMALL
November 1999

GRACE SHIMIZU, director of the Japanese Peruvian Oral History Project, contributed to the research for this essay.

References

Barnhart, Edward N. "Japanese Internees from Peru," *Pacific Historical Review,* vol. 31, June 1962.

Commission on Wartime Relocation and Internment of Civilians. *Personal Justice Denied.* Appendix D. Seattle and London: University of Washington Press and The Civil Liberties Public Education Fund, 1997.

Daniels, Roger, ed. *Japanese Americans: From Relocation to Redress.* Revised edition. Seattle and London: University of Washington Press, 1991.

Emmerson, John K. *The Japanese Thread: A Life in the U.S. Foreign Service.* New York: Holt, Rinehart and Winston, 1978.

Gardiner, C. Harvey. "The Latin-American Japanese and World War II." In *From Relocation to Redress,* ed. Roger Daniels, pp. 142-45. Seattle and London: University of Washington Press, 1991.

_____. *Pawns in a Triangle of Hate: The Peruvian Japanese and the United States.* Seattle and London: University of Washington Press, 1981.

Weglyn, Michi Nishiura. *Years of Infamy: The Untold Story of America's Concentration Camps.* Updated edition. Seattle and London: University of Washington Press, 1996.

Index

Acosta, Marta, 107, 108
  riots after death of, 108-112
air transportation, Peruvian, 121-122
alcoholic beverages, in Peru, 51-52, 65, 87
Anderson, Ms. (INS officer), 178
"anti-citizenship" detainees, 167, 176
anti-Japanese movement. *See also*
  arrests of Japanese; deportation of Japanese; relocation of Japanese, within Peru
  Acosta riots, 108-112
  and blacklist, 114-116, 117, 118, 120
  Chinese response to, 110-111
  and earthquake, 111-112
  effect on Japanese businesses, 126
  origins of, 77, 103-105, 108-111
  U.S. influence in, 103, 104, 105, 113-114
Araki, Mr., 48-49, 53, 65-66
Araki Company, 53, 56, 58, 65-67, 68, 78
arrests of Japanese
  of "people's uniform" wearers, 127-128
  random, 125, 128-129
  of S. Higashide, 135-139
Aspengren, Deanna (neé Higashide), 220, 239
Banno, Akio, 107
Barber's Trade Association, Japanese, 105-108
baseball in Peru, 70
Bazar Bienvenida (Ica store)
  closing of, 151-154
  establishment of, 86, 88-95, 101-102
  theft from, 189-190
  during wartime, 116-117, 120, 126, 134
blacklist, in Peruvian anti-Japanese movement, 114-116, 117, 118, 120
bribes, 123, 125, 129
Bridgeton, description of, 189
Buddhism, 11-12, 171
burial
  of detainees in U.S., 171
  Incan (calaveras), 66-67
  of Japanese immigrants in Peru, 148-149
business practices, Japanese vs. American, 186-188, 190-191
calaveras, 66-67
Camp Kenedy, 157-160, 176
camps. *See* detention camps
CCC (Civilian Conservation Corps), 182
censorship of detainees' letters, 149
Central Japanese Association, 106, 113
Cerro revolution, 60-62
Chicago. *See* Higashide, Seiichi, in Chicago; housing, in Chicago
Chinese, and anti-Japanese movement, 110-111
citizenship, U.S. *See also* "anti-citizenship" detainees
  for detainees, 179
  detainees' movement against, 167, 176
  Higashide's attainment of, 223-224
Civilian Conservation Corps (CCC), 182
Collins, Wayne M., 179
Commercio, El, 114, 134
Consulate, Japanese. *See* Japanese Consulate, in Peru
contract workers, in Peru, 53-55, 97, 148
cotton growing, 71-72
Crystal City camp, 157, 158, 161, 164-171, 176, 179, 180
deportation of Japanese. *See also* Higashide, Seiichi, deportation of
  from Peru to Japan, 117, 119-120
  from Peru to U.S.
    in general, 125, 126, 127, 128-129, 132, 136, 140-141
    Peruvian government role in, 126-127, 142-143
  from U.S. to Japan, 178
depression, in Peru, 60-61, 68
detainees, German, 155, 164
detainees, Japanese. *See also* Higashide, Angelica (neé Yoshinaga) (wife), detainment of; Higashide, Seiichi, detainment of

anti-citizenship group of, 167, 176
attitude to U.S., 171-172
censorship of correspondence of, 149
children of, activities of, 165, 168-170
families of
reunion with detainees, 149-150, 155, 157, 160
separated families, problems of, 161-164
food for, 140, 146, 157, 166
funerals for, 171
health care for, 16
Japanese community leaders as, 117, 144, 146
leisure activities of, 166, 169-171
number of, 176, 177
in Panama, 144-147, 149-150, 155
in Peru, 117, 139-140
in post-war period
illegal immigrant status of, 163, 178, 223
prohibition of reentry to Peru, 162-163
release of, 176-177, 179
return to Japan by, 172-175
U.S. citizenship for, 179
reparations for Latin American, lack of, 245-246
resistance activities of, 159
schools for children of, 165, 168-170
self-government of, 164-165, 170
treatment of
at Camp Kenedy, 158-160
at Crystal City camp, 164-171
in New Orleans, 156-157
in Panama, 144-146, 149
in Peru, 139-140
on shipboard, 142, 155-156, 161
work assignments of, 145, 159-161, 164-165, 170
detention camps
Camp Kenedy, 157-160, 176
Crystal City camp, 157, 158, 161, 164-171, 176, 179, 180
Tule Lake camp, 176
Dongo, Juan, 102-103, 121, 123
earthquakes, in Peru, 111-112, 124
elderly Japanese in Peru, 69-70

elementary schools, Japanese
in detention camp, 165, 168-170
in Japan, 10, 21-22
in Peru, 68-70, 74, 79-81
Emerson, John K., 125
Executive Orders, 176,178
families of detainees. See detainees, Japanese, families of
food
for detainees, 140, 146, 157, 166
in Hokkaido, 12-14
at Seabrook Farms, 184
Francisca, Madre, 231
"free" immigrants, 97
Fujii, Chuzo, 55
Fukazawa, Kichihei, 11, 24
Fukazawa, Mr. (detainee at Camp Kenedy), 160-161
funerals for detainees, 171
Furuya, Tokijiro, 106-108
Furuya (detainee from Arequipa), 141
generation gap among immigrants
in Peru, 217-219
in U.S., 219-220
Guadalupe Middle School, 108
Hamano, Torakichi, 37, 43
Hatta, Ichiro, 199-200, 208
Hawaii
conflict between Japanese Americans in, 240-242
cultural aspects of, 242-243
exclusivity and discrimination in, 239-242
S. Higashide in, 235-237, 238, 243-244
Hayasaka, Hisashi, 105, 107
Hayashi, Heitaro, 88-90
Hayashi, Kishiro, 90
Hayashi Company, 88-91
health care
for detainees in U.S., 168
for immigrants in Peru, 231
Higa, Keiji, 105-107
Higashide, Angelica (neé Yoshinaga) (wife)
adjustment to American work ethic, 214
business activities of, in Peru, 94, 97, 101, 116-117, 134
in Chicago, 197, 198-199, 214
citizenship of, U.S., 223-224

detainment of, 150-154, 161
and detainment of husband, 123,
  130-131, 137, 140-141, 142
education of, 83-84, 86
marriage of, 78-79, 80-81, 86-87
neuralgia of, 235
at Seabrook Farms, 182, 183, 184
Higashide, Arthur (Arturo) (son)
  in Chicago, 197, 216, 222
  education of, 216, 222
  employment of, 222, 235
  in Hawaii, 235-236, 240
  at Seabrook Farms, 183-184
Higashide, Carlos (son)
  birth of, 103
  in Chicago, 216, 239
  in detention camp, 169
  education of, 169, 183, 216
  employment of, 216
  marriages of, 222
  at Seabrook Farms, 183
Higashide, Chie (neé Ishiwari), 222
Higashide, Deanna (daughter), 220,
  239
Higashide, Elsa (daughter). See Kudo,
  Elsa (neé Higashide)
Higashide, Irma (daughter). See Kudo,
  Irma (neé Higashide)
Higashide, Iwamatsu (father), 9-12, 17,
  19, 21, 22, 24, 202-203
Higashide, Mark (son), 220, 239
Higashide, Martha (daughter). See
  Shigio, Martha (Marta) (neé
  Higashide)
Higashide, Misao (sister), 12, 21, 27, 32
Higashide, Norio (cousin), 199-202, 201
Higashide, Richard (Ricardo) (son),
  195, 197, 220, 239
Higashide, Riyo, 9
Higashide, Seiichi
  birth of, 12
  businesses of
    apartment houses, 206-212, 225-
      230, 235
    Otani Company, 72-75, 81, 84-
      85
    (see also Bazar Bienvenida)
  in Chicago
    apartment house ownership,
      206-212, 225-230, 235
    early years, 197-204

employment, 194-195, 198-199
housing problems, 195-196, 197,
  205
move to, 194-197
relationships with other
  Japanese, 228-232
citizenship of, U.S., 223-224
decision to remain in U.S., 174,
  177-178
deportation of
  from Peru to Japan, attempted,
    62-65, 119-120
  from Peru to U.S., actual, 136,
    140-142
  from Peru to U.S., attempted,
    129-132, 136, 140-141
detainment of
  arrest, 135-139
  at Camp Kenedy, 157-161
  at Crystal City, 161, 164-171,
    179
  hiding to avoid, 133-135
  in Panama, 143-150, 155
  in Peru, 139-140
  release from, 179-180
  travels to, 140-142, 155-157
education of, 10, 21-22, 24-25, 28-33
immigration from Japan to Peru,
  35-43
employment of
  with Araki Company in Peru,
    53, 56, 58, 65-67, 68, 78
  architectural, 33-35, 58-59
  in Chicago, 194-195, 198-199
  in detention camp, 169
  in Japan, 24, 28, 32-35
  at Seabrook Farms (New
    Jersey), 181-188
  as teacher in Peru, 68, 69-70,
    74, 79-81
family history of, 9-10
in Hawaii, 235-237, 238, 243-244
illnesses of, 32, 33, 59-60, 231
in Japan
  childhood years, 10-11, 12-22
  education, 10, 21-22, 24-25, 28-
    33
  for visit, in later life, 234-235
marriage of, 77, 78-79, 80-81, 86-87
military obligations of, 62-65
in Peru

with Araki Company, 53, 56-58, 65-67, 68, 78
arrival, 44-46
on blacklist of "Axis Nationals," 114-116, 117, 118, 120
and Cerro Revolution, 60-62
deportation to Japan, attempts, 62-65, 119-120
deportation to U.S., 129-132, 136, 140-142
in detainment, 135-140
employment search, 46-49
in hiding, 133-135
in Japanese Association of Ica, 95-101, 114
malaria, 59-60
marriage of, 77, 78-79, 80-81, 86-87
and military obligations, 62-65
Otani Company ownership, 72-75, 81, 84-85
political acquaintances of, 102-103, 115-116
teaching employment, 68, 69-70, 74, 79-81
tour of Peru, 121-124
(*see also* Bazar Bienvenida)
retirement of, 233-237, 238, 243-244
at Seabrook Farms (New Jersey), 181-191, 193, 194, 196-197
sixtieth birthday, 233
sports activities of, 25, 70, 80
Washington, D.C. visit by, 191-192
Higashide, Shinyuemon (great-grandfather), 9
Higashide, Shinzaemon (grandfather), 9-10
Higashide, Shizue (sister), 12, 21
Higashide, Yonu (neé Itakura) (mother), 9-10, 12, 20, 202
Higashide, Yoshitaka (brother), 12, 19-21, 22, 202
Hokkaido, 10-22
housing
in Chicago, 195-196, 197, 205, 211-212
in detention camps, 144, 158, 167
at Seabrook Farms, 182
Hozen Technical School, 30-32
Ica, description of, 88

Ica Japanese Association. *See* Japanese Association of Ica
Ica Rifle Club, 102
Ichikawa Company, 91-92
Iida, Mr., 196, 197
Ikenaga, Mrs. Yahei, 174
illegal immigrants, former detainees as, 163, 178, 223
immigrants, Japanese in America, 216, 219-220, 228
immigrants, Japanese in Hawaii, 237, 240-242
immigrants, Japanese in Peru. *See also* anti-Japanese movement; immigration
attacks on, during Cerro revolution, 61-62
burial of, 148-149
conflicts between, 97, 105-108, 218-219
contract labor immigrants, 53-55, 97, 148
elderly, 69-70
exclusiveness of, 76-77, 104
generation gap among, 217-219
health care for, 231
marriage of, 75-76, 80
prohibition of reentry for, 162-163, 177
social customs of, 50-52
working guests, 52-53, 70-71
immigration. *See also* immigrants, Japanese in Peru
Japanese immigrants in America in general, 216, 219-220, 228
Japanese immigrants in Hawaii, 237, 240-242
Peruvian prohibition of, 77, 162-163, 177
U.S. law on, history of, 223
Immigration and Naturalization Service (INS), 156, 177-179
Incan calaveras, 66-67
Ishida, Shuzo, 41
Ishiwari, Chie, 222
Ishiwari, Roy, 222
Ishizu, Yogoro, 132
Itakura, Yonu, 9-10, 12, 20, 202
Japanese Association, Central, 106, 113
Japanese Association of Ica, 95-101,

114, 115, 118
Japanese Barber's Trade Association, 105-108
Japanese Consulate, in Peru
    in business disputes, 99-100, 106-107, 113
    response to Acosta riots, 109
    and S. Higashide's military obligations, 62-65
Japan National Youth Improvement Organization, 24-25
Kamizono, Mr., 47-48
Kanashiro, Kotaro, 127
Kato, Mr., 73-74, 84-85
Kim, Rev., 229-230
Koyama, Junko (neé Sakaguchi), 230
Koyama, Yukinori, 230
Kubose, Rev., 231-232
Kudo, Eigo, 215-216, 221, 238
Kudo, Elsa (neé Higashide)
    birth of, 103
    in Chicago, 214-215
    in detention camp, 169
    education of, 169, 183, 215
    employment of, 214-215, 221-222
    family role of, 214
    marriage of, 215-216, 221
    move to Hawaii, 238
    at Seabrook Farms, 183, 184
Kudo, Irma (neé Higashide)
    birth of, 103
    in Chicago, 216, 239
    in detention camp, 169
    education of, 169, 183, 216
    employment of, 222
    marriage of, 216, 222
    at Seabrook Farms, 183
Kudo, Rokuichi, 138-139, 215, 238
Kudo, Shiro, 222, 223
Kudo, Suketsune, 72
Kurihara, Mr., 49-50
Kuroiwa, Masami, 79-80, 82
Kuroiwa, Shigeyuki, 80, 82
Kurotobi, Isamu, 138
Kurotobi, Tatsujiro, 46, 47, 55, 83-84, 86, 88, 138
Kurusu, Saburo, 61-62
Leguia regime, 60-61
Lima Jiho, 106
Lima Nippo, 106
marriage of Japanese

in Peru, 75-76, 80
    in U.S., 221
Masaki, Yodokawa, 62-65
Miyamoto, Eikichi, 87
Morimoto, Ichitaro, 42, 146
Nagano, Hiroyuki, 82
Nakaya, Dr., 204-205
Narita, Victor, 137
Nazca, description of, 122
nicknames, use in Peru, 50-51
Nimura, Genji, 146
Nippon Yusen Company, 107, 110
nisei, discrimination against, 218-219
Nishihira, Shuei, 109
Nishii, Jorge, 230
Nishii, Tajiemon, 55, 230
Nishimichi family, 17
Ogawa, Mr., 228
Oreck, J.L., 164
Ota, Mosaburo, 40
Otani, Choichi, 68, 72-75
Otani Company, 72-75, 81, 84-85
"people's uniforms", 127-128
Peru Jiho, 47, 86
Peruvian government
    and anti-Japanese movement, 60-61, 125, 126
    in deportation of Japanese, 126-127, 142-143
    prohibition of imigration/reentry by, 77, 162-163, 177
    WWII loyalities of, 103
police, in Peru
    in actions against Japanese, 109, 117, 119, 124-125, 127, 128-132, 136-140
    friendly actions toward Japanese, 103, 131
Prensa, La, 114
racial discrimination
    in Chicago, 196, 210
    in Peru (*see* anti-Japanese movement)
Reagan, Ronald, 245
Red Cross Association, Japanese, 106
relocation camps. *See* detainees, Japanese; detention camps
relocation of Japanese, within Peru, 126-127
reparations for internees, 245-246
repatriation to Japan, 117, 119-120,

178
Roosevelt, Franklin Delano, 176, 182
Sakaguchi, Junko, 230
Sakaguchi, Misao (neé Higashide), 12, 21, 27, 32
Sakaguchi, Sotojiro, 27-29, 32, 33
San Vincente Japanese Elementary School, 68, 69-70, 74, 79-81
Sasaki, Mr., 35
Sato, Shun, 106-107
schools, elementary. *See* elementary schools, Japanese
Seabrook Farms, 179, 181-188, 193, 194, 196-197
Self-governing Association, 164-165, 170
Shigio, Don, 222, 239
Shigio, Martha (Marta) (neé Higashide)
  birth of, 150
  in Chicago, 197, 216
  education of, 216, 222
  marriage of, 216, 222
  move to Hawaii, 239
  at Seabrook Farms, 183
Shioya, Yoshiko, 42, 146
Shochi, Professor, 231-232
Smith, Adam, 213-214
social welfare system, in U.S., 225-227
Suetomi Company, 91-92
Suwa, Mr., 132
Tachibana, Shozo, 72
Takahashi, Mr. (of Kurotobi Company), 45, 46
Takahashi, Seitsu (of Crystal City camp), 169
Takeshita, Kunio, 194, 195, 196
Taniguchi, Tadao, 106
Tateishi, Victor K., 218
Taura, Shizuo, 49, 52
Teran, Mr., 121, 122, 124-125
Tokuno, Kakichi, 37-38
Tominaga, Shintaro, 39, 46, 47
Tule Lake camp, 176
Uchimura, Gun'ichi, 38, 40, 43, 47, 59
Umehara, Jitsutaro, 37, 38, 40, 41, 42, 43
United States government
  in anti-Japanese movement in Peru, 103, 104, 105, 113-114
  and legal status of detainees, 163, 176-179

Wakabayashi, Dr., 99
War Relocation Authority, 176
Washington, D.C., 191-192
Watanabe, Kenzo (of Watanabe Company), 48-49, 71, 162, 163
Watanabe, Mr. (detainee at Camp Kenedy), 160-161
Watanabe, Sengoro (of Watanabe Company), 55, 70-71
work ethic, American, 213-214
working guests, 52-53, 70-71
World War II. *See also* anti-Japanese movement; detainees, Japanese
  defeat of Japan, 172-173
  economic effects on Peru, 95, 128
  Peruvian government loyalties in, 103
Yagi, Sentei, 146-149
Yamada, Tatsumi, 39-40, 45, 46
Yamamoto, Kuninosuke, 47, 86
Yamasaki, Paul, 229
Yamashiro, Mr., 118
Yamashita, Juan, 152
Yasuda, Mr., 69
Yokota, Mr., 138
Yoshinaga, Angelica. *See* Higashide, Angelica (neé Yoshinaga) (wife)
Yoshinaga, Fumiko, 203-205
Yoshinaga, Kahei, 55, 56, 78-79, 85, 175
Yoshinaga, Mrs. Kahei, 55-56
Youth Improvement Organization, Japan National, 24-25